MTEL
Early Childhood (02) Exam

SECRETS

Study Guide
Your Key to Exam Success

Dear Future Exam Success Story:

First of all, **THANK YOU** for purchasing Mometrix study materials!

Second, congratulations! You are one of the few determined test-takers who are committed to doing whatever it takes to excel on your exam. **You have come to the right place.** We developed these study materials with one goal in mind: to deliver you the information you need in a format that's concise and easy to use.

In addition to optimizing your guide for the content of the test, we've outlined our recommended steps for breaking down the preparation process into small, attainable goals so you can make sure you stay on track.

We've also analyzed the entire test-taking process, identifying the most common pitfalls and showing how you can overcome them and be ready for any curveball the test throws you.

Standardized testing is one of the biggest obstacles on your road to success, which only increases the importance of doing well in the high-pressure, high-stakes environment of test day. Your results on this test could have a significant impact on your future, and this guide provides the information and practical advice to help you achieve your full potential on test day.

Your success is our success

We would love to hear from you! If you would like to share the story of your exam success or if you have any questions or comments in regard to our products, please contact us at **800-673-8175** or **support@mometrix.com**.

Thanks again for your business and we wish you continued success!

Sincerely,
The Mometrix Test Preparation Team

Need more help? Check out our flashcards at: http://MometrixFlashcards.com/MTEL

TABLE OF CONTENTS

Introduction

Thank you for purchasing this resource! You have made the choice to prepare yourself for a test that could have a huge impact on your future, and this guide is designed to help you be fully ready for test day. Obviously, it's important to have a solid understanding of the test material, but you also need to be prepared for the unique environment and stressors of the test, so that you can perform to the best of your abilities.

For this purpose, the first section that appears in this guide is the **Secret Keys**. We've devoted countless hours to meticulously researching what works and what doesn't, and we've boiled down our findings to the five most impactful steps you can take to improve your performance on the test. We start at the beginning with study planning and move through the preparation process, all the way to the testing strategies that will help you get the most out of what you know when you're finally sitting in front of the test.

We recommend that you start preparing for your test as far in advance as possible. However, if you've bought this guide as a last-minute study resource and only have a few days before your test, we recommend that you skip over the first two Secret Keys since they address a long-term study plan.

If you struggle with **test anxiety**, we strongly encourage you to check out our recommendations for how you can overcome it. Test anxiety is a formidable foe, but it can be beaten, and we want to make sure you have the tools you need to defeat it.

Secret Key #1 – Plan Big, Study Small

There's a lot riding on your performance. If you want to ace this test, you're going to need to keep your skills sharp and the material fresh in your mind. You need a plan that lets you review everything you need to know while still fitting in your schedule. We'll break this strategy down into three categories.

Information Organization

Start with the information you already have: the official test outline. From this, you can make a complete list of all the concepts you need to cover before the test. Organize these concepts into groups that can be studied together, and create a list of any related vocabulary you need to learn so you can brush up on any difficult terms. You'll want to keep this vocabulary list handy once you actually start studying since you may need to add to it along the way.

Time Management

Once you have your set of study concepts, decide how to spread them out over the time you have left before the test. Break your study plan into small, clear goals so you have a manageable task for each day and know exactly what you're doing. Then just focus on one small step at a time. When you manage your time this way, you don't need to spend hours at a time studying. Studying a small block of content for a short period each day helps you retain information better and avoid stressing over how much you have left to do. You can relax knowing that you have a plan to cover everything in time. In order for this strategy to be effective though, you have to start studying early and stick to your schedule. Avoid the exhaustion and futility that comes from last-minute cramming!

Study Environment

The environment you study in has a big impact on your learning. Studying in a coffee shop, while probably more enjoyable, is not likely to be as fruitful as studying in a quiet room. It's important to keep distractions to a minimum. You're only planning to study for a short block of time, so make the most of it. Don't pause to check your phone or get up to find a snack. It's also important to **avoid multitasking**. Research has consistently shown that multitasking will make your studying dramatically less effective. Your study area should also be comfortable and well-lit so you don't have the distraction of straining your eyes or sitting on an uncomfortable chair.

The time of day you study is also important. You want to be rested and alert. Don't wait until just before bedtime. Study when you'll be most likely to comprehend and remember. Even better, if you know what time of day your test will be, set that time aside for study. That way your brain will be used to working on that subject at that specific time and you'll have a better chance of recalling information.

Finally, it can be helpful to team up with others who are studying for the same test. Your actual studying should be done in as isolated an environment as possible, but the work of organizing the information and setting up the study plan can be divided up. In between study sessions, you can discuss with your teammates the concepts that you're all studying and quiz each other on the details. Just be sure that your teammates are as serious about the test as you are. If you find that your study time is being replaced with social time, you might need to find a new team.

Secret Key #2 – Make Your Studying Count

You're devoting a lot of time and effort to preparing for this test, so you want to be absolutely certain it will pay off. This means doing more than just reading the content and hoping you can remember it on test day. It's important to make every minute of study count. There are two main areas you can focus on to make your studying count:

Retention

It doesn't matter how much time you study if you can't remember the material. You need to make sure you are retaining the concepts. To check your retention of the information you're learning, try recalling it at later times with minimal prompting. Try carrying around flashcards and glance at one or two from time to time or ask a friend who's also studying for the test to quiz you.

To enhance your retention, look for ways to put the information into practice so that you can apply it rather than simply recalling it. If you're using the information in practical ways, it will be much easier to remember. Similarly, it helps to solidify a concept in your mind if you're not only reading it to yourself but also explaining it to someone else. Ask a friend to let you teach them about a concept you're a little shaky on (or speak aloud to an imaginary audience if necessary). As you try to summarize, define, give examples, and answer your friend's questions, you'll understand the concepts better and they will stay with you longer. Finally, step back for a big picture view and ask yourself how each piece of information fits with the whole subject. When you link the different concepts together and see them working together as a whole, it's easier to remember the individual components.

Finally, practice showing your work on any multi-step problems, even if you're just studying. Writing out each step you take to solve a problem will help solidify the process in your mind, and you'll be more likely to remember it during the test.

Modality

Modality simply refers to the means or method by which you study. Choosing a study modality that fits your own individual learning style is crucial. No two people learn best in exactly the same way, so it's important to know your strengths and use them to your advantage.

For example, if you learn best by visualization, focus on visualizing a concept in your mind and draw an image or a diagram. Try color-coding your notes, illustrating them, or creating symbols that will trigger your mind to recall a learned concept. If you learn best by hearing or discussing information, find a study partner who learns the same way or read aloud to yourself. Think about how to put the information in your own words. Imagine that you are giving a lecture on the topic and record yourself so you can listen to it later.

For any learning style, flashcards can be helpful. Organize the information so you can take advantage of spare moments to review. Underline key words or phrases. Use different colors for different categories. Mnemonic devices (such as creating a short list in which every item starts with the same letter) can also help with retention. Find what works best for you and use it to store the information in your mind most effectively and easily.

Secret Key #3 – Practice the Right Way

Your success on test day depends not only on how many hours you put into preparing, but also on whether you prepared the right way. It's good to check along the way to see if your studying is paying off. One of the most effective ways to do this is by taking practice tests to evaluate your progress. Practice tests are useful because they show exactly where you need to improve. Every time you take a practice test, pay special attention to these three groups of questions:

- The questions you got wrong
- The questions you had to guess on, even if you guessed right
- The questions you found difficult or slow to work through

This will show you exactly what your weak areas are, and where you need to devote more study time. Ask yourself why each of these questions gave you trouble. Was it because you didn't understand the material? Was it because you didn't remember the vocabulary? Do you need more repetitions on this type of question to build speed and confidence? Dig into those questions and figure out how you can strengthen your weak areas as you go back to review the material.

Additionally, many practice tests have a section explaining the answer choices. It can be tempting to read the explanation and think that you now have a good understanding of the concept. However, an explanation likely only covers part of the question's broader context. Even if the explanation makes sense, **go back and investigate** every concept related to the question until you're positive you have a thorough understanding.

As you go along, keep in mind that the practice test is just that: practice. Memorizing these questions and answers will not be very helpful on the actual test because it is unlikely to have any of the same exact questions. If you only know the right answers to the sample questions, you won't be prepared for the real thing. **Study the concepts** until you understand them fully, and then you'll be able to answer any question that shows up on the test.

It's important to wait on the practice tests until you're ready. If you take a test on your first day of study, you may be overwhelmed by the amount of material covered and how much you need to learn. Work up to it gradually.

On test day, you'll need to be prepared for answering questions, managing your time, and using the test-taking strategies you've learned. It's a lot to balance, like a mental marathon that will have a big impact on your future. Like training for a marathon, you'll need to start slowly and work your way up. When test day arrives, you'll be ready.

Start with the strategies you've read in the first two Secret Keys—plan your course and study in the way that works best for you. If you have time, consider using multiple study resources to get different approaches to the same concepts. It can be helpful to see difficult concepts from more than one angle. Then find a good source for practice tests. Many times, the test website will suggest potential study resources or provide sample tests.

Practice Test Strategy

If you're able to find at least three practice tests, we recommend this strategy:

Untimed and Open-Book Practice

Take the first test with no time constraints and with your notes and study guide handy. Take your time and focus on applying the strategies you've learned.

Timed and Open-Book Practice

Take the second practice test open-book as well, but set a timer and practice pacing yourself to finish in time.

Timed and Closed-Book Practice

Take any other practice tests as if it were test day. Set a timer and put away your study materials. Sit at a table or desk in a quiet room, imagine yourself at the testing center, and answer questions as quickly and accurately as possible.

Keep repeating timed and closed-book tests on a regular basis until you run out of practice tests or it's time for the actual test. Your mind will be ready for the schedule and stress of test day, and you'll be able to focus on recalling the material you've learned.

Secret Key #4 – Pace Yourself

Once you're fully prepared for the material on the test, your biggest challenge on test day will be managing your time. Just knowing that the clock is ticking can make you panic even if you have plenty of time left. Work on pacing yourself so you can build confidence against the time constraints of the exam. Pacing is a difficult skill to master, especially in a high-pressure environment, so **practice is vital**.

Set time expectations for your pace based on how much time is available. For example, if a section has 60 questions and the time limit is 30 minutes, you know you have to average 30 seconds or less per question in order to answer them all. Although 30 seconds is the hard limit, set 25 seconds per question as your goal, so you reserve extra time to spend on harder questions. When you budget extra time for the harder questions, you no longer have any reason to stress when those questions take longer to answer.

Don't let this time expectation distract you from working through the test at a calm, steady pace, but keep it in mind so you don't spend too much time on any one question. Recognize that taking extra time on one question you don't understand may keep you from answering two that you do understand later in the test. If your time limit for a question is up and you're still not sure of the answer, mark it and move on, and come back to it later if the time and the test format allow. If the testing format doesn't allow you to return to earlier questions, just make an educated guess; then put it out of your mind and move on.

On the easier questions, be careful not to rush. It may seem wise to hurry through them so you have more time for the challenging ones, but it's not worth missing one if you know the concept and just didn't take the time to read the question fully. Work efficiently but make sure you understand the question and have looked at all of the answer choices, since more than one may seem right at first.

Even if you're paying attention to the time, you may find yourself a little behind at some point. You should speed up to get back on track, but do so wisely. Don't panic; just take a few seconds less on each question until you're caught up. Don't guess without thinking, but do look through the answer choices and eliminate any you know are wrong. If you can get down to two choices, it is often worthwhile to guess from those. Once you've chosen an answer, move on and don't dwell on any that you skipped or had to hurry through. If a question was taking too long, chances are it was one of the harder ones, so you weren't as likely to get it right anyway.

On the other hand, if you find yourself getting ahead of schedule, it may be beneficial to slow down a little. The more quickly you work, the more likely you are to make a careless mistake that will affect your score. You've budgeted time for each question, so don't be afraid to spend that time. Practice an efficient but careful pace to get the most out of the time you have.

Secret Key #5 – Have a Plan for Guessing

When you're taking the test, you may find yourself stuck on a question. Some of the answer choices seem better than others, but you don't see the one answer choice that is obviously correct. What do you do?

The scenario described above is very common, yet most test takers have not effectively prepared for it. Developing and practicing a plan for guessing may be one of the single most effective uses of your time as you get ready for the exam.

In developing your plan for guessing, there are three questions to address:

- When should you start the guessing process?
- How should you narrow down the choices?
- Which answer should you choose?

When to Start the Guessing Process

Unless your plan for guessing is to select C every time (which, despite its merits, is not what we recommend), you need to leave yourself enough time to apply your answer elimination strategies. Since you have a limited amount of time for each question, that means that if you're going to give yourself the best shot at guessing correctly, you have to decide quickly whether or not you will guess.

Of course, the best-case scenario is that you don't have to guess at all, so first, see if you can answer the question based on your knowledge of the subject and basic reasoning skills. Focus on the key words in the question and try to jog your memory of related topics. Give yourself a chance to bring the knowledge to mind, but once you realize that you don't have (or you can't access) the knowledge you need to answer the question, it's time to start the guessing process.

It's almost always better to start the guessing process too early than too late. It only takes a few seconds to remember something and answer the question from knowledge. Carefully eliminating wrong answer choices takes longer. Plus, going through the process of eliminating answer choices can actually help jog your memory.

Summary: Start the guessing process as soon as you decide that you can't answer the question based on your knowledge.

How to Narrow Down the Choices

The next chapter in this book (**Test-Taking Strategies**) includes a wide range of strategies for how to approach questions and how to look for answer choices to eliminate. You will definitely want to read those carefully, practice them, and figure out which ones work best for you. Here though, we're going to address a mindset rather than a particular strategy.

Your chances of guessing an answer correctly depend on how many options you are choosing from.

How many choices you have	How likely you are to guess correctly
5	20%
4	25%
3	33%
2	50%
1	100%

You can see from this chart just how valuable it is to be able to eliminate incorrect answers and make an educated guess, but there are two things that many test takers do that cause them to miss out on the benefits of guessing:

- Accidentally eliminating the correct answer
- Selecting an answer based on an impression

We'll look at the first one here, and the second one in the next section.

To avoid accidentally eliminating the correct answer, we recommend a thought exercise called **the $5 challenge**. In this challenge, you only eliminate an answer choice from contention if you are willing to bet $5 on it being wrong. Why $5? Five dollars is a small but not insignificant amount of money. It's an amount you could afford to lose but wouldn't want to throw away. And while losing $5 once might not hurt too much, doing it twenty times will set you back $100. In the same way, each small decision you make—eliminating a choice here, guessing on a question there—won't by itself impact your score very much, but when you put them all together, they can make a big difference. By holding each answer choice elimination decision to a higher standard, you can reduce the risk of accidentally eliminating the correct answer.

The $5 challenge can also be applied in a positive sense: If you are willing to bet $5 that an answer choice *is* correct, go ahead and mark it as correct.

Summary: Only eliminate an answer choice if you are willing to bet $5 that it is wrong.

Which Answer to Choose

You're taking the test. You've run into a hard question and decided you'll have to guess. You've eliminated all the answer choices you're willing to bet $5 on. Now you have to pick an answer. Why do we even need to talk about this? Why can't you just pick whichever one you feel like when the time comes?

The answer to these questions is that if you don't come into the test with a plan, you'll rely on your impression to select an answer choice, and if you do that, you risk falling into a trap. The test writers know that everyone who takes their test will be guessing on some of the questions, so they intentionally write wrong answer choices to seem plausible. You still have to pick an answer though, and if the wrong answer choices are designed to look right, how can you ever be sure that you're not falling for their trap? The best solution we've found to this dilemma is to take the decision out of your hands entirely. Here is the process we recommend:

Once you've eliminated any choices that you are confident (willing to bet $5) are wrong, select the first remaining choice as your answer.

Whether you choose to select the first remaining choice, the second, or the last, the important thing is that you use some preselected standard. Using this approach guarantees that you will not be enticed into selecting an answer choice that looks right, because you are not basing your decision on how the answer choices look.

This is not meant to make you question your knowledge. Instead, it is to help you recognize the difference between your knowledge and your impressions. There's a huge difference between thinking an answer is right because of what you know, and thinking an answer is right because it looks or sounds like it should be right.

Summary: To ensure that your selection is appropriately random, make a predetermined selection from among all answer choices you have not eliminated.

Test-Taking Strategies

This section contains a list of test-taking strategies that you may find helpful as you work through the test. By taking what you know and applying logical thought, you can maximize your chances of answering any question correctly!

It is very important to realize that every question is different and every person is different: no single strategy will work on every question, and no single strategy will work for every person. That's why we've included all of them here, so you can try them out and determine which ones work best for different types of questions and which ones work best for you.

Question Strategies

Read Carefully

Read the question and answer choices carefully. Don't miss the question because you misread the terms. You have plenty of time to read each question thoroughly and make sure you understand what is being asked. Yet a happy medium must be attained, so don't waste too much time. You must read carefully, but efficiently.

Contextual Clues

Look for contextual clues. If the question includes a word you are not familiar with, look at the immediate context for some indication of what the word might mean. Contextual clues can often give you all the information you need to decipher the meaning of an unfamiliar word. Even if you can't determine the meaning, you may be able to narrow down the possibilities enough to make a solid guess at the answer to the question.

Prefixes

If you're having trouble with a word in the question or answer choices, try dissecting it. Take advantage of every clue that the word might include. Prefixes and suffixes can be a huge help. Usually they allow you to determine a basic meaning. Pre- means before, post- means after, pro - is positive, de- is negative. From prefixes and suffixes, you can get an idea of the general meaning of the word and try to put it into context.

Hedge Words

Watch out for critical hedge words, such as *likely, may, can, sometimes, often, almost, mostly, usually, generally, rarely*, and *sometimes*. Question writers insert these hedge phrases to cover every possibility. Often an answer choice will be wrong simply because it leaves no room for exception. Be on guard for answer choices that have definitive words such as *exactly* and *always*.

Switchback Words

Stay alert for *switchbacks*. These are the words and phrases frequently used to alert you to shifts in thought. The most common switchback words are *but, although*, and *however*. Others include *nevertheless, on the other hand, even though, while, in spite of, despite, regardless of*. Switchback words are important to catch because they can change the direction of the question or an answer choice.

Face Value

When in doubt, use common sense. Accept the situation in the problem at face value. Don't read too much into it. These problems will not require you to make wild assumptions. If you have to go beyond creativity and warp time or space in order to have an answer choice fit the question, then you should move on and consider the other answer choices. These are normal problems rooted in reality. The applicable relationship or explanation may not be readily apparent, but it is there for you to figure out. Use your common sense to interpret anything that isn't clear.

Answer Choice Strategies

Answer Selection

The most thorough way to pick an answer choice is to identify and eliminate wrong answers until only one is left, then confirm it is the correct answer. Sometimes an answer choice may immediately seem right, but be careful. The test writers will usually put more than one reasonable answer choice on each question, so take a second to read all of them and make sure that the other choices are not equally obvious. As long as you have time left, it is better to read every answer choice than to pick the first one that looks right without checking the others.

Answer Choice Families

An answer choice family consists of two (in rare cases, three) answer choices that are very similar in construction and cannot all be true at the same time. If you see two answer choices that are direct opposites or parallels, one of them is usually the correct answer. For instance, if one answer choice says that quantity x increases and another either says that quantity x decreases (opposite) or says that quantity y increases (parallel), then those answer choices would fall into the same family. An answer choice that doesn't match the construction of the answer choice family is more likely to be incorrect. Most questions will not have answer choice families, but when they do appear, you should be prepared to recognize them.

Eliminate Answers

Eliminate answer choices as soon as you realize they are wrong, but make sure you consider all possibilities. If you are eliminating answer choices and realize that the last one you are left with is also wrong, don't panic. Start over and consider each choice again. There may be something you missed the first time that you will realize on the second pass.

Avoid Fact Traps

Don't be distracted by an answer choice that is factually true but doesn't answer the question. You are looking for the choice that answers the question. Stay focused on what the question is asking for so you don't accidentally pick an answer that is true but incorrect. Always go back to the question and make sure the answer choice you've selected actually answers the question and is not merely a true statement.

Extreme Statements

In general, you should avoid answers that put forth extreme actions as standard practice or proclaim controversial ideas as established fact. An answer choice that states the "process should be used in certain situations, if…" is much more likely to be correct than one that states the "process should be discontinued completely." The first is a calm rational statement and doesn't even make a definitive, uncompromising stance, using a hedge word *if* to provide wiggle room, whereas the second choice is a radical idea and far more extreme.

Benchmark

As you read through the answer choices and you come across one that seems to answer the question well, mentally select that answer choice. This is not your final answer, but it's the one that will help you evaluate the other answer choices. The one that you selected is your benchmark or standard for judging each of the other answer choices. Every other answer choice must be compared to your benchmark. That choice is correct until proven otherwise by another answer choice beating it. If you find a better answer, then that one becomes your new benchmark. Once you've decided that no other choice answers the question as well as your benchmark, you have your final answer.

Predict the Answer

Before you even start looking at the answer choices, it is often best to try to predict the answer. When you come up with the answer on your own, it is easier to avoid distractions and traps because you will know exactly what to look for. The right answer choice is unlikely to be word-for-word what you came up with, but it should be a close match. Even if you are confident that you have the right answer, you should still take the time to read each option before moving on.

General Strategies

Tough Questions

If you are stumped on a problem or it appears too hard or too difficult, don't waste time. Move on! Remember though, if you can quickly check for obviously incorrect answer choices, your chances of guessing correctly are greatly improved. Before you completely give up, at least try to knock out a couple of possible answers. Eliminate what you can and then guess at the remaining answer choices before moving on.

Check Your Work

Since you will probably not know every term listed and the answer to every question, it is important that you get credit for the ones that you do know. Don't miss any questions through careless mistakes. If at all possible, try to take a second to look back over your answer selection and make sure you've selected the correct answer choice and haven't made a costly careless mistake (such as marking an answer choice that you didn't mean to mark). This quick double check should more than pay for itself in caught mistakes for the time it costs.

Pace Yourself

It's easy to be overwhelmed when you're looking at a page full of questions; your mind is confused and full of random thoughts, and the clock is ticking down faster than you would like. Calm down and maintain the pace that you have set for yourself. Especially as you get down to the last few minutes of the test, don't let the small numbers on the clock make you panic. As long as you are on track by monitoring your pace, you are guaranteed to have time for each question.

Don't Rush

It is very easy to make errors when you are in a hurry. Maintaining a fast pace in answering questions is pointless if it makes you miss questions that you would have gotten right otherwise. Test writers like to include distracting information and wrong answers that seem right. Taking a little extra time to avoid careless mistakes can make all the difference in your test score. Find a pace that allows you to be confident in the answers that you select.

Keep Moving

Panicking will not help you pass the test, so do your best to stay calm and keep moving. Taking deep breaths and going through the answer elimination steps you practiced can help to break through a stress barrier and keep your pace.

Final Notes

The combination of a solid foundation of content knowledge and the confidence that comes from practicing your plan for applying that knowledge is the key to maximizing your performance on test day. As your foundation of content knowledge is built up and strengthened, you'll find that the strategies included in this chapter become more and more effective in helping you quickly sift through the distractions and traps of the test to isolate the correct answer.

Now it's time to move on to the test content chapters of this book, but be sure to keep your goal in mind. As you read, think about how you will be able to apply this information on the test. If you've already seen sample questions for the test and you have an idea of the question format and style, try to come up with questions of your own that you can answer based on what you're reading. This will give you valuable practice applying your knowledge in the same ways you can expect to on test day.

Good luck and good studying!

Knowledge of Child Development

Sensorimotor Stage of Piaget's Theory of Cognitive Development

From birth until about 2 years of age, infants are in what Piaget termed the Sensorimotor stage of cognitive development. They learn through environmental input they receive through their senses; motor actions they engage in; and through feedback they receive from their bodies and the environment about their actions. For example, a baby kicks his legs, sees his feet moving, and reaches for them. He sees objects, reaches for them, and grasps them. Eventually, babies learn they can make some objects move by touching or hitting them. They learn through repeated experiences that when they throw objects out of their cribs, their parents retrieve them. They will seem to make a game of this, not to annoy parents, but as a way of learning rules of cause and effect by repeating actions to see the same results. They also enjoy their ability to be causal agents and their power to achieve effects through their actions.

<u>First Three Substages of the Sensorimotor Stage</u>

From birth to 1 month old, infants learn to comprehend their environment through their inborn reflexes, such as the sucking reflex and the reflex of looking at their surroundings. From 1–4 months old, babies begin to coordinate their physical sensations with new schemas, i.e. mental constructs/concepts they form to represent elements of reality. For example, an infant might suck her thumb by chance and feel pleasure from the activity; in the future, she will repeat thumb-sucking because the pleasure is rewarding. Piaget called this second substage "Primary Circular Reactions." In the third substage, around 4–8 months, which he called "Secondary Circular Reactions," children also repeat rewarding actions, but now they are focused on things in the environment that they can affect, rather than just the child's own person. For example, once a baby learns to pick up an object and mouth it, s/he will repeat this. Thus, babies learn an early method of environmental exploration through their mouths, an extension of their initial sucking reflex.

<u>Last Three Substages of the Sensorimotor Stage</u>

According to Piaget, babies about 8–12 months are in the "Coordination of Reactions" substage of the Sensorimotor stage. Having begun repeating actions purposely to achieve environmental effects during the previous substage of Secondary Circular Reactions, in Coordination of Reactions, infants begin further exploring their surroundings. They frequently imitate others' observed behaviors. They more obviously demonstrate intentional behaviors. They become able to combine schemas (mental constructs) to attain certain results. They develop object permanence, the understanding that unseen objects still exist. They learn to associate certain objects with their properties. For example, once a baby realizes a rattle makes a noise when shaken, s/he will deliberately shake it to produce the sound. In "Tertiary Circular Reactions," at about 12–18 months, children begin experimenting through trial-and-error. For instance, a child might test various actions or sounds for getting parents' attention. From 18–24 months, in the substage of "Early Representational Thought," children begin representing objects and events with symbols. They begin to understand the world via not only actions, but mental operations.

<u>Object Permanence</u>

One of the landmarks of infant cognitive development is learning that concrete objects are not "out of sight, out of mind"; in other words, things still continue to exist even when they are out of our sight. Babies generally develop this realization around 8–9 months old, though some may be earlier or later. Some researchers after Piaget have found object permanence in babies as young as 3½ months. Younger infants typically attend to an object of interest only when they can see it; if it is removed or hidden, they are upset/confused at its disappearance and/or shift their attention to something else. A sign that they have developed object permanence is if they search for the object after it is moved or hidden. Babies only become interested in "hide and seek" types of games once they have developed this understanding that the existence of objects and people persist beyond their immediate vision or proximity. Another example of emerging object permanence is the delight babies begin to take in "peek-a-boo" games.

Schema and Schemata Development in Infants

Piaget proposed we form mental constructs or concepts that he called schemata, representing elements of the environment, beginning in infancy. A schema does not represent an individual object, but a category or class of things. For example, a baby might form a schema representing "things to suck on," initially including her bottle, her thumb, and her pacifier. Piaget said assimilation is when we can fit something new into an existing schema: the child in this example assimilates "Daddy's knee" into her schema of things she can suck on when she discovers this action. When something new cannot be assimilated into an existing schema, we either modify that schema or form a new schema, which both constitute accommodation. The baby in our example, becoming a toddler, might modify her schema of things to suck to include straws, which require a different sucking technique. Piaget said assimilation and accommodation combined constitute the process of adaptation, i.e. adjusting, to our environment through interacting with it.

Piaget's Schema Examples

A toddler on an airplane sees a nearby stranger who is male, about 5'8", with white hair and eyeglasses. Both of his grandfathers have these same general appearances. He murmurs to himself, "Hi, Granddaddy." Explain this according to Piaget's concept of the schema in his cognitive-developmental theory.

> The toddler in this example did not actually mistake a complete stranger for either one of his grandfathers. Notice that he did not directly address the stranger as "Granddaddy" with conversational loudness, but murmured it to himself. He recognized this man was not someone he knew. However, he recognized common elements with his grandfathers in the man's appearance. According to Piaget's theory of cognitive development, the explanation for this is that the child had formed a schema, i.e. a mental construct, to represent men about 5'8" with white hair and eyeglasses, based initially on his early knowledge of two such men he knew, his grandfathers, and then extending to include other similar-appearing men, through the process of assimilation of new information into an existing schema. His description did not mean he thought the stranger was named "Granddaddy." Rather, the word "Granddaddy" was not only the name he called one grandfather, but also the word he used to label his schema for all men who appeared to fit into this category.

A toddler sees a large, brown dog through the window and says, "Moo." Explain this according to Piaget's theory of cognitive development.

> Piaget found that forming schemas, or mental constructs to represent objects and actions, is how babies and children learn about themselves and the world through their interactions with their bodies and the environment. If they can fit a new experience into an existing schema, they assimilate it; or when necessary, they change an existing schema or form a new one to accommodate a new stimulus. Therefore, in this example, the toddler had seen cows in picture books, photos, or on

a farm, and learned to associate the sound "Moo" with cows, reinforced by the teaching of toys, books, and adults. She had formed a schema for large, brown, four-legged, furry animals. Because the dog she saw fit these properties, she assimilated the dog into her cow schema. If she were then told this was a dog that says "Bow-wow," she would either form a new schema for dogs; or, if she had previously only seen smaller dogs, accommodate (modify) her existing dog schema to include larger dogs.

Conservation

Conservation is the cognitive ability to understand that objects or substances retain their properties of numbers or amounts even when their appearance, shape, or configuration changes. Piaget found from his experiments with children that this ability develops around the age of five years. He also found children develop conservation of number, length, mass, weight, volume, and quantity respectively at slightly different ages. One example of a conservation experiment is with liquid volume: the experimenter pours the same amount of liquid into a short, wide container and a tall, thin one. Children who have not developed conservation of liquid volume typically say one container has more liquid, even though they saw both amounts were equal, based on one container's looking fuller. Similarly, children who have not developed conservation of number, shown equal numbers of beads, usually say a group arranged in a long row has more beads than a group clustered together. Children having developed conservation recognize the amounts are the same regardless of appearance.

Preoperational Versus Concrete Operational Stages

Piaget called the stage of most children aged 2–6 years Preoperational because children these ages cannot yet perform mental operations, i.e. manipulate information mentally. At around 6–7 years old, children begin to develop Concrete Operations. A key aspect of this stage is the ability to think logically. This ability first develops relative to concrete objects and events. Concrete Operational children still have trouble understanding abstract concepts or hypothetical situations, but they can apply logical sequences and cause and effect to things they can see, feel, and manipulate physically. For example, Concrete Operational children develop the understanding that things have the same amount or number regardless of their shape or arrangement, which Piaget termed conservation. They develop proficiency in inductive logic, i.e. drawing generalizations from specific instances. However, deductive logic, i.e. predicting specific results according to general principles, is not as well-developed until the later stage of Formal Operations involving abstract thought. Another key development of Concrete Operations is reversibility, i.e. the ability to reverse an action or operation.

The different thinking found between Piaget's Preoperational and Concrete Operations stages is exemplified in experiments he and others conducted to prove his theory. For example, the absence/presence of ability to conserve liquid volume across shape/appearance has been shown in experiments with differently aged children. A preschooler is shown a tall, thin beaker and a short, wide one. The experimenter also shows the child two identically sized and shaped containers with identical amounts of liquid in each. The experimenter then pours the equal amounts of liquid into the two differently shaped beakers. The preschooler will say either the thin beaker holds more liquid because it is taller or the short beaker holds more because it is wider. Piaget termed this "centration"—focusing on only one property at a time. An older child "decentrates," can "conserve" the amount, and knows both beakers hold identical amounts. Older children also use reversibility and logic, e.g. "I know they are still equal, because I just saw you pour the same amount into each beaker."

17

Preoperational Stage of Piaget's Theory of Cognitive Development

Children between (roughly) two and six years old are in Piaget's Preoperational stage of cognitive development. Having begun to use objects to represent other things, i.e. symbolic representation, near the end of the previous Sensorimotor stage, children now further develop this ability during pretend/make-believe play. They may pretend a broom is a guitar or a horse; or talk using a block as a phone. Toddlers begin to play "house," pretending they and their playmates are the mommy, the daddy, the mailman, the doctor, etc. The reason Piaget called this stage Preoperational is that children are not yet capable of performing mental "operations," including following concrete logic or manipulating information mentally. Their thinking is intuitive rather than following logical steps. Piaget termed Preoperational children "egocentric" in that they literally cannot adopt another's point of view, even concretely: in experiments, after seeing pictures of a scene as viewed from different positions, children could not match a picture to another person's position, selecting the picture showing the scene from their own viewpoint.

Animism and Magical Thinking

Piaget found that children in the Preoperational stage are not yet able to perform logical mental operations. Their thinking is intuitive during the toddler and preschool years. One characteristic of the thinking of young children is animism, or assigning human qualities, feelings, and actions to inanimate objects. For example, a child seeing an autumn leaf fall off of a tree might remark, "The tree didn't like that leaf and pushed it off of its branch." Or a child with a sunburn might say, "The sun was angry at me and burned me." A related characteristic is magical thinking, which is attributing cause and effect relationships between their own feelings and thoughts and environmental events where none exists. For example, if a child says "I hate you" to another person or secretly dislikes and wishes the other gone, and something bad then happens to that person, the child is likely to believe what s/he said/felt/thought caused the other's unfortunate event. This is related to egocentrism—seeing everything as revolving around oneself.

Stages of Growth and Development in Art

Austrian and German art scholars established six stages in art. (1) The Scribble stage: from 2–4 years, children first make uncontrolled scribbles; then controlled scribbling; then progress to naming their scribbles to indicate what they represent. (2) The Preschematic stage: from ages 4–6, children begin to develop a visual schema. Schema, meaning mental representation, comes from Piaget's cognitive-developmental theory. Without complete comprehension of dimensions and sizes, children may draw people and houses the same height; they use color more emotionally than logically. They may omit or exaggerate facial features, or they might draw sizes by importance, e.g. drawing themselves as largest among people or drawing the most important feature, e.g. the head, as the largest or only body part. (3) The Schematic stage: from 7–9 years, drawings more reflect actual physical proportions and colors. (4) Dawning Realism: from ages 9–11, drawings become increasingly representational. (5) Children aged 11–13 are in the Pseudorealistic stage, reflecting their ability to reason. (6) Children 14+ are in the Period of Decision stage, reflecting the adolescent identity crisis.

Viktor Lowenfeld

Viktor Lowenfeld (1903–1960) taught art to elementary school students and sculpture to blind students. Lowenfeld's acquaintance with Sigmund Freud, who was interested in his work with people with visual impairments, motivated Lowenfeld to pursue scientific research. He published several books on using creative arts activities therapeutically. Lowenfeld was familiar with six stages previously identified in the growth of art. He combined these with principles of human development drawn from the school of psychoanalytic psychology founded by Freud. In his adaptation, he named the six stages reflecting the development of children's art as Scribble, Preschematic, Schematic, Dawning Realism, Pseudorealistic, and Period of Decision. Lowenfeld identified adolescent learning styles as haptic, focused on physical sensations and subjective emotional experiences, and as visual, focused on appearances, each demanding corresponding instructional approaches. Lowenfeld's book Creative and Mental Growth (1947) was the most influential text in art education during the later 20th century. Lowenfeld's psychological emphasis in this text gave scientific foundations to creative and artistic expression, and identified developmentally age-appropriate art media and activities.

Involvement of Music in the Development of Infants and Young Children

Long before they can speak, and before they even comprehend much speech, infants respond to the sounds of voices and to music. These responses are not only to auditory stimulation, but moreover to the emotional content in what they hear. Parents sing lullabies to babies; not only are these sounds pleasant and soothing, but they also help children develop trust in their environment as secure. Parents communicate their love to children through singing and introduce them to experiences of pleasure and excitement through music. As children grow, music progresses to be not only a medium of communication but also one of self-expression as they learn to sing/play musical sounds. Music facilitates memory, as we see through commercial jingles and mnemonic devices. Experiments find music improves spatial reasoning. Children's learning of perceptual and logical concepts like beginning/ending, sequences, cause-and-effect, balance, harmony/dissonance and mathematical number and timing concepts is reinforced by music. Music also promotes language development. Children learn about colors, counting, conceptual relationships, nature, and social skills through music.

Enhancing the Emotional, Social, Aesthetic, and School Readiness Skills with Music

Young children who are just learning to use spoken language often cannot express their emotions very well verbally. Music is a great aid to emotional development in that younger children can express happiness, sadness, anger, etc., through singing and/or playing music more easily than they can with words. Children of preschool ages not only listen to music and respond to what they hear, they also learn to create music through singing and playing instruments together with other children. These activities help them learn crucial social skills for their lives, like cooperating with others, collaborating, and making group or team efforts to accomplish something. When children are given guided musical experiences, they learn to make their own judgments of what is good or bad music; this provides them with the foundations for developing an aesthetic sense. Music promotes preliteracy skills by enhancing phonemic awareness. As growing children develop musical appreciation and skills, these develop fundamental motor, cognitive, and social skills they need for language, school readiness, literacy, and life.

Premathematical Learning Experiences

Preschool children do not think in the same ways as older children and adults do, as Piaget observed. Their thinking is strongly based upon and connected to their sensory perceptions. This means that in solving problems, they depend mainly on how things look, sound, feel, smell, and taste. Therefore, preschool children should always be given concrete objects that they can touch, explore, and experiment with in any learning experience. They are not yet capable of understanding abstract concepts or manipulating information mentally, so they must have real things to work with to understand premath concepts. For example, they will learn to count solid objects like blocks, beads, or pennies before they can count numbers in their heads. They cannot benefit from rote math memorization, or "sit still and listen" lessons. Since young children "centrate" on one

19

characteristic/object/person/event at a time, adults can offer activities encouraging decentration/incorporating multiple aspects, e.g. not only grouping all triangles, but grouping all red triangles separately from blue triangles.

Activities Assisting Children Develop Cognitive Abilities

As shown by Piaget, young children have difficulty reversing operations. Adults can ask them to build block structures, for example, and then dismantle them one block at a time to reverse the construction. They can ask children to retell rhymes or stories backward. They can take small groups of children for walks and ask them if they can return by the same route as they came. Young children often assume causal relationships where none exist. Adults can provide activities to produce and observe results, e.g. pouring water into different containers; knocking over bowling pins by swinging a pendulum; rolling wheeled toys down ramps; or blowing balls through mazes, and then asking them, "What happened when you did this? What would happen if you did this? What could you do to make this happen?" Young children are also often egocentric, seeing everything from their own viewpoint. Adults can help them take others' perspectives through guessing games wherein they must give each other clues to guess persons/objects and dramatic role-playing activities, where they pretend to be others.

Salient Aspects of Typical Early Childhood Physical Development

Early childhood physical growth, while significant, is slower than infant growth. From birth to 2 years, children generally grow to four times their newborn weight and 2/3 their newborn length/height. From 2–3 years, however, children usually gain only about 4 lbs. and 3.5 inches. From 4–6 years, growth slows more; gains of 5–7 lbs. and 2.5 inches are typical. Due to slowing growth rates, 3- and 4-year-olds appear to eat less food, but do not; they actually just eat fewer calories per pound of body weight. Brain growth is still rapid in preschoolers: brains attain 55 percent of adult size by 2 years, and 90 percent by 6 years. The majority of brain growth is usually by 4–4.5 years, with a growth spurt around 2 years and growth rates slowing significantly between 5 and 6 years. Larger brain size indicates not more neurons, but larger sizes; differences in their organization; more glial cells nourishing and supporting neurons; and greater myelination (development of the sheath protecting nerve fibers and facilitating their efficient intercommunication).

Gender Differences in Motor Development

On average, preschool boys have larger muscles than preschool girls, so they can run faster, climb higher, and jump farther. Boys at these ages tend to be more muscular physically. Preschool girls, while less muscular, are on the average more mature physically for their ages than boys. While boys usually exceed girls in their large-muscle, gross-motor abilities like running, jumping, and climbing, girls tend to surpass boys in small-muscle, fine-motor abilities like buttoning buttons, using scissors, and similar activities involving the manipulation of small tools, utensils, and objects. While preschool boys exhibit more strength in large-muscle, gross-motor actions, preschool girls are more advanced than preschool boys in large-muscle, gross-motor skills that do not demand strength so much as coordination, like hopping, balancing on one foot, and skipping. While these specific gender differences in preschoolers' physical and motor development have been observed consistently in research, it is also found that preschool girls' and boys' physical and motor development patterns are generally more similar than different overall.

Abilities in Perceptual Development Occurring in Infancy

In normal development, babies have usually established the ability to see, hear, smell, taste, and feel and also the ability to integrate such sensory information by the age of six months. Additional perceptual abilities, which are less obvious and more complex, continue to emerge throughout the early childhood years. For instance, young children develop increasing precision in recognizing visual concepts like size and shape. This development allows children to identify accurately the shape and size of an object no matter from what angle they perceive it. Infants have these capacities in place, but have not yet developed accuracy in using them. For example, a baby might realize that objects farther away occupy less of their visual fields than nearer objects; however, the baby has yet to learn just how much less of the visual field is taken up by the farther object. Young children attain this and similar kinds of learning by actively, energetically exploring their environments. Such activity is crucial for developing accurate perception of size, shape, and distance.

Signs of Progress in Typical Motor Development

Genetics, physiological maturation, nutrition, and experience through practice combine to further preschoolers' motor skills development. Newborns' reflexive behaviors progress to preschoolers' voluntary activities. Also, children's perception of the size, shape, and position of the body and body parts becomes more accurate by preschool ages. In addition, increases in bilateral coordination of the body's two sides enhance preschoolers' motor skills. Motor skills development entails both learning new movements and gradually integrating previously learned movements into smooth, continuous patterns, as in learning to throw a ball with skill. Both large muscles, for gross-motor skills like climbing, running, and jumping, and small muscles, for fine-motor skills like drawing and tying knots, develop. Eye-hand coordination involves fine-motor control. Preschoolers use visual feedback, i.e. seeing whether they are making things go where and do what they want them to, in learning to manipulate small objects with their hands and fingers.

Nature-Nurture Interaction in Early Childhood Physical Development

The physical development of babies and young children is a product of the interactions between genetic and environmental factors. Also, a child's physical progress is equally influenced by environmental and psychological variables. For the body, brain, and nervous system to grow and develop normally, children must live in healthy environments. When the interaction of hereditary and environmental influences is not healthful, this is frequently reflected in abnormal patterns of growth. Failure to thrive syndrome is a dramatic example. When children are abused or neglected for long periods of time, they actually stop growing. The social environments of such children create psychological stress. This stress makes the child's pituitary gland stop releasing growth hormones, and growth ceases. When such environmental stress is relieved and these children are given proper care, stimulation, and affection, they begin growing again. They often grow rapidly enough to catch up on the growth they missed earlier. Normal body and brain growth—as well as psychological development—depend upon the collaboration of nature and nurture.

Visual Perceptual Aspects of Interpreting Pictures and Eye Movements

As adults, our ability to look at pictures of people and things in the environment is something we usually take for granted. Researchers have established that 3-year-old children's responses indicate their ability to recognize shading, line convergence, and other cues of depth in two-dimensional pictures. However, scientists have also found that children's sensitivity to these kinds of visual cues increases as they grow older. The eye movements and eye fixation patterns of young children affect their ability to get the most complete and accurate information from pictorial representations of reality. When viewing pictures, adults sweep the entire picture to see it as a whole, their eye movements leaping around; to focus on specific details, adults use shorter eye movements. Preschool children differ from adults in using shorter eye movements overall, and focusing on small parts of the picture near the center or an edge. They therefore disregard, or do not see, a lot of the picture's available information.

Characteristics in Art Reflecting Perceptual, Cognitive, and Motor Development

Observations of young children find that while a 2½-year-old can grasp a crayon and scribble with it, by the age of 4 years, s/he can draw a picture we recognize as human. The typical 4-year-old drawing of a human being is called the "tadpole person" because it has no body, a large head, and stick limbs. Between the ages of 3 and 4 years, children typically make a transition from scribbling to producing tadpole person drawings. This development is enabled by greater development in motor control and eye-hand coordination, among other variables. Between the ages of 4 and 5 years, children make another transition by progressing from drawing tadpole persons to drawing complete figures with heads and bodies. Howard Gardner, psychologist and author of the Multiple Intelligences theory, stated that children achieve a "summit of artistry" by the end of their preschool years. He describes their drawings as "characteristically colorful, balanced, rhythmic, and expressive, conveying something of the range and...vitality associated with artistic mastery." (1980)

Self-Concept and Self-Esteem

Young children's self-concepts are founded on observable, readily defined, mainly concrete factors. Many young children also experience much adult encouragement. Because their self-concepts are more simple and concrete than those of older children and adults and because they typically receive abundant encouragement and positive reinforcement, preschoolers often have fairly high self-esteem, i.e. judgment regarding their own value. In general, young children tend to have positive, optimistic attitudes that they can learn something new, finish tasks, and succeed if they persist in their attempts. Self-esteem related specifically to one's ability to perform a given task is sometimes called "achievement-related attribution." Albert Bandura called it "self-efficacy." Young children derive self-esteem from multiple sources, including their relationships with their parents; their friendships; their abilities and achievements in tasks involving playing and helping others; their physical/athletic abilities; and their achievements in preschool/school.

Basic Temperament Types Influencing Personalities of Children

Psychologists studied the behavior of infants and classified their characteristics into three types of temperaments: easy, difficult, and slow to warm up. The majority of infants are easy babies. When they cry from hunger/needing changing/being tired/feeling discomfort/needing cuddling/attention, they are easily soothed by having these needs met. They typically sleep well. While they experience normal negative emotions, their predominant mood is good. Other than normal stranger anxiety at applicable ages, they respond positively to meeting people. In contrast, difficult babies are more likely to cry longer and be much harder to soothe. It is often hard to get them to sleep, and they may sleep fitfully, with many interruptions and/or for shorter times. They are more easily frightened by strange/new people and things, and more easily upset overall. Slow to warm up babies can initially seem difficult by not being as immediately responsive to people other than their parents like easy babies. However, given some time to adjust, they eventually "warm up" to new people and situations.

External Variables Influencing Self-Concepts, Self-Esteem, and Self-Efficacy

The way young children see themselves is affected by the feedback they receive from other people. When adults like parents, caregivers, and teachers give young children positive responses to their efforts—whether they succeed initially or not—the children are more likely to develop positive self-concepts, engendering higher self-esteem, and greater self-efficacy, the belief that they have the competency to succeed at a specific task or activity. On the other hand, when adults frequently give punitive/judgmental/indifferent/otherwise negative responses to young children's efforts, children develop poorer self-images. They feel they are not valued/good/important/worthy. They develop lower self-esteem, and their self-efficacy is weaker; they come to expect failure when they attempt tasks and may not even try. Peers also affect young children's self-concepts and self-esteem. When friends and classmates include a child in activities, this promotes a positive self-image and higher self-esteem and self-efficacy. If peers exclude, tease, or bully a young child, this can cause low self-esteem, make their self-concepts more negative, and lower their self-efficacy.

Learning Styles and Implications for Early Childhood Education

Young children with normal development learn in the same chronological sequences and learn the same types of skills. Even those with delayed development, as with intellectual disabilities, learn the same things in the same order, but simply at a slower rate and hence at later ages; and those with severe/profound impairment may never achieve certain developmental milestones. However, one aspect of learning that varies is learning style. For example, some children approach learning in a primarily visual manner. They focus on what they see and how things look. They learn best given visual stimuli, like colorful objects, pictures, and graphics. They understand abstract concepts and relationships better when these are illustrated visually. Other children approach learning in a primarily haptic or tactile way. They focus on textures and movements, learning through touch and kinesthetic senses. They learn best given concrete things to explore and manipulate, and physical activities to perform. They learn abstract concepts and relationships better through handling materials and engaging in physical movements and actions.

Internal Variable Influencing Self-Concepts, Self-Esteem, and Self-Efficacy

One major internal influence on self-concept is a child's basic temperament. Easy, difficult, and slow-to-warm-up temperaments in babies continue into early childhood (and throughout life). For example, children having easy temperaments are better prepared for coping with challenges and frustration. When they encounter difficulty attempting new tasks, they do not give up as easily and are more persistent. They are thus more likely to develop self-concepts of being good, valuable, and successful and hence have higher self-esteem. Since they experience more success through persistence, they develop greater self-efficacy, i.e. belief in their competence to perform specific tasks. Children with more difficult temperaments become frustrated more easily, after fewer attempts, and give up trying in discouragement or require extra help to perform new or challenging tasks. They are more at risk for believing they cannot succeed and hence are not valuable, leading to their developing lower self-esteem. This also affects self-efficacy: they are more likely to doubt their ability to perform a specific proposed task.

Locus of Control

Psychologist Julian Rotter originated the term and concept of locus of control. It refers to the place (locus) where we attribute causes for outcomes we experience, either externally or internally. An external locus control is something outside of us—another person and/or his/her actions; an environmental event; or an unknown but exterior influence, like good/bad luck or random chance.

An internal locus of control is something inside of us—our native ability, our motivation, or our effort. For example, blaming another for failing—"The teacher gave me something too hard/wouldn't help me/didn't tell me how to do it" or "Johnny was bothering me" are examples of external locus of control. Blaming conditions, e.g. "It was too dark/hot/cold/noisy/the sun was in my eyes" is also external. Individuals may also attribute successes externally: "The teacher helped me" or "Johnny showed me how" or "I was lucky." Blaming/crediting oneself for failure/success is internal locus of control: "I didn't study the new words" or "I'm stupid" with failures or "I worked hard"/"I'm smart" with successes.

First Stage of Freud's Psychoanalytic Theory of Personality Development

Freud's orientation toward personality development was psychosexual. He believed the most important factors were the focus of erotic energy, which shifted in each developmental stage, and the child's early relationship with parents. Freud formulated five stages of development: Oral, Anal, Phallic, Latency, and Genital. He found if infants and children successfully complete each stage, they are well-adjusted; if not, they become fixated on one stage. Freud said infants from birth to 18 months are in the first Oral stage: their focus of pleasure is on the mouth as they suck to nurse. If a baby's oral need to nurse is met appropriately, s/he will progress to the following stage. However, if an infant's feeding needs are met either inadequately or excessively, s/he can develop an oral fixation. Signs of this in later life include tendencies to overeat, drink too much, smoke, bite one's nails, talk excessively, and other orally focused activities. Oral personalities either become overly dependent and gullible; or, when resisting oral compulsions, become pessimistic and aggressive to others.

Second Stage of Freud's Psychoanalytic Theory of Personality Development

Freud's theory divided personality development into five stages, each based on the corresponding erogenous zone: Oral, Anal, Phallic, Latency, and Genital. Infants 0–18 months are in the Oral stage as the focus is on nursing. Children 18–36 months are in the second Anal stage. The focus of pleasure sensations is on the anus as they are engaged in toilet training. Society and parents demand they control retaining/expelling waste; they must learn to control anal stimulation. This can be a power struggle between child and parents. Children this age are also learning to assert their individual independence and will, mirroring the battle of wills over toileting. Success contributes to healthy development; when unsuccessful, individuals develop anal fixation. Signs of this in later life take two extremes: those who resisted parental control and asserted personal control by retaining their feces develop anal-retentive personalities, becoming rigid, controlling, and overly preoccupied with neatness and cleanliness. Conversely, those who asserted themselves by expelling their feces develop anal-expulsive personalities, with sloppy, messy, disorganized, defiant behavior.

Effect of the Oedipal Conflict on Later Development

In his theory of personality development, Freud placed children ages 3–6 in his third Phallic stage when pleasure is focused on the genitals. He proposed that boys undergo an Oedipal conflict at this age, which he named after Greek tragedian Sophocles' Oedipus Rex, wherein the title character killed his father and married his mother. He said a boy unconsciously desires his mother, competing for her affection with his father, which equals aggression toward the father, and fears retaliation by the father through castration. He resolves these unacceptable impulses by "identifying with the aggressor," wanting to be like his father. Unsuccessful conflict resolution/fixation leads to later confusion/weakness of sexual identity, and either excessive or insufficient sexual activity. Because Freud focused only on males, later psychologists proposed a female counterpart, the Electra conflict. They pointed out how girls at the same ages become "Daddy's girls," often rejecting their mothers, and then around ages 4–5 want to be "just like Mommy," adopting feminine behaviors, paralleling male development. Freud rejected this notion.

Functions of the Basic Personality Structures in Freud's Developmental Theory

Freud proposed that the personality is governed by three structures or forces: the Id, the Ego, and the Superego. The Id, the "pleasure principle," represents the source of our powerful, instinctual urges, such as sexual and aggressive impulses. It is necessary as it energizes us to act, but cannot go unrestrained. The Ego, the "reality principle," represents our sense of self within reality. It is necessary for telling us what will happen if we act on the Id's impulses and knowing how to control them to protect ourselves. The Superego, the "conscience," represents our sense of morality. It is necessary when Ego protects ourselves but not others, so we also control our social interactions to be ethical and nonharmful to others. For example, when a young child sees a cookie or a toy belonging to someone else, his Id says, "I want that." His Ego says, "If I take that and get caught, I will be in trouble." His Superego says, "Whether I get caught or not, stealing is wrong."

Third Stage of Freud's Psychoanalytic Theory of Personality Development

Freud described developmental stages as focusing on particular erogenous zones. Nursing infants are in his Oral stage; toilet-training toddlers are in his Anal stage. His third stage, when children are aged 3–6 years, is the Phallic stage. Pleasure is focused on the genitals as children discover these. Freud focused his theory on males, proposing that at this age, boys develop unconscious sexual desires for their mothers and corresponding unconscious rivalries with their fathers for mother's attention. The rivalry represents aggression toward the father. Therefore they also unconsciously fear retaliation by the father in the form of castration. Freud named this the Oedipal conflict after the Greek tragic hero Oedipus, who unwittingly slew his father and married his mother. Since these unconscious impulses are socially unacceptable, boys resolve the conflict through a process Freud called "identification with the aggressor." This explains the common behavior of boys around ages 4–5, imitating and wanting to be "just like Daddy." They repress desires for mother and adopt masculine characteristics.

Fourth and Fifth Stages of Freud's Psychoanalytic Theory of Personality Development

Each of the stages in Freud's theory centered on an erogenous zone. Infants are in the Oral stage as they nurse; toddlers in the Anal stage as they are toilet-trained; preschoolers are in the Phallic stage as they focus on genital discovery, unconscious sexual impulses toward their opposite-sex parent, and unconscious aggressive impulses toward their same-sex parent, and resolving conflicts over these urges. Freud labeled the stage when children are six years old to puberty the Latency stage. During this time, children begin school. They are occupied with making new friends, developing new social skills; participating in learning, developing new academic skills; and learning school rules, developing acceptable societal behaviors. Freud said that children in the Latency stage repress their sexual impulses, deferring them while developing their cognitive and social skills takes priority. Thus sexuality is latent. From puberty on, children are in Freud's Genital stage, when sexuality reemerges with physical maturation and adolescents are occupied with developing intimate relationships with others.

Ego Defense Mechanisms of Freud's Psychoanalytic Theory of Personality Development

Freud identified and described many ego defense mechanisms in his theory. He said these are ways the ego finds to cope with impulses threatening it, and hence the person. Just a few of these that can be apparent in young children's behavior include the following. Regression—for example, if a child has received parental attention exclusively for four years, but then the parents introduce a new baby, not only is parental attention divided between two children, but the baby naturally needs and gets more attention by being a helpless infant. If the child feels displaced/threatened by the younger sibling, s/he may regress from normal four-year-old behaviors to more infantile ones in a bid for similar attention. Projection—if a child feels threatened by experiencing inner aggressive impulses, e.g. hating another person, s/he may project these feelings onto that person, accusing, "You hate me!" Denial—if a child cannot accept feelings triggered by losing a loved one through divorce or death, s/he may deny reality: "S/he will come back."

Key Differences Between Freud's and Erikson's Developmental Theories

Erikson's theory was based on Freud's, but whereas Freud's focus was psychosexual, Erikson's was psychosocial. Both emphasized early parent-child relationships. Freud believed the personality was essentially formed in childhood and proposed five stages through puberty and none thereafter; Erikson depicted lifelong development through nine stages. Each stage centers on a "nuclear conflict" to resolve, with positive/negative outcomes of successful/unsuccessful resolutions. Erikson's first, infancy stage (birth—18 months) is Basic Trust vs. Mistrust. When an infant's basic needs—such as being fed, changed, bathed, held/cuddled, having discomfort relieved, and receiving attention, affection, and interaction are met sufficiently and consistently, the baby develops basic trust in the world, gaining a sense of security, confidence, and optimism. The positive outcomes are hope and drive; negative outcomes are withdrawal and sensory distortion. If infant needs are inadequately and/or inconsistently met, the baby develops basic mistrust, with a sense of insecurity, worthlessness, and pessimism.

Second Stage in Erikson's Psychosocial Theory of Human Development

In each of Erikson's developmental stages, a central conflict must be resolved; success/failure dictates outcomes. Babies first develop basic trust or mistrust in the world during the first stage. Toddlers are in Erikson's second stage of Autonomy vs. Shame and Self-Doubt. In this stage, children 18 months—3 years are learning muscular control (walking, toilet-training) and developing moral senses of right/wrong. As they gain skills, they want to do more things independently, and they begin to assert their individual wills. Parents are familiar with the associated tantrums, "No!" and other common "Terrible Twos" behaviors. Children receiving appropriate parenting during this stage develop a sense of autonomy through being allowed to attempt tasks realistic for them; to fail and try again; and eventually to master them. Positive outcomes are will/willpower and self-control; negative outcomes are impulsivity and compulsion. Children with parenting at either extreme—being ignored and given no guidance or support; or overly controlled/directed, having everything done for them and never allowed freedom—develop shame, doubting their abilities.

Third Stage in Erikson's Psychosocial Theory of Human Development

Each of Erikson's nine developmental stages involves a "nuclear crisis" the individual must resolve; success or failure results in positive or negative outcomes. Babies develop basic trust or mistrust; toddlers develop autonomy or shame and self-doubt. Erikson's third stage, Initiative vs. Guilt, involves preschoolers. At this age, young children are exploring the environment further commensurately with their increasing physical/motor, cognitive, emotional, and social skills. They exercise imagination in make-believe/pretend play and pursue adventure. Having gained some control over their bodies in the previous stage, they now attempt to exercise control over their environments. When they succeed in this stage, the positive outcomes are purpose and direction. Children who receive adult disapproval for exerting control over their surroundings—either because they try to use too much control or because parents are overly controlling—feel guilt. Negative outcomes include excessive inhibition against taking action or ruthless, inconsiderate behavior at the opposite extreme.

Fourth Stage in Erikson's Psychosocial Theory of Human Development

Erikson formulated nine stages encompassing the entire human lifespan. The fourth stage corresponds to the end of the early childhood years, when children begin formal schooling. Erikson named this stage, which lasts from around ages 5–6 to puberty, Industry vs. Inferiority. Children in this stage are primarily occupied with learning new academic and social competencies as they attend school, meet more peers and adults, make new friends, and learn to interact in a wider environment. Whereas the focus of Stage 2, Autonomy vs. Shame and Doubt, was self-control and parents were the main relationship; and the focus of Stage 3, Initiative vs. Guilt, was environmental exploration and family was the main relationship; in Stage 4, Industry vs. Inferiority, the focus is on achievements and accomplishments. Friends, neighbors, school, and teachers are the most important relationships. Children's successful resolutions bring positive outcomes of competence and method; negative outcomes are narrowness of abilities and inertia (lack of activity).

Children's Development of Sexual/Gender Identification

Freud's View of Children's Development of Sexual/Gender Identification

While different psychological theories/schools of thought agree that sex as a social identity develops through the process of identification, they have different views and explanations for how children develop their social identities as boys or girls. In Freud's view, gender identity develops through processes of differentiation and affiliation. He said once children observe that certain other people have characteristics in common with themselves, they "endeavor to mold the ego after one that had been taken as a model." In other words, they identify with similar other people and try to attain the same attributes. Freud proposed that boys resolve their Oedipal conflicts through identification with the aggressor, i.e. adopting their fathers' characteristics and suppressing sexual impulses toward their mothers. While he focused exclusively on males in this respect, Neo-Freudian psychologists later proposed a female counterpart, the Electra conflict, wherein girls resolve desires for fathers by identifying with mothers and adopting their characteristics. In either case, children differentiate from their opposite-sex parent and identify/affiliate with their same-sex parent.

Explanation of Social Learning and Behaviorist Theories

Albert Bandura and other proponents of social learning theory maintain that children learn through a process of observing other people's behavior, observing certain behaviors of others that are rewarded, and then imitating those behaviors to obtain similar rewards. The concept of rewards reinforcing behaviors, i.e. increasing the probability of repeating them, comes from behaviorism or learning theory. Social learning theory is based on behaviorism, but includes additional emphasis on the ideas that learning occurs within a social context and that social interactions are primary influences on learning. According to social learning theory, children observe that males and females engage in different behaviors. They additionally observe that boys and girls receive different rewards for their behaviors. Based on these observations, children then imitate the behaviors appropriate to their own sex that they have seen rewarded in others of their sex to obtain the same rewards. Both behaviorist and social learning theories view gender identity development as being environmentally shaped by consequences; social learning theory focuses on the social environment.

Kohlberg's Cognitive-Developmental Theory

Kohlberg had developed a cognitive theory of moral development, based upon and expanding the concepts of morality Piaget included in his theory of cognitive development. Kohlberg also proposed a cognitive-developmental approach to children's acquisition of sex/gender roles. Piaget and Kohlberg discussed classification or categorization as one of the cognitive abilities that children develop. Just as they learn to categorize various things, e.g. foods, animals, people, etc., they learn that people include female and male categories. They then learn to categorize themselves as either female/girls or male/boys. When children are around 2 years old, they each begin to develop their distinctive sense of self. Once they have differentiated self from the rest of the world, they also begin to be able to develop complex mental concepts. These abilities enable them to develop self-concepts of gender. According to the cognitive-developmental view, once children have developed concepts of their sex/gender, these are maintained despite social contexts and are difficult to change.

Contribution of Psychoanalytic Theory to Early Childhood Care and Educational Practices

In his development of psychoanalytic theory, Freud (a physician) identified stages of childhood development according to the particular bodily zones where pleasure is focused during each age period. This identification still regularly informs early childhood care and educational practices. For example, infants are in the Oral stage, when nursing provides pleasure as well as nutrition and satisfying hunger. Knowing this, caregivers recognize that babies begin exploring their environments through oral routes. They thus will not punish mouthing of objects; will anticipate and prevent mouthing of unsafe/unsanitary objects; provide suitable objects and activities for oral inspection and orally oriented rewards. Toddlers engaged in toilet-training are in Freud's Anal stage. As they learn to control their bladders and bowels, they also learn to control their impulses and behaviors. Adults knowing this recognize toddlers' willful, stubborn behaviors as normal parts of the process of establishing individual identities and asserting their wishes. Thus, they will not punish these behaviors harshly/inappropriately, but strike a balance between permitting exploration and providing limits, guidance, and support.

Application of Freud's Third Stage of Psychoanalytic Theory

According to Freud's theory, preschoolers are in his Phallic stage of psychosexual development. This is the time when they discover their own genitals, so caregivers and educators knowing this will not be distressed at young children's attention to and manipulation of their genitals, and their curiosity and interest in others' genitals as these are not abnormal (unless excessive). Adults who are also aware of Freud's Oedipal conflict in boys and other Neo-Freudian psychologists' corresponding Electra conflict in girls should be neither surprised nor upset when little boys first focus more attention on mothers/female caregivers, and later abandon these attentions to focus on imitating fathers/male caregivers. Freud would say they are demonstrating the Oedipal desire for the mother, which includes fear of castration by the father, and then resolving this conflict through identification with the aggressor/father. Neo-Freudians would say little girls are undergoing a similar process in favoring their fathers and subsequently identifying with their mothers.

Fourth Stage of Psychosexual Development of Freud's Psychoanalytic Theory of Personality Development

Freud theorized that children are in his fourth Latency stage of development at around the same ages when they begin to attend formal schooling. Since Freud's emphasis on development was psychosexual, he identified an erogenous zone where pleasure was focused in each stage of development. The mouth, anus, and genitals are erogenous zones central to Freud's other developmental stages. However, in the stage he termed Latency, there is no erogenous zone of focus. This is because Freud believed that children's sexuality is repressed or submerged during this period. The child's attention is occupied at this time with learning new social and academic skills in the new environment of the school setting. Adults familiar with Freud's basic psychoanalytic concepts realize that children's focus shifts from their relationships with parents to their relationships with friends, classmates, teachers, and other adults during the Latency stage. Children are not rejecting/abandoning parents, but responding to widening social environments. They are more able to learn academic concepts and structures and more complex social interactions and behaviors.

Salient Characteristics of Piaget's Second Stage of Child Cognitive Development

Piaget's second cognitive-developmental stage is Preoperational. Toddlers and preschoolers in this stage typically begin to recognize rudimentary symbolic representation, i.e. that some objects represent other things. This understanding of symbols allows them to begin using words to represent things, people, feelings, and thoughts. Adults can support early childhood language development by frequently conversing with young children, reading books to them, introducing and explaining new vocabulary words, and playing games involving naming and classifying things. Children in this stage also begin pretend/make-believe play through understanding symbols; adults can encourage and support this play, which develops imagination and planning abilities. Preoperational children's thinking is intuitive, not logical; adults understanding this will not expect them to follow/use logical sequences such as doing arithmetic, as they cannot yet perform mental operations. Adults familiar with Piaget's concept of egocentrism realize Preoperational children cannot see others' viewpoints. They thus engage children's attention/interest by beginning from topics related to children's personal selves and activities.

Magical Thinking Concept of Piaget's Theory of Cognitive Development

According to Piaget, magical thinking is the belief that one's thoughts make external events happen. He identified this as a common characteristic of the way children in his Preoperational stage think. Piaget said that preschool children have not yet developed the cognitive ability to perform mental operations. Because they cannot follow or apply logical thought processes, their thinking is irrational and intuitive rather than organized and based on real-world, empirical observations. For example, a Preoperational child may believe that something good happened because s/he wished hard enough for it. Preschoolers also commonly believe their saying/thinking/feeling/wishing something bad toward another caused the other's misfortune. They often blame themselves for divorce or death in the family, thinking these happened because they were "bad." Adults should explain to young children that what they wished, thought, felt, or said did not cause good or bad events, and reassign causes external to the child, e.g. "Mommy and Daddy were not getting along with each other"/"Grandpa was sick"/"It was an accident, not anybody's fault."

Major Characteristics of Piaget's Theory of Cognitive Development

According to Piaget's theory, infants are in the Sensorimotor stage of cognitive development. This means they learn through sensory input they get from the environment, motor actions they perform, and environmental feedback they receive from those actions. They also eventually coordinate their actions and reactions. For example, babies hear and attend to sounds; visually locate sound sources; and learn that some objects make sounds, like rattles. They learn to reach for, grasp, and manipulate objects. They learn when they shake a rattle, it makes a sound, and then repeat this action purposefully to generate the sound. Adults knowing these characteristics will provide infants with many toys they can manipulate, including toys that make noises/music, spin/twirl, or roll/bounce/fly; experiences affording input through all sensory modalities; and positive reinforcement when babies discover new body parts, objects, sights, sounds, textures, smells, and tastes; and demonstrate new behaviors interacting with these. They will not punish repetitious behaviors, like repeatedly throwing items from cribs/high-chair trays, which are part of learning in this stage.

Piaget's Egocentrism and Animism Concepts of Preoperational Children

Preoperational children are egocentric, i.e. they view everything as revolving around themselves. Adults aware of this understand that most two-year-olds, for example, neither want to share with others nor understand why they should. Egocentrism also means being unable to see others' perspectives. Adults who take this ability for granted may not realize the simplicity of both some early childhood problems and their solutions. For example, when a preschooler does something physically or emotionally hurtful to another, adults can guide identification of consequences: "Look at her face now. How do you think she feels?" and then guide perspective-taking: "How would you feel if somebody hit you like you just hit Sally?" This has not occurred to the preschooler, but once s/he is guided to think of it, it can be a revelation. Animism is Preoperational children's attributing human qualities to inanimate objects. Many children's books and TV shows accordingly appeal to young children by animating letters, numbers, or objects (e.g. SpongeBob SquarePants).

Piaget's New Developments of the Concrete Operations Stage Versus Previous Preoperational Stage

Piaget said that while preschoolers are in the Preoperational stage and do not think logically because they cannot yet perform mental operations, this ability emerges in the Concrete Operations stage, which tends to coincide with elementary school ages. Concrete Operational children can follow and apply logical sequences to concrete objects they can see and manipulate. This is why they can begin learning mathematical concepts and procedures like addition and subtraction, and grammatical paradigms like verb conjugations. While Preoperational children "centrate" or focus on one attribute of an object, like its appearance, Concrete Operational children "decentrate," accommodating multiple attributes, and can perform and reverse mental operations. For example, a Preoperational child can count pennies, but not understand ten pennies spread into a long row equal ten pennies clustered together. Children in Concrete Operations, instead of focusing on appearance, will use logic and simply count the pennies, showing that each group has the same number regardless of how they look.

Conservation in Piaget's Theory of Cognitive Development

Piaget identified conservation as a key ability, which Preoperational preschoolers have not yet developed. Piaget found elementary school-age Concrete Operational children develop conservation—the understanding that an object or substance conserves, or retains, its essential properties despite changes in appearance or configuration. For example, adults know a cup of liquid is the same amount regardless of the size or shape of the container holding it. Preoperational children, seeing equal amounts of liquid poured from a tall thin glass to a short wide one or vice versa, will "centrate" (focus exclusively) on either height or width and say one glass holds more. Concrete operational children know logically that the amounts are equal regardless of container shape/appearance. When asked how they know, they use empirical evidence and logic: "Of course it's the same amount; I just saw you pour it from the tall glass to the short one." A universal phenomenon is that after developing conservation, we take it for granted and cannot remember or believe our earlier Preoperational thinking.

Key Concepts of Bandura's Social Learning Theory

Psychologist Alfred Bandura developed the primary theory of social learning. While his theory incorporates elements of behaviorism in that environmental rewards and punishments that shape the behaviors and learning of children, Bandura focused more on the social dimension of learning in that he found the context of social interactions the most important medium and influence for learning. Bandura's theory also incorporates elements of cognitive theory by emphasizing the roles played by the cognitive processes of attention, memory, and motivation in learning. Bandura found children learn by observing and imitating the behaviors of models, including adults, older children, and peers. He proposed four conditions required for this learning: Attention, Retention, Reproduction, and Motivation. Adults understanding Bandura's theory realize children can learn new behaviors by seeing others be rewarded for performing these, and then imitating them; this greatly expands children's learning potential. Bandura also proved that children viewing violent video content engage in more aggressive behaviors, informing adults of the importance of monitoring and controlling children's exposure to media influences.

How Erikson's First Stage Informs Early Childhood Caregiving

Erikson's theory is based on Freud's, but focuses on psychosocial rather than psychosexual development. Erikson proposed infants are in his first stage, named for its nuclear conflict of Basic Trust vs. Mistrust. Erikson found if an infant's needs are met adequately and consistently, the baby will form a sense of trust in the world; but if they are not fully and/or regularly met, the baby will form a sense of mistrust in the environment and people. Erikson proposed a positive outcome for resolving the nuclear crisis in each stage; in this stage it is Hope. Caregivers understanding this theory and stage will feed a baby on a regular schedule and not leave the child crying from hunger for long times. They will change the baby's diaper timely when needed rather than letting him/her experience discomfort and cry too long. Moreover, caregivers will meet infant needs for interaction, especially holding and cuddling. Making care/nurturing predictable for babies establishes optimism. The negative outcome of Mistrust is linked to worthless feelings, even suicide.

How Erikson's Second Stage Informs Early Childhood Caregiving

Erikson's second stage of psychosocial development centers on the nuclear conflict of Autonomy vs. Shame and Doubt. Toddlers in this stage are engaged in learning to walk and toilet-training, involving motor control and self-control. They are also learning to assert themselves. This is one reason for tantrums characteristic of this age group. Toddlers who begin loudly saying "No!" are not merely obstinate or difficult, but are learning to express their wills. Erikson designated Will as the positive outcome of resolving the conflict in this stage, as well as self-control and courage. Children allowed to use their emerging skills to try things on their own become more independent, developing autonomy. Those not allowed to practice and progress in making choices and/or are made to feel ashamed during toilet-training/while learning other new skills, learn to doubt themselves and their abilities instead of developing independence. Adults appreciating this theory and stage let children express preferences and practice new skills, supplying needed encouragement, support, and positive reinforcement without overly restricting, controlling, or punishing them.

Relation of Erikson's Third Stage to Early Childhood Education

In his theory of psychosocial development, Erikson proposed his third stage revolves around the nuclear conflict of Initiative vs. Guilt. Erikson described 3- to 5-year-olds in this stage as being at the "play age." Having developed the ability for make-believe/pretend play, children imitate parents and other adults in their activities. At these ages, children begin taking the initiative to plan and enact scenarios wherein they play roles and use objects to symbolize other things. Through creating situations and stories, they experiment and identify socially with adult roles and behaviors. They are also more actively exploring their environments. Relationships expand from parents to family. The positive outcome/strength of this stage is Purpose. Children thwarted in fulfilling their natural goals and desires develop the negative outcome of Guilt through adults' punishing them for trying to control their environments and/or adults' controlling them too much. Adults understanding this encourage and support pretend play. They encourage and approve children for initiating activities rather than inhibiting or always directing their actions.

Relation of Erikson's Fourth Stage to Early Childhood Education

Erikson termed the fourth stage of his psychosocial theory of development as centering on the nuclear conflict of Industry vs. Inferiority. Children commonly enter this stage around the years beginning school, also coinciding with the close of the early childhood years. Children at elementary school ages acquire a great many new skills and much new knowledge. This enables them to attempt and accomplish many more things, which they are expected to do in school. Their increased ability and accomplishment engender a positive sense of Industry. Children's most important relationships are no longer only with their parents and family, but with friends, neighbors, classmates, teachers, and other school staff. Hence social interactions are central during this stage. Children feeling unequal to new tasks develop a sense of Inferiority compared to peers. Parents and educators who encourage and reinforce children's desires and attempts to learn and practice new skills and perform tasks help them develop senses of method and competence. Unsupportive/punitive adult responses result in restricted competencies and/or lack of motivation.

Hierarchy of Needs in Maslow's Humanistic Theory of Self-Actualization

Maslow proposed humans are driven by needs, and meeting the most basic needs is prerequisite to meeting more advanced needs. Maslow's needs hierarchy is depicted as a pyramid, with the most fundamental needs at the base. Its five levels are (1) physiological needs: air, water, sleep, and food necessary for survival; (2) security needs: shelter and a safe environment; (3) social needs: feeling loved, receiving affection, and belonging to a family and/or group; (4) esteem needs: feeling personal value, accomplishment, and social recognition; and (5) self-actualizing needs: achieving optimal personal growth and realizing one's full potential. For example, babies and young children must have clean air to breathe and be fed and rested to survive before other needs can be addressed. Children must have safe places to live, then their needs for love and belonging can be met. Once a child feels loved and part of a family/group, s/he can develop self-esteem through accomplishments and feeling valued by society. After satisfying these, children can self-actualize.

Organismic Valuing, Conditions of Worth, the Real Self, the Ideal Self, and Incongruence in Carl Rogers' Theory

Rogers said all organisms naturally pursue a tendency to actualize or make the best of life. Organismic valuing is the natural tendency to value what is healthy, e.g. avoiding bad-tasting foods, which can be poisonous or rotten. Organismic valuing leads to positive regard/esteem, engendering positive self-regard/self-esteem, reflecting what Rogers called the real self—the person one becomes under optimal conditions. Rogers observed society substitutes conditions of worth for organismic valuing, giving us things based not on our needs but on meeting society's required conditions. Children are taught early they will receive something they want on the condition they do what adults want. This establishes conditional positive regard, meaning children only feel esteemed by others on others' conditions; this develops conditional positive self-regard, or self-esteem dependent on others' esteem. This creates an unattainable ideal self-based on others' standards rather than the real self. For Rogers, incongruence between real and ideal self-causes neurosis. Rogers' required qualities for effective therapists—congruence/genuineness, empathy, and respect—are equally effective in early childhood education.

Rogers believed in actualization or realizing one's full potential as did fellow humanist Abraham Maslow. While Maslow applied self-actualization to humans, Rogers applied the "actualization tendency" to all life forms. Rogers gave the name "conditions of worth" to the process he observed whereby others give individuals things based not on need but worthiness. For example, while babies usually receive care based on need, as they grow older, adults establish conditions of worth: children get dessert if they finish dinner/vegetables; they get drinks or snacks after finishing a task/activity/lesson/class; and most significantly, they often get affection on condition of acceptable/desirable behavior. In behaviorism, this is called contingencies of reinforcement: rewards are given contingent on desired behaviors. Rogers would likely disagree with this practice, which he called conditional positive regard. He felt it makes children do what others want, not what they want or need, and teaches them conditional positive self-regard, i.e. self-esteem dependent on external standards. Rogers' remedy was unconditional positive regard—unconditional love and acceptance.

Fundamental Principles of Behaviorist or Learning Theory

Major principles of behaviorism include these: Organisms learn through interacting with the environment. Environmental influences shape behavior. Environmental stimuli elicit responses from organisms. Hypothetical constructs like the mind and/or inner physiological changes are unnecessary for scientifically describing behaviors—everything organisms do, including feeling and thinking. Learning and behavior change are achieved through arranging the learner's environment to elicit certain responses, increasing the probability of repeating those responses by rewarding them (positive reinforcement) and decreasing repetition of unwanted behaviors by punishing (positive punishment) or ignoring them (extinction). Just as Thorndike previously found all animals including humans learn the same way, Skinner also found his principles applied equally to rats, pigeons, and people. His methods have become so popular that early childhood educators routinely give positive reinforcement—verbal praise, treats, and privileges—for performing new skills and demonstrating socially desirable behaviors; teach young children complex tasks in steps (shaping/chaining/task analysis); take away privileges to punish unwanted behaviors (negative punishment); and remove aversive stimuli for complying (negative reinforcement).

Lev Vygotsky and the Zone of Proximal Development

Vygotsky identified an area or range of skills wherein a learner can complete a task s/he could not yet complete independently, given some help. He termed this area the Zone of Proximal Development. Vygotsky found if a child is given assistance, guidance, or support from someone who knows more—especially another child just slightly more advanced in knowledge and/or skills—the first child can not only succeed at a task s/he is still unable to do alone; but that child also learns best through accomplishing something just slightly beyond his/her limits of expertise to do alone. Jerome Bruner coined the term "scaffolding" to describe temporary support that others give learners for achieving tasks. Scaffolding is closely related to the ZPD in that only the amount of support needed is given, and it allows the learner to accomplish things s/he could not complete autonomously. Scaffolding is gradually withdrawn as the child's skills develop, until the child reaches the level of expertise needed to complete the task on his/her own.

Montessori Method

Sections of the Montessori Method of Early Childhood Instruction

The Practical Life area of Montessori classes helps children develop care for self, others, and the environment. Children learn many daily skills, including buttoning, pouring liquids, preparing meals, and cleaning up after meals and activities. The Sensorial area gives young children experience with learning through all five senses. They participate in activities like ordering colors from lightest to darkest; sorting objects from roughest to smoothest texture; and sorting items from biggest to smallest/longest to shortest. They learn to match similar tastes, textures, and sounds. The Language Arts area encourages young children to express themselves in words, and they learn to identify letters, match them with corresponding phonemes (speech sounds), and manually trace their shapes as preparation for learning reading, spelling, grammar, and writing. In the Mathematics and Geometry area, children learn to recognize numbers, count, add, subtract, multiply, divide, and use the decimal system via hands-on learning with concrete materials. In the Cultural Subjects area, children learn science, art, music, movement, time, history, geography, and zoology.

Aspects of the Philosophy of the Montessori Method as a Curriculum Approach

Maria Montessori's method emphasizes children's engagement in self-directed activities, with teachers using clinical observations to act as children's guides. In introducing and teaching concepts, the Montessori Method also employs self-correcting ("autodidactic") equipment. This method focuses on the significance and interrelatedness of all life forms, and the need for every individual to find his/her place in the world and to find meaningful work. Children in Montessori schools learn complex math skills and gain knowledge about diverse cultures and languages. Montessori philosophy puts emphasis on adapting learning environments to individual children's developmental levels. The Montessori Method also believes in teaching both practical skills and abstract concepts through the medium of physical activities. Montessori teachers observe and identify children's movements into sensitive periods when they are best prepared to receive individual lessons in subjects of interest to them that they can grasp readily. Children's senses of autonomy and self-esteem are encouraged in Montessori programs. Montessori instructors also strive to engage parents in their children's education.

General Practices in the Montessori Method

What Montessori calls "work" refers to developmentally appropriate learning materials. These are set out so each student can see the choices available. Children can select items from each of Montessori's five sections: Practical Life, Sensorial, Language Arts, Mathematics and Geometry, and Cultural Subjects. When a child is done with a work, s/he replaces it for another child to use and selects another work. Teachers work one on one with children and in groups; however, the majority of interactions are among children, as Montessori stresses self-directed activity. Not only teachers but also older children help younger ones in learning new skills, so Montessori classes usually incorporate 2- or 3-year age ranges. Depending on students' ages and the individual school, Montessori schooldays are generally half-days, e.g. 9 a.m.–noon or 12:30 p.m. Most Montessori schools also offer afternoon and/or early evening options. Children wanting to "do it myself" benefit from Montessori, as do special-needs children. Individualized attention, independence, and hands-on learning are emphasized. Montessori schools prefer culturally diverse students and teach about diverse cultures.

Schedules of Reinforcement in Behaviorism

Continuous schedules of presenting rewards or punishments are fixed. Fixed ratio schedules involve introducing reinforcement after a set number of instances of the targeted behavior. For example, when asking a preschooler to put away materials, a teacher might present punishment for noncompliance only after making three consecutive requests. The disadvantage is, even young children know they can get away with ignoring the first two requests, only complying just before the third. Fixed interval schedules introduce reinforcement after set time periods. Again, the disadvantages are, even multiply disabled infants quickly learn when to expect reinforcement, rather than associating it with how long they have engaged in a desired behavior; young children only change their behavior immediately before the teacher will observe and reward it. Variable ratio and variable interval schedules apply reinforcement following irregular numbers of responses or irregular time periods, respectively. The advantage of variable schedules is, since children cannot predict when they will receive reinforcements, they are more likely to repeat/continue desired behaviors more and for longer times.

Bank Street Curriculum Approach to Early Childhood Education

Lucy Sprague Mitchell founded the Bank Street Curriculum, applying theoretical concepts from Jean Piaget, Erik Erikson, John Dewey, and others. Bank Street is called a Developmental Interaction Approach. It emphasizes children's rich, direct interactions with wide varieties of ideas, materials, and people in their environments. The Bank Street method gives young children opportunities for physical, cognitive, emotional, and social development through engagement in various types of child care programs. Typically, multiple subjects are included and taught to groups. Children can learn through a variety of methods and at different developmental levels. By interacting directly with their geographical, social, and political environments, children are prepared for lifelong learning through this curriculum. Using blocks, solving puzzles, going on field trips, and doing practical lab work are among the numerous learning experiences Bank Street offers. Its philosophy is that school can simultaneously be stimulating, satisfying, and sensible. School is a significant part of children's lives, where they inquire about and experiment with the environment and share ideas with other children as they mature.

Classroom Characteristics for 5- to 6-Year-Olds

The Bank Street Developmental Interaction Approach to teaching recommends that children at the oldest early childhood ages of 5–6 years should have classrooms that are efficient, organized, conducive to working, and designed to afford them sensory and motor learning experiences. Classrooms should include rich varieties of appealing colors, which tend to energize children's imaginations and activity and encourage them to interact with the surroundings and participate in the environment. "Interest corners" in classrooms are advocated by the Bank Street approach. These are places where children can display their art works, use language, and depict social life experiences. This approach also recommends having multipurpose tables in the classroom that children can use for writing, drawing, and other classroom activities. The Bank Street Developmental Interaction Approach also points out the importance of libraries in schools, not just for supporting classroom content, but for providing materials for children's extracurricular reading.

Requirements and Roles of Classrooms and Teachers

The Bank Street Developmental Interaction Approach requires educators to create well-designed classrooms: this curriculum approach finds children are enabled to develop discipline by growing up in such controlled environments. Teachers are considered to be extremely significant figures in their young students' lives. The Bank Street Approach requires that teachers always treat children with respect, to enable children to develop strong senses of self-respect. Teachers' having faith in their students and believing in their ability to succeed are found to have great impacts on young children's performance and their motivation to excel in school and in life. The Bank Street Curriculum emphasizes the importance of providing transitions from one type of activity to another. It also stresses changing the learning subjects at regular time intervals. This facilitates children's gaining a sense of direction and taking responsibility for what they do. Bank Street views these practices as helping children develop internal self-control, affording them discipline for dealing with the external world.

Froebel's Educational Theory Regarding Learning and Teaching

Froebel, 19th-century inventor of Kindergarten, developed an influential educational theory. He found that observation, discovery, play, and free, self-directed activity facilitated children's learning. He observed that drawing/art activities develop higher level cognitive skills and that virtues are taught through children's games. He also found nature, songs, fables, stories, poems, and crafts effective learning media. He attributed reading and writing development to children's self-expression needs. Froebel recommended activities to develop children's motor skills and stimulate their imaginations. He believed in equal rather than authoritarian teacher-student relationships, and advocated family involvement/collaboration. He pointed out the critical nature of sensory experiences, and the value of life experiences for self-expression. He believed teachers should support students' discovery learning rather than prescribing what to learn. Like Piaget, Dewey, and Montessori, Froebel embraced constructivist learning, i.e. children construct meaning and reality through their interactions with the environment. He stressed the role of parents, particularly mothers, in children's educational processes.

Froebel's Famous Achievement

Friedrich Froebel (1782–1852) invented the original concept and practice of Kindergarten. His theory of education had widespread influences, including using play-based instruction with young children. Froebel's educational theory emphasized the unity of humanity, nature, and God. Froebel believed the success of the individual dictates the success of the race, and that school's role is to direct students' will. He believed nature is the heart of all learning. He felt unity, individuality, and diversity were important values achieved through education. Froebel said education's goals include developing self-control and spirituality. He recommended curricula include math, language, design, art, health, hygiene, and physical education. He noted school's role in social development. According to Froebel, schools should impart meaning to life experiences; show students relationships among external, previously unrelated knowledge; and associate facts with principles. Froebel felt human potential is defined through individual accomplishments. He believed humans generally are productive and creative, attaining completeness and harmony via maturation.

Salient Aspects Regarding Society, Educational Opportunity, and Consensus

Friedrich Froebel originated the concept and practice of Kindergarten (German for "child's garden") in 1837. His educational theory had great influence on early childhood education. Froebel's theory addressed society's role in education. He saw education as defined by the "law of divine unity," which stated that everything is connected and humanity, nature, and God are unified. Froebel believed all developments are by God's plan; he found the social institution of religion an important part of children's education. He emphasized parental and sibling involvement in child education. He theorized that culture is changed not by acquiring ideas, but by the productivity, work, and actions of the individual. Froebel believed all children deserve respect and individual attention; should develop their individual potentials; and can learn, irrespective of social class or religion, providing they are developmentally ready for given specific content. Regarding consensus, Froebel's view was religious: he believed God's supreme plan determined social and moral order. He felt people should share common experiences and learn unity, while also respecting diversity and individuality.

Siegfried Engelmann's Contributions to Early Childhood Education

Engelmann (b. 1931) cofounded the Bereiter-Engelmann Program with Carl Bereiter with funding from the U.S. Office of Education. This project demonstrated the ability of intensive instruction to enhance cognitive skills in disadvantaged preschool-aged children, establishing the Bereiter-Engelmann Preschool Program. Bereiter and Engelmann also conducted experiments reexamining Piaget's theory of cognitive development, specifically concerning the ability to conserve liquid volume. They showed, contrary to Piaget's contention that this ability depended solely on a child's cognitive-developmental stage, it could be taught. Engelmann researched curriculum and instruction, including preschoolers with Down syndrome and children from impoverished backgrounds, establishing the philosophy and methodology of Direct Instruction. He designed numerous reading, math, spelling, language, and writing instruction programs, and also achievement tests, videos, and games. Engelmann worked with Project Head Start and Project Follow Through. The former included his and Wesley Becker's comparison of their Engelmann-Becker model of early childhood instruction with other models in teaching disadvantaged children. The latter is often considered the biggest controlled study ever comparing teaching models and methods.

Engelmann's Methods and Features of His Curricula

In the 1960s, Siegfried Engelmann noted a lack of research into how young children learn. Wanting to find out what kinds of teaching effected retention, and what the extent was of individual differences among young learners, Engelmann conducted research, as Piaget had done, using his own children and those of colleagues and neighbors. With a previous advertising background, Engelmann formed focus groups of preschool children to test-market teaching methods. Main features of the curricula Engelmann developed included emphasizing phonics and computation early in young children's instruction; using a precise logical sequence to teach new skills; teaching new skills in small, separate, "child-sized" pieces; correcting learners' errors immediately; adhering strictly to designated teaching schedules; constantly reviewing to integrate new learning with previously attained knowledge; and scrupulous measurement techniques for assessing skills mastery. To demonstrate the results of his methods for teaching math, Engelmann sent movies he made of these to educational institutions. They showed that with his methods, toddlers could master upper-elementary-grade-level computations, and even simple linear equations.

Direct Instruction Method of Teaching Children

Direct Instruction (DI) is a behavioral method of teaching. Therefore, learner errors receive immediate corrective feedback, and correct responses receive immediate, obvious positive reinforcement. DI has a fast pace—10–14 learner responses per minute overall—affording more attention and less boredom; reciprocal teacher-student feedback; immediate indications of learner problems to teachers; and natural reinforcement of teacher activities. DI thus promotes more mutual student and teacher learning than traditional "one-way" methods. Children are instructed in small groups according to ability levels. Their attention is teacher-focused. Teacher presentations follow scripts designed to give instruction the proper sequence, including prewritten prompts and questions developed through field-testing with real students. These optimized prepared lessons allow teachers to attend to extra instructional and motivational aspects of learning. Cued by teachers, who control the pace and give all learners with varying response rates chances for practice, children respond actively in groups and individually. Small groups are typically seated in semicircles close to teachers, who use visual aids like blackboards and overhead projectors.

Project Follow Through

In 1967, President Lyndon B. Johnson declared his War on Poverty. This initiative included Project Follow Through, funded by the U.S. Office of Education and Office of Economic Opportunity. Research had previously found that Project Head Start, which offered early educational interventions to disadvantaged preschoolers, had definite positive impacts; but these were often short-lived. Project Follow Through was intended to discover how to maintain Head Start's benefits. Siegfried Engelmann and Wesley Becker, who had developed the Engelmann-Becker instructional model, invited others to propose various other teaching models in communities selected to participate in Project Follow Through. The researchers asked parents in each community to choose from among the models provided. The proponents of each model were given funds to train teachers and furnish curriculum. Models found to enhance disadvantaged children's school achievement were to be promoted nationally. Engelmann's Direct Instruction model showed positive results surpassing all other models. However, the U.S. Office of Education did not adopt this or other models found best.

Approaches to Remedial or Compensatory Education

A huge comparative study of curriculum and instruction methods, Project Follow Through incorporated three main approaches: Affective, Basic Skills, and Cognitive. Affective approaches used in Project Follow Through included the Bank Street, Responsive Education, and Open Education models. These teaching models aim to enhance school achievement by emphasizing experiences that raise children's self-esteem, which is believed to facilitate their acquisition of basic skills and higher-order problem-solving skills. Basic Skills approaches included the Southwest Labs, Behavior Analysis, and Direct Instruction models. These models find that mastering basic skills facilitates higher-order cognitive and problem-solving skills, and higher self-esteem. Cognitive approaches included the Parent Education, TEEM, and Cognitively Oriented Curriculum models. These models focus on teaching higher-order problem-solving and thinking skills as the optimal avenue to enhancing school achievement, and to improving lower-order basic skills and self-esteem. Affective and Cognitive models have become popular in most schools of education. Basic Skills approaches are less popular, but are congruent with other, very effective methods of specialized instruction.

Contributions of Constance Kamii to Early Childhood Education

Professor of early childhood education Constance Kamii, of Japanese ancestry, was born in Geneva, Switzerland. She attended elementary school in both Switzerland and Japan, completing secondary school and higher education degrees in the United States. She studied extensively with Jean Piaget, also of Geneva. She worked with the Perry Preschool Project in the 1960s, fueling her subsequent interest in theoretically grounded instruction. Kamii believes in basing early childhood educational goals and objectives upon scientific theory of children's cognitive, social, and moral development; and moreover that Piaget's theory of cognitive development is the sole explanation for child development from birth to adolescence. She has done much curriculum research in the U.S., and published a number of books, on how to apply Piaget's theory practically in early childhood classrooms. Kamii agrees with Piaget that education's overall, long-term goal is developing children's intellectual, social, and moral autonomy. Kamii has said, "A classroom cannot foster the development of autonomy in the intellectual realm while suppressing it in the social and moral realms."

Theoretical Orientation, Philosophy, and Approach of the Kamii-DeVries Approach

Constance Kamii and Rhetta DeVries formulated the Kamii-DeVries Constructivist Perspective model of preschool education. It is closely based upon Piaget's theory of child cognitive development and on the Constructivist theory to which Piaget and others subscribed, which dictates that children construct their own realities through their interactions with the environment. Piaget's particular constructivism included the principle that through their interacting with the world within a logical-mathematical structure, children's intelligence, knowledge, personalities, and morality develop. The Kamii-DeVries approach finds that children learn via performing mental actions, which Piaget called operations, through the vehicle of physical activities. This model favors using teachers experienced in traditional preschool education, who employ a child-centered approach, and establish active learning settings, are in touch with children's thoughts, respond to children from children's perspectives, and facilitate children's extension of their ideas. The Kamii-DeVries model has recently been applied to learning assessments using technology (2003) and to using constructivism in teaching physics to preschoolers (2011).

High/Scope Curriculum

David Weikart and colleagues developed the High/Scope Curriculum in the 1960s and 1970s, testing it in the Perry Preschool and Head Start Projects, among others. The High/Scope philosophy is based on Piaget's Constructivist principles that active learning is optimal for young children; that they need to become involved actively with materials, ideas, people, and events; and that children and teachers learn together in the instructional environment. Weikart and colleagues' early research focused on economically disadvantaged children, but the High/Scope approach has since been extended to all young children and all kinds of preschool settings. This model recommends dividing classrooms into well-furnished, separate "interest areas," and regular daily class routines affording children time to plan, implement, and reflect upon what they learn, and to participate in large and small group activities. Teachers establish socially supportive atmospheres; plan group learning activities; organize settings and set daily routines; encourage purposeful child activities, problem-solving, and verbal reflection; and interpret child behaviors according to High/Scope's key child development experiences.

High/Scope Curriculum's Key Experiences for Preschoolers

The High/Scope Curriculum, developed by David P. Weikart and colleagues, takes a constructivist approach influenced by Piaget's theory, advocating active learning. The High/Scope curriculum model identified a total of 58 "key experiences" it finds critical for preschool child development and learning. These key experiences are subdivided into ten main categories: (1) Creative representation, which includes recognizing symbolic use, imitating, and playing roles; (2) Language and literacy, which include speaking, describing, scribbling, and narrating/dictating stories; (3) Initiative and social relations, including solving problems, making decisions and choices, and building relationships; (4) Movement, including activities like running, bending, stretching, and dancing; (5) Music, which includes singing, listening to music, and playing musical instruments; (6) Classification, which includes sorting objects, matching objects or pictures, and describing object shapes; (7) Seriation, or arranging things in prescribed orders (e.g. by size or number); (8) Numbers, which for preschoolers focuses on counting; (9) Space, which involves activities like filling and emptying containers; and (10) Time, including concepts of starting, sequencing, and stopping actions.

Technology Use, School Day Durations and Settings, and Targets for Its Application

The High/Scope Curriculum frequently incorporates computers as regular program components, including developmentally appropriate software, for children to access when they choose. School days may be full-day or part-day, determined by each individual program. Flexible hours accommodate individual family needs and situations. High/Scope programs work in both child care and preschool settings. High/Scope was originally designed to enhance educational outcomes for young children considered at-risk due to socioeconomically disadvantaged, urban backgrounds, and was compatible with Project Head Start. This model of early childhood curriculum and instruction advocates individualizing teaching to each child's developmental level and pace of learning. As such, the High/Scope approach is found to be effective for children who have learning disabilities, and also for children with developmental delays. It works well with all children needing individual attention. High/Scope is less amenable to highly structured settings that use more adult-directed instruction.

Head Start Program

Head Start was begun in 1964, extended by the Head Start Act of 1981, and revised in its 2007 reauthorization. It is a program of the U.S. Department of Health and Human Services designed to give low-income families and their young children comprehensive services of health, nutrition, education, and parental involvement. While Head Start was initially intended to "catch up" low-income children over the summer to reach kindergarten readiness, it soon became obvious that a six-week preschool program was inadequate to compensate for having lived in poverty for one's first five years. Hence the Head Start Program was expanded and modified over the years with the aim of remediating the effects of system-wide poverty upon child educational outcomes. Currently, Head Start gives local public, private, nonprofit, and for-profit agencies grants for delivering comprehensive child development services to promote disadvantaged children's school readiness by improving their cognitive and social development. It particularly emphasizes developing early reading and math abilities preschoolers will need for school success.

Genesis and Rationale of the Head Start Program

The Early Head Start program developed as an outgrowth of the original Head Start Program. Head Start initially aimed to remediate the deprivation of poor preschool-aged children by providing educational services over the summer to help them attain school readiness by kindergarten. Because educators and researchers soon discovered the summer program was insufficient to make up for poor children's lack of preparation, Head Start was expanded to become more comprehensive. Head Start was established in 1964 and expanded by the Head Start Act in 1981. After research had accumulated considerable evidence of how important children's earliest years are to their ensuing growth and development, the U.S. Department of Health and Human Services Administration for Children and Families' Office of Head Start established the Early Head Start Program in 1995. Early Head Start works to improve prenatal health; improve infant and toddler development; and enhance healthy family functioning. It serves children from 0–3 years. Like the original program, Early Head Start stresses parental engagement in children's growth, development, and learning.

Emergent Literacy Theory

Emergent Literacy Versus Reading Readiness

Historically, early childhood educators viewed "reading readiness" as a time during young children's literacy development when they were ready to start learning to read and write, and taught literacy accordingly. However, in the late 20th and early 20th centuries, research has found that children have innate learning capacities and that skills emerge under the proper conditions. Educational researchers came to view language as developing gradually within a child rather than a child's being ready to read at a certain time. Thus, the term "emergent" came to replace "readiness," while "literacy" replaced "reading" as referring to all of language's interrelated aspects of listening, speaking, writing, and viewing, as well as reading. Traditional views of literacy were based only on children's reading and writing in ways similar to those of adults. However, more recently, the theory of emergent literacy has evolved through the findings of research into the early preschool reading of young children and their and their families' associated characteristics.

Emergent Literacy Theory's Principles About How Young Children Learn to Read and Write

Through extensive research, emergent literacy theorists have found that: (1) Young children develop literacy through being actively involved in reading and rereading their favorite storybooks. When preschoolers "reread" storybooks, they have not memorized them; rather, theorists find this activity to exemplify young children's reconstruction of a book's meaning. Similarly, young children's invented spellings are examples of their efforts to reconstruct what they know of written language; they can inform us about a child's familiarity with specific phonetic components. (2) Adults' reading to children, no matter how young, is crucial to literacy development. It helps children gain a "feel" for the character, flow, and patterns of written/printed language, and an overall sense of what reading feels like and entails. It fosters positive attitudes toward reading in children, strongly motivating them to read when they begin school. Being read to also helps children develop print awareness and formulate concepts of books and reading. (3) Influenced by Piaget and Vygotsky, emergent literacy theory views reading and writing as developmental processes having successive stages.

Perspective Regarding Instructional Models

The emergent literacy theoretical perspective yields an instructional model for the learning and teaching of reading and writing in young children that is founded on building instruction from the child's knowledge. Emergent literacy theory's assumption is that young children already know a lot about language and literacy by the time they enter school. This theory furthermore regards even 2- and 3-year-olds as having information about how the reading and writing processes function, and as having already formed particular ideas about what written/printed language is. From this perspective, emergent literacy theory then dictates that teaching should build upon what a child already knows and should support the child's further literacy development. Researchers conclude that teachers should furnish open-ended activities allowing children to show what they already know about literacy; to apply that knowledge; and to build upon it. From the emergent literacy perspective, teachers take the role of creating a learning environment with conditions that are conducive to children's learning in ways that are ideally self-motivated, self-generated, and self-regulated.

How Babies and Young Children Learn to Read and Write

(1) According to the theory of emergent literacy, even infants encounter written language. Two- and three-year-old's commonly can identify logos, labels, and signs in their homes and communities. Also, young children's scribbles show features/appearances of their language's specific writing system even before they can write. For example, Egyptian children's scribbles look more like Egyptian writing; American children's scribbles look more like English writing. (2) Young children learn to read and write concurrently, not sequentially; the two abilities are closely interrelated. Moreover, though with speech, receptive language comprehension seems easier/sooner to develop than expressive language production, this does not apply to reading and writing: first learning activities involving writing are found easier for preschoolers than those involving reading. (3) Research finds that form follows function, not the opposite: young children's

literacy learning is mostly through meaningful, functional, purposeful/goal-directed real-life activities. Literacy comprises not isolated, abstract skills learned for their own sake, but rather authentic skills applied to accomplish real-life purposes, the way children observe adults using literacy.

Developmentally Inappropriate Kindergarten and Preschool Literacy Practices

Research finds some preschools are like play centers, but not optimal for literacy because their curricula exclude natural reading and writing activities. Researchers have also identified a trend in many kindergartens to ensure children's "reading readiness" by providing highly academic programs, influencing preschool curricula to get children "ready" for such kindergartens. Influenced and even pressured by kindergarten programs' academic expectations, parents have also come to expect preschools to prepare their children for kindergarten. However, experts find applying elementary-school programs to kindergartens and preschools developmentally inappropriate. Formal instruction in reading and writing and worksheets are not suitable for younger children. Instead, research finds print-rich preschool environments both developmentally appropriate and more effective. For example, when researchers changed classrooms from having a "book corner" to having a centrally located table with books plus paper, pencils, envelopes, and stamps, children spent 3 to 10 times more time on direct reading and writing activities. Children are found to take naturally to these activities without prior formal reading and writing lessons.

Planning a Play-Based Curriculum

To plan a curriculum based on children's natural play with building blocks (Hoisington, 2008), a teacher can first arrange the environment to stimulate further such play. Then s/he can furnish materials for children to make plans/blueprints for and records and models of buildings they construct. The teacher can make time during the day for children to reflect upon and discuss their individual and group building efforts. Teachers can also utilize teaching strategies that encourage children to reflect on and consider in more depth the scientific principles related to their results. A teacher can provide building materials of varied sizes, shapes, textures, and weights, and props to add realism, triggering more complex structures and creative, dramatic, emotional, and social development. Teachers can take photos of children's structures as documents for discussions, stimulating language and vocabulary development. Supplying additional materials to support and stick together blocks extends play-based learning. Active teacher participation by offering observations and asking open-ended questions promotes children's standards-based learning of scientific, mathematical, and linguistic concepts, processes, and patterns.

Supporting and Integrating Standards-Based Learning in Scientific, Mathematical, and Linguistic Domains

When children play at building with blocks, for example, they investigate material properties such as various block shapes, sizes, and weights and the stability of carpet vs. hard floor as bases. They explore cause-and-effect relationships; make conclusions regarding the results of their trial-and-error experiments; draw generalizations about observed patterns; and form theories about what does and does not work to build high towers. Ultimately, they construct their knowledge of how reality functions. Teachers support this by introducing relevant learning standards in the play context meaningful to children. For example, math standards including spatial awareness, geometry, number, operations, patterns, and measurement can be supported through planning play. By encouraging and guiding children's discussion and documentation of their play constructions, and supplying nonfictional and fictional books about building, a teacher also integrates learning goals and objectives for language and literacy development. Teachers can plan activities specifically to extend learning in these domains, like counting blocks;

comparison/contrast; matching; sorting; sequencing; phonological awareness; alphabetic awareness; print awareness; book appreciation; listening, comprehension, speech, and communication.

Using Thematic Teaching Units

To develop a thematic teaching unit, a teacher designs a collection of related activities around certain themes or topics that crosses several curriculum areas or domains. Thematic units create learning environments for young children that promote all children's active engagement, as well as their process learning. By studying topics children find relevant to their own lives, thematic units build upon children's preexisting knowledge and current interests, and also help them relate information to their own life experiences. Varied curriculum content can be more easily integrated through thematic units, in ways that young children can understand and apply meaningfully. Children's diverse individual learning styles are also accommodated through thematic units. Such units involve children physically in learning; teach them factual information in greater depth; teach them learning process-related skills, i.e. "learning how to learn"; holistically integrate learning; encourage cohesion in groups; meet children's individual needs; and provide motivation to both children and their teachers.

Project Approach

The Project Approach (Katz and Chard, 1989) entails having young children choose a topic interesting to them, studying this topic, researching it, and solving problems and questions as they emerge. This gives children greater practice with creative thinking and problem-solving skills, which supports greater success in all academic and social areas. For example, if a class of preschoolers shows interest in the field of medicine, their teacher can plan a field trip to a local hospital to introduce a project studying medicine in depth. During the trip, the teacher can write down/record children's considerations and questions, and then use these as guidelines to plan and conduct relevant activities that will further stimulate the children's curiosity and imagination. Throughout this or any other in-depth project, the teacher can integrate specific skills for reading, writing, math, science, social studies, and creative thinking. This affords dual benefits: enabling both children's skills advancement, and their gaining knowledge they recognize is required and applies in their own lives. Children become life-long learners with this recognition.

Integrated Curriculum and Early Childhood Education

An integrated curriculum organizes early childhood education to transcend the boundaries between the various domains and subject content areas. It unites different curriculum elements through meaningful connections to allow study of wider areas of knowledge. It treats learning holistically and mirrors the interactive nature of reality. The principle that learning consists of series of interconnections is the foundation for teaching through use of an integrated curriculum. Benefits of integrated curricula include an organized planning mechanism; greater flexibility; and the ability to teach many skills and concepts effectively, include more varied content, and enable children to learn most naturally. By identifying themes children find most interesting, teachers can construct webs of assorted themes, which can provide the majority of their curriculum. Research has proven the effectiveness of integrated teaching units for both children and their teachers. Teachers can also integrate new content into existing teaching units they have identified as effective. Integrated units enable teachers to ensure children are learning pertinent knowledge and applying it to real-life situations.

Skills, Topics, Strategies, and Benefits Related to Creating Thematically-Based Teaching Units

EC teachers can incorporate many skills into units organized by theme. This includes state governments' educational standards/benchmarks for various skills. Teachers can base units on topics of interest to young children, e.g. building construction, space travel, movie-making, dinosaurs, vacations, nursery rhymes, fairy tales, pets, wildlife, camping, the ocean, and studies of particular authors and book themes. Beginning with a topic that motivates the children is best; related activities and skills will naturally follow. In planning units, teachers should establish connections among content areas like literacy, physical activity, dramatic play, art, music, math, science, and social studies. Making these connections permits children's learning through their strongest/favored modalities and supports learning through meaningful experiences, which is how they learn best. Theme-based approaches effectively address individual differences and modality-related strengths, as represented in Gardner's theory of Multiple Intelligences. Thematic approaches facilitate creating motivational learning centers and hands-on learning activities, and are also compatible with creating portfolio assessments and performance-based assessments. Teachers can encompass skill and conceptual benchmarks for specific age/developmental levels within engaging themes.

Guidelines for Indoor and Outdoor Space Use

Indoor and outdoor EC learning environments should be safe, clean, and attractive. They should include at least 35' square indoors and 75' square outdoors of usable play space per child. Staff must have access to prepare spaces before children's arrival. Gyms/other larger indoor spaces can substitute if outdoor spaces are smaller. The youngest children should be given separate outdoor times/places. Outdoor scheduling should ensure enough room, plus prevent altercations/competition among different age groups. Teachers can assess if enough space exists by observing children's interactions and engagement in activities. Children's products and other visuals should be displayed at child's-eye level. Spaces should be arranged to allow individual, small-group, and large-group activity. Space organization should create clear pathways enabling children to move easily among activities without overly disturbing others, should promote positive social interactions and behaviors; and activities in each area should not distract children in other areas.

Arrangement of Learning Environments

Arranging Indoor Learning Environments According to Curricular Activities

EC experts indicate that rooms should be organized to enable various activities, but not necessarily to limit activities to certain areas. For example, mathematical and scientific preschool activities may occur in multiple parts of a classroom, though the room should still be laid out to facilitate their occurrence. Sufficient space for infants to crawl and toddlers to toddle are necessary, as are both hard and carpeted floors. Bolted-down/heavy, sturdy furniture is needed for infants and toddlers to use for pulling up, balancing, and cruising. Art and cooking activities should be positioned near sinks/water sources for cleanup. Designating separate areas for activities like block-building, book-reading, musical activities, and dramatic play facilitates engaging in each of these. To allow ongoing project work and other age-appropriate activities, school-aged children should have separate areas. Materials should be appropriate for each age group and varied. Equipment/materials for sensory stimulation, manipulation, construction, active play, dramatic play, and books, recordings, and art supplies, all arranged for easy, independent child access and rotated for variety, are needed.

Arranging Learning Environments to Children's Personal, Privacy, and Sensory Needs

In any EC learning environment, the indoor space should include easily identifiable places where children and adults can store their personal belongings. Since EC involves children in groups for long time periods, they should be given indoor and outdoor areas allowing solitude and privacy while still easily permitting adult supervision. Playhouses and tunnels can be used outdoors, small interior rooms and partitions indoors. Environments should include softness in various forms like grass outdoors; carpet, pillows, and soft chairs indoors; adult laps to sit in and be cuddled; and soft play materials like clay, Play-Doh, finger paints, water, and sand. While noise is predictable, even desirable in EC environments, undue noise causing fatigue and stress should be controlled by noise-absorbing elements like rugs/carpets, drapes, acoustical ceilings and other building materials. Outdoor play areas supplied/arranged by school/community playgrounds should be separated from roadways and other hazards by fencing and/or natural barriers. Awnings can substitute for hills, and inclines/ramps for shade, when these are not naturally available. Surfaces and equipment should be varied.

Principles Related to Early Childhood Behavior Management

Repetition and consistency are two major elements for managing young children's behavior. Adults must always follow and enforce whichever rules they designate. They must also remember that they will need to repeat their rules over and over to make them effective. Behaviorism has shown it is more powerful to reward good behaviors than punish bad behaviors. Consistently rewarding desired behaviors enables young children to make the association between behavior and reward. Functional behavior analysis can inform adults: knowing the function of a behavior is necessary to changing it. For example, if a toddler throws a tantrum out of frustration, providing support/scaffolding for a difficult task, breaking it down to more manageable increments via task analysis, and giving encouragement would be appropriate strategies; but if the tantrum was a bid for attention, adults would only reinforce/strengthen tantrum recurrence by paying attention. Feeling valued and loved within a positive relationship greatly supports young children's compliance with rules. The "10:1 Rule" prescribes at least 10 positive comments per 1 negative comment/correction.

Including Families in Children's Education

First, ECE personnel can make sure that communication between the school/program and family is reciprocal and regular. EC educators should promote and support the enhancement and application of parenting skills. They should also acknowledge that parents have an integral part in supporting children's learning. All school personnel should make parents feel welcome in school, and moreover should seek parents' help and support. When school administrators, teachers, and other staff make educational decisions that affect the children and their families, they should always be sure that the children's parents are involved in these decisions. In addition, educational personnel should not just work on children's educational goals, learning objectives, and curricular and instructional planning and design on their own, keeping the school or program isolated; they should make use of all available community resources. Instead of trying to educate young children within a school bubble, educators who collaborate with their communities realize benefits of stronger families, schools, and child learning.

Managing the Normal Behavior of Young Children

Before reacting to young children's behaviors, adults should make sure children understand the situation. They should state rules simply and clearly; repeat them frequently for a long time for young children to remember and follow them; and state and enforce rules very consistently to avoid confusion. Adults should tell children clearly what they expect of them. They should never assume they need do nothing when children follow rules; they should consistently give rewards for compliance. Adults should also explain to young children why they are/are not receiving rewards by citing the rule they did/did not follow. Adults can arrange the environment to promote success. For example, if a child throws things that break windows, adults can remove such objects and substitute softer/more lightweight items. Organization is also important. Adults should begin with a simple, easy-to-implement plan and adhere to it. They should record children's progress; analyzing the records shows what does/does not work and why, enabling new/revised plans.

Effect of Maturational Factors on the Development and Learning

Many physiological factors affect the development of babies and young children. These dictate which kinds of learning activities are appropriate or ineffective for certain ages. For example, providing a newborn with visual stimuli from several feet away is wasted, as newborns cannot yet focus on distant objects. Adults cannot expect infants younger than about 5 months to sit up unsupported, as they have not yet developed the strength for it. Adults cannot expect toddlers who have not yet attained stable walking gaits to hop or balance upon one foot successfully. It is not coincidental that first grade begins at around 6 years: younger children cannot physically sit still for long periods and have not developed long enough attention spans to prevent distraction. This is also why kindergarten classes feature varieties of shorter term activities and more physical movement. Younger children also have not yet developed the self-regulation to keep from shouting out on impulse, getting up and running around, etc.—behaviors disruptive to formal schooling but developmentally normal.

Relationship of Sleep Quality to Blood Sugar Control in Children with Type 1 Diabetes

Researchers find blood sugar stability problematic for many children with Type 1 (juvenile) diabetes, despite all efforts by parents and children to follow diabetic health care rules, because of sleep differences. Diabetic children spend more time in lighter than deeper stages of sleep compared to nondiabetic children. This results in higher levels of blood sugar and poorer school performance. Lighter sleep and resulting daytime sleepiness tend to increase blood sugar levels. Sleep apnea is a sleep disorder that causes a person's breathing to be interrupted often during sleeping. These breathing interruptions result in poorer sleep quality, fatigue, and daytime sleepiness. Sleep apnea has previously been associated with Type 2 diabetes—historically adult-onset, though now children are developing it, too. It is now known that apnea is also associated with Type 1 diabetes in children: roughly one-third of diabetic children studied have sleep apnea, regardless of their weight (being overweight can contribute to apnea). Sleep apnea is additionally associated with much higher blood sugars in diabetic children.

Considerations for Early Childhood Nutrition

Raw or lightly steamed vegetables are best because excess heat destroys nutrients and frying adds fat calories. Fresh, in-season and flash-frozen fruits are more nutritious/less processed than canned. Adults should monitor young children's diets to limit highly processed produce, which can have excessive sugar, salt, or preservatives. Good protein sources include legumes, nuts, lean poultry, and fish. Adults should take care with young children to avoid choking hazards by cutting foods into bite-sized pieces. Serving nut butters instead of whole nuts is safer, but spread thinly on whole-grain breads/crackers or vegetable pieces, because young children can choke on large globs of nut butter as well. Omega-3 fatty acids from salmon, mackerel, herring, flaxseeds, and walnuts control inflammation, prevent heart arrhythmias, and lower blood pressure. Monounsaturated fats from avocados, olives, peanuts, their oils, and canola oil prevent heart disease, lower bad

46

cholesterol, and raise good cholesterol. Polyunsaturated fats from nuts, seeds, and corn, soy, sesame, sunflower, and safflower oils lower cholesterol. These fats/oils should be served in moderation, avoiding saturated fats.

Nutritional Factors in Diet Affecting Early Childhood Development

Babies are typically nourished via mother's milk or infant formula, and then with baby food; however, young children mostly eat the same foods as adults by the age of 2 years. Though they eat smaller quantities, young children have similar nutritional needs to those of adults. Calcium can be more important in early childhood to support the rapid bone growth occurring during this period; young children should receive 2–3 servings of dairy products and/or other calcium-rich foods. For all ages, whole-grain foods are nutritionally superior for their fiber and nutrients than refined flours, which have had these removed. Refined flours provide "empty calories" causing wider blood-sugar fluctuations and insulin resistance—Type 2 diabetes risks—than whole grains, which stabilize blood sugar and offer more naturally occurring vitamins and minerals. Darkly and brightly colored produce are most nutritious. Adults should cut foods into small, bite-sized pieces to prevent choking in young children, who have not yet perfected their biting, chewing, and swallowing skills.

Considerations for Feeding Young Children

Saturated fats from meats and full-fat dairy should be limited; they can cause health problems like high cholesterol, cardiovascular disease, obesity, and diabetes. Trans fats are produced chemically by hydrogenating normally liquid unsaturated fats and converting them to solid, saturated fats as in margarine and shortening used in many baked goods. These are considered even unhealthier than regular saturated fats and should be avoided. (The words "partially hydrogenated" in the ingredients signal trans fats.) Infants derive enough water from mother's milk/formula, but young children should be given plenty of water and/or milk in "sippy cups" to stay hydrated. The common practice of giving young children fruit juice should be avoided. Even without added sugars, fruit juices crowd out room in small stomachs for food nutrients and cause dental cavities and weaken permanent teeth before they erupt. Children can also gain weight, as juice calories do not replace food calories the way actual fruit does with its fiber and solids. Young children should eat two-thirds of adult-sized portions.

Characteristics of Young Children's Nutritional Needs

Young children have smaller stomachs than adults and cannot eat as much at one time as teens or adults. However, it is common practice for today's restaurants to provide oversized portions. The historical tradition of encouraging young children to "clean their plates" is ill-advised considering these excessive portions and the abundance of food in America today. Adults can help young children by teaching them instead to respond to their own bodies' signals and eat only until they are satisfied. Adults can also place smaller portions of food on young children's plates and request to-go containers at restaurants to take leftovers home. Because young children cannot eat a lot at once, they must maintain their blood sugar and energy throughout the day by snacking between meals. However, "snack foods" need not be high in sugar, salt, and unhealthy fats. Cut pieces of fresh fruits and vegetables, whole-grain crackers and low-fat cheeses, and portable yogurt tubes make good snacks for young children.

General Sleep Needs and Behaviors of Young Children

Sleep allows the body to become repaired and recharged for the day and is vital for young children's growth and development. Children aged 2–5 years generally need 10–12 hours of sleep daily. Children 5–7 years old typically need 9–11 hours of sleep. Their sleep schedules should be

47

fairly regular. While occasionally staying up later or missing naps for special events is not serious, overall inconsistent/disorganized schedules cause lost sleep and lethargic and/or cranky children. Some young children sleep fewer hours at night but need long daytime naps, while others need longer, uninterrupted nighttime sleep but seldom nap. Young children are busy exploring and discovering new things; they have a lot of energy and are often excited even when tired. Because they have not developed much self-regulation, they need adult guidance to calm down enough to go to sleep and will often resist bedtimes. Adults should plan bedtime routines. These can vary, but their most important aspect is consistency. Children then expect routines' familiar steps, and anticipating these comfort them.

Considerations in Children's Bedrooms and Family Beds

The majority of early childhood experts think young children should not have adults in their rooms every night while they fall asleep. They believe this can interfere with young children's capacity for "self-soothing" and falling asleep on their own, making them dependent on an adult presence to fall asleep. Parents/caregivers are advised to help children relax until sleepy, and then leave, saying "Good night" and "I love you." Young children frequently feel more comfortable going to bed with a favorite blanket or stuffed animal and/or a night light. Regardless, fears and nightmares are still fairly common in early childhood. "Family beds," i.e. children sleeping in the same bed or adjacent beds with parents, are subject to controversy. However, this is traditional in many developing countries and was historically so in America. Whatever the individual family choice, it should be consistent as young children will be frustrated by inconsistent practices and less likely to develop good sleeping habits.

Feeding Strategies Supporting Development of Nutritious Eating Habits and Attitudes

Early childhood is an age range often associated with "finicky" eaters. Adults can experiment by substituting different foods that are similar sources of protein or other nutrients to foods young children dislike. Preparing meals to look like happy faces, animals, or have appealing designs can entice young children to eat varied foods. Engaging children age-appropriately in selecting and preparing meals with supervision can also motivate them to consume foods when they have participated in their preparation. Adults should model healthy eating habits for young children, who imitate admired adults' behaviors. Early childhood is when children form basic food-related attitudes and habits and so is an important time for influencing these. Children are exposed to unhealthy foods in advertising, at school, in restaurants, and with friends, so adult modeling and guidance regarding healthy choices are important to counteract these influences. However, adults should also impart the message early that no foods are "bad"/forbidden, allowing some occasional indulgences in small amounts, to prevent the development of eating disorders.

Components and Characteristics of Good Bedtime Routines

Bedtime routines serve as transitions from young children's exciting, adventurous daytime activities to the tranquility needed for healthful rest. Adults should begin routines by establishing and enforcing a rule that daytime activities like rough-and-tumble physical play or TV watching stop at a specific time. While preschoolers may be less interested in computer/video games than older children, establishing limits early will help parents enforce stopping these activities at bedtime when they are older, too. Bath time is one good way to begin bedtime routines. Toys and games make baths fun, and bath washes with lavender and other soothing ingredients are now available to relax young children. Also, since young children eat smaller meals, healthy bedtime snacks are important. Too much/too little food will disrupt sleep, and too much liquid can cause bedwetting. Adults should plan nighttime snacks appropriately for the individual child. Bedtime reading promotes interest in books and learning, adult-child/family bonding, and calms children. Singing lullabies, hugging, and cuddling also support bonding, relax children, and make them feel safe and secure.

Helping Young Children Transition from Cribs to Regular Beds

One of young children's significant transitions from infancy is moving from a crib to a "big bed." Some become very motivated to escape cribs. For example, some bright, adventurous toddlers and even babies have untied padded crib bumpers, stacked them, and climbed out of the crib. For such children, injury is a greater danger from a crib than a bed. Others, whose cognitive and verbal skills are more developed than motor skills, may stand/jump up and down, repeatedly calling, "Hey, I'm up!" until a parent comes. These children should be moved to regular beds, with guardrails and/or body pillows to prevent rolling/falling-out accidents. If a child is moved to a bed to free the crib for a new baby, this should be done weeks ahead of the infant's arrival if possible, to separate these two significant life events. Most young children are excited about "grown-up" beds. Some, if hesitant, can sleep in the crib and nap in the bed for a gradual transition until ready for the bed full-time.

Hygiene in Early Childhood

Importance of Hand-Washing

A major change during early childhood is that hygiene transforms from something adults do for children to something children learn to do themselves. Toddlers are typically learning toilet-training, getting many germs on their hands. Preschoolers today are also often exposed to germs in daycare or school settings. Adults must explain to young children using concrete, easily understood terms how germs spread; how hand-washing removes germs; and when and how to wash their hands. Adults also need to remind children frequently to wash their hands until it becomes a habit. Remind them hand-washing is required before eating, after toileting, after being outdoors, after sneezing/coughing, and after playing with pets. Because young children have short attention spans and can be impatient, they are unlikely to wash long or thoroughly enough. Adults can encourage this by teaching children to sing "Happy Birthday" or other 15- to 20-second songs/verses while washing, both assuring optimal hand-washing duration and making the process more fun.

Bathing

While infants are bathed by adults, by the time they are toddlers or preschoolers, they generally have learned to sit in a bathtub and wash themselves. However, regardless of their ability to bathe, young children should never be left unsupervised by adults in the bath. Young children can drown very quickly, even in an inch of water; an adult should always be in the bathroom. Also, adults should not let young children run bathwater: they are likely to make it too cold or hot. Adults can prevent scalding accidents by turning down the water heater temperature. The adult should adjust water temperature and test it on his/her own inner arm (an area with more sensitive skin). Parents/caregivers should choose baby shampoos, soaps, and washes that do not irritate young eyes or skin, and keep adult bath products out of children's reach and sight. Very active children may need to bathe daily; others suffering dry, itchy skin should bathe every other day and/or have parents/caregivers apply mild moisturizing lotion.

Promoting and Teaching Dental Hygiene

Even while young children still have their deciduous/"baby" teeth, dental hygiene practices can affect their permanent/adult teeth before they erupt. For example, excessive sugar can weaken adult teeth before they even appear above the gumline. Adults should not only teach young children how important it is to brush their teeth twice and floss once daily at a minimum; moreover, they should model these behaviors. Children are far more likely to imitate parents' dental hygiene practices than do what parents only tell them but do not do themselves. Integrating tooth brushing into morning and bedtime routines promotes the habit. Adults can help motivate resistant children with entertaining toothbrushes that play music, spin, light up, and/or have cartoon illustrations. Young children have not developed the fine motor skills sufficient for flossing independently and will need adult supervision until they are older. Individual flossers are easier for them to use with help than traditional string dental floss.

Exercise Benefits for Young Children

Young children need daily physical exercise to strengthen their bones, lungs, hearts, and other muscles. Throwing, catching, running, jumping, kicking, and swinging actions develop young children's gross motor skills. Children sleep better with regular physical activity and are at less risk for obesity. Playing actively with other children also develops social skills, including empathy, sharing, cooperation, and communication. Family playtimes strengthen bonding and let parents model positive exercise habits. Outdoor play is fun for youngsters; running and laughing lift children's moods. Pride at physical attainments moreover boosts children's self-images and self-esteem. At least 60 minutes of physical activity most days is recommended for children. This includes jungle gyms, slides, swings, and other playground equipment; family walks, bike-riding, playing backyard catch, baseball, football, or basketball; adult-supervised races or obstacle courses; and age-appropriate community sports activities/leagues. Adults should plan and supervise activities to prevent injuries. They should also provide repeated sunscreen applications for outdoor activities to prevent sunburn and long-term skin damage.

Exposure to TV/Other Media and Optimal Environmental Conditions for Leisure Activities

Preschool-aged children are not yet cognitively able to distinguish between reality and fantasy. Therefore, overly violent or intense content in TV or other media can frighten them. Additionally, exposure to video violence has been proven to increase aggressive behaviors in young children. Moreover, using TV as a babysitter for long times excludes more cognitively stimulating and interactive pursuits. Parents/caregivers can provide young children with paints, crayons, and modeling clay. They can play board games and simple card games, do puzzles, sing songs, and read stories with young children. Pretend/make-believe play develops during early childhood, so adults can encourage their playing "house," "dress-up," or "auto shop." Park/playground trips afford outdoor play and physical activity/exercise. Visiting local museums, zoos, or planetariums combine education and entertainment with outings. In multiple-child families, it is important for each child to get some one on one time with parents regularly, even in unstructured activities like going to the hardware store with Daddy or keeping Mommy company while she washes dishes.

Disadvantages/Advantages and Risk/Protective Factors in Economically Deprived and Culturally Diverse Environments

Historically, disadvantages of poverty have been the focus of research; e.g. lack of toys, inadequate verbal interactions limiting visual discrimination and linguistic development or risk factors like less education, poorer nutrition, family stressors, medical illness, inadequate social stimulation, and insufficient social-service support leading to school dropouts, delinquency, unemployment, and perpetuated poverty. However, more recent research also identifies poverty's advantages, including opportunities for young children to play with peers and older children with little adult intervention, promoting empathy, cooperation, self-control, self-reliance, and sense of belonging; experience with multiple teaching styles, especially modeling, observation, and imitation; and language acquisition within a culturally-specific context through rich cultural traditions of stories, songs, games, and toys. These findings illuminate the resiliency or stress resistance of some children. Recent research also identifies protective factors against risk factors. These protections contribute to child resiliency, including the child's personality traits; having stable, supportive, cohesive family units; and having external support systems promoting positive values and coping skills.

Influence of Cultures and Cultural Values on Early Childhood Development

The culture in a society influences, even determines, our individual values, as do both historical and current social and political occurrences. Our values then influence the ways in which children are valued and raised. As American educators, we can understand the "American" perspective on early childhood better through understanding cultural diversity. We tend to fixate on our own culture's beliefs of truth as the only existing reality, but depending on our personal histories and values and current conditions, there can actually be multiple right ways of doing things. For example, Western cultures value children's early attainment of independence and individuality, but Eastern cultures value interdependence and group harmony more than individualism. In affluent societies, letting children explore the environment early and freely is valued, but in poor and/or developing societies, parents protect children, keeping them close and even carrying them while working, and thus do not value early freedom and exploration.

Effect of Age, Ethnicity, and Income on Health and School Outcomes

Research traces many variations in well-being and health to early childhood. These differences come from inequities in service access and treatment, congenital health problems, and early exposure to greater familial and community risk factors. Child groups at risk that are overrepresented in our population include young children, low-income children, and minority children. More young children than older children are likely to live in economically disadvantaged families. As of 2005, more than 10 million children aged 0–5 years lived in the U.S. 20 percent of these were in families classified as poor, i.e. with income below the federal poverty level (FPL), and 42 percent were in families designated low-income, i.e. with income below double the FPL. Of more than 2 million American children aged 0–5 living in families identified as extremely poor, i.e. with income less than half the FPL, minority groups were also overrepresented. The younger the children are, the greater the adverse effects of poverty are on their developmental outcomes.

Environment, Social and Emotional Support, Self-Image, and Success

Researchers have recently found that a child's sense of self is significant in predicting success in life. Even when a child's family environment involves multiple stressors, having a good relationship with one parent mitigates a child's psychosocial risks. As a child grows older, a close, supportive, lasting relationship with an adult outside the family can confer similar protection. Such relationships promote self-esteem in a child. Children with positive self-esteem are more able to develop feelings of control, mastery, and self-efficacy to achieve tasks, and they are more able to manage stressful life experiences. Such children demonstrate more initiative in forming relationships and accomplishing tasks. They reciprocally derive more positive experiences from their environments. Children with positive self-concepts pursue, develop, and sustain experiences and relationships that support success. Their positive self-images are further enhanced by these successes, generating additional supportive relationships and experiences. While we often hear about negative cycles of poverty, abuse, or failure, positive cycles of success can be equally as self-perpetuating.

Individualistic Versus Collectivistic Cultures

Anthropologists have classified various world cultures along a continuum of how individualistic or interdependent their structures and values are. Investigating these differences is found to afford much insight and application for early childhood education. The predominant culture in America is considered very individualistic. Children are encouraged to assert themselves and make their own choices to realize their highest potentials, with the ultimate goal of individual self-fulfillment. Collectivistic/sociocentric cultures, however, place the highest importance on group well-being; if collective harmony is disrupted by individual assertiveness, such self-assertion is devalued. Some educators characterize this contrast as the difference between standing out (individualist) and fitting in (collectivist). Researchers note that when asked to finish "I am…" statements, members of interdependent cultures tend to supply a family role, religion, or organization (e.g. "a father/a Buddhist"); whereas members of individualistic cultures cite personal qualities (e.g. "intelligent/hardworking"). Research finds American culture most individualistic, Latin American and Asian cultures most interdependent, and European cultures in the middle.

Health Risks and Results Related to Racial and Ethnic Origins

Children are at higher risk for inadequate development when they are born prematurely or with low birth weights. Recent research found racial and ethnic disparities in these birth conditions. For example, rates of low birth weights in 2004 were almost double for African-Americans as for whites (13.4 percent versus 7.1 percent). Latinos had similar but slightly lower risk than whites for low birth weight (6.9 percent versus 7.1 percent). Native American/Alaska Natives had slightly higher risk than white (7.5 percent versus 7.1 percent), as did Asian/Pacific Islanders (7.9 percent versus 7.1 percent). In oral health, 28 percent of preschoolers have had tooth decay. Moreover, data show that in children aged 2–5 years, oral disease increased 15.2 percent from 1994–2002, equaling 600,000 more children. It was found 13.9 percent of children aged 2–5 years were overweight or obese. Risk for overweight/obesity is higher for low-income and minority children. These groups are also at higher risk for poorer quality and continuity in asthma treatment. Asthma's prevalence as well as asthma-related morbidity and deaths are higher in African-American children than white children.

Effect of Racial/Ethnic, Economic, Educational, and Mental Health Factors on the Emotional, Mental Health, and Social Outcomes

Proportionately more mothers in minority and low-income groups—up to 40 percent—suffer maternal depression than in other parts of the population. Maternal depression is associated with poor mother-child bonding; lower child scores in language and reading; and higher prevalence of depression and other mental health problems later in children. Low-income and minority families are at higher risk for developmental difficulties and mental health issues. According to U.S. surveys, about one-third or over 3 million of young children have two or more health and developmental risk factors. These risk factors include maternal mental health, maternal education, family poverty, and race/ethnicity. Each added risk factor increases the probability of either greater developmental risk or worse health status. Risk increases exponentially with multiple factors. One risk factor doubles risk; two factors more than triple it; three causes almost five times the risk; and four risk factors represent 14 times the risk of developmental delay or poor health.

Effects of Racial, Ethnic, and Economic Disparities Upon Parenting, Home Safety, and School Readiness

According to the National Survey on Early Childhood Health, significant differences are reported in Latino and African-Americans' parenting practices, home routines, and home safety measures. These differences are associated with differing degrees of positive early childhood development. Research studies have also revealed that American children in minority groups, on the average, demonstrate lower school readiness levels when they begin formal education than white American children do. The research furthermore shows that most of these differences in school readiness levels are associated with differences in family income. Researchers also comment that disparities among racial and ethnic groups in their school readiness and subsequent academic achievement in school may be additional contributors to discrimination against minority racial and ethnic groups by teachers and other educational personnel.

Effects of Income and Race/Ethnicity Upon Health Care Aspects

Although the disparity in childhood immunizations between white and minority infants and toddlers has decreased, still, fewer minority children are receiving standard immunizations than white children in America. For example, the preschool rates for receiving each major vaccination from 2003–2004 in America were the lowest among non-Latino black, Native American, and Alaskan Native children. One sign of health service quality and continuity is having a regular health care provider. Recent national surveys have found that while more than 80 percent of children under the age of 5 in economically affluent families are seen at physicians' offices or HMOs for care when sick, not much more than 54 percent of children under age 5 in economically poor families are seen for sick care. The National Survey of Early Childhood Health has found African-American and Latino parents report more dissatisfaction with pediatricians and more unmet needs for early childhood development services than white parents. Twice as many Latino as white parents felt providers never or only occasionally understood their individual child's needs.

Socioeconomic and Racial Effects on Mental, Emotional, and Social Health

According to the National Survey of Child and Adolescent Well-Being, in recent years over 40 percent of toddlers and over 68 percent of preschoolers who were in contact with the child welfare system had high levels of need, developmentally and behaviorally. But overall, fewer than 23 percent of these children were getting services to address these needs. Thus, young children of socioeconomically disadvantaged families were found to have more developmental and behavioral problems than children in other socioeconomic groups, yet were also less likely to receive help with such problems. Another social and emotional difference related to racial group membership has been reflected by levels of violence in the family. 2003 data found that over 15 percent of African-American families experienced violent conflicts, compared to below 9 percent of white families and over 11 percent of Latino families. Racial groups classified as "other" constituted over 12 percent. Experts concede that styles of disagreeing can be influenced by cultural and demographic variables. However, they find the strongest influence on conflicts becoming violent to be parental stress.

Inequity in Health Insurance Coverage for Children of Minority Groups

Research has demonstrated that after taking health insurance status into account, there are no significant socioeconomic differences in how family organization and doctor/health care practitioner visits are related. Furthermore, research has shown that having health insurance coverage decreases differences in developmental and health outcomes for young children. However, despite these findings, children of minority groups are less likely than their nonminority

53

peers to have either private or public health care coverage. Regarding access to health care services, it has been found that parents whose first language was not English were only half as likely to get preventive health care for their infants as native English-speaking families. This inequity in service delivery was found to be constant across white, African-American, and Latino families that had infants, but not in Asian-American families having infants.

According to data collected by the National Survey of Early Childhood Health, minority families have less communication and guidance from pediatric health care providers than white families. For example, African-American parents were found to make significantly fewer phone calls than white parents to pediatric health care practices. Latino parents made fewer than half the calls that white parents did; African-American parents made fewer than three-fourths of the calls white parents did. This survey also found that pediatricians and other pediatric health care service providers were more likely to emphasize topics of household alcohol and drug use and community violence when they talked with minority patient families than they did in discussions with white patient families. African-American children are found far more likely to have special health care needs than white children; yet researchers find that even after controlling for health status, insurance, and other pertinent variables, health care providers are still nearly twice as likely not to refer minority children to specialists and consultants.

Early Childhood Comprehensive Systems

Decreasing Socioeconomically and Racially Influenced Health Care Inequities

According to the National Center for Children in Poverty, Early Childhood Comprehensive Systems (ECCS) initiatives in each U.S. state have the ability to further methods that can decrease socioeconomically related health care inequities in early childhood, which generates positive impacts for the rest of children's lives. To raise and shape consciousness of health care issues affected by income and race, experts recommend that ECCS establish connections between projects/programs designed to eradicate poverty and racism and efforts in developing early childhood systems. Another consciousness-raising strategy recommended for ECCS is to work at increasing the general public's awareness of racial, ethnic, and economic disparities in early childhood health care and to work at increasing such awareness in health professionals, educators, early care providers, and other significant stakeholders who regularly provide services to young children. ECCS can also include racial/ethnic data in performance monitoring; encourage state CHIP and Medicaid agencies to do the same; analyze state data for disparities in risk, access, and outcomes, including small-area analyses, geocoding, etc.; and identify and measure unequal treatment through data analysis.

Improving and Equalizing Health Care for All American Demographic Groups

Enhancing Community Support

Experts in early childhood development find that state ECCS should target their support toward communities with larger populations of minority and low-income families. Inasmuch as local systems have limited resources, some state ECCS might need to allocate more of these resources to communities having higher risks of adverse outcomes for children. ECCS can also provide assistance to communities by helping them assess their local assets, strengths, needs, and risk factors. Early childhood development experts emphasize that state ECCS should focus their efforts on improving the quality of health care services that are available within communities where all or the majority of residents are members of minority groups and/or have low socioeconomic status. Another way in which state ECCS can strengthen the supports available in communities for citizens who are subject to unequal health care treatment according to their demographic groups is to offer and provide incentives for community development projects that are designed to decrease health care treatment disparities based on racial/ethnic and economic differences.

Reducing Unequal Treatment of Cultural/Linguistic Minorities

Early childhood experts advise that each U.S. state's ECCS should implement strategies designed to monitor health care providers and services for cultural and linguistic competency, and to improve these competencies. One example of such improvement is ensuring that specific training in cultural and linguistic competency and cross-cultural competency is integrated into the training of both health care providers and early childhood educators. ECCS can also be responsible for seeing that parent education materials and resources in health care are translated into the native languages of local families who are not native English speakers, and supporting interpreter and translator services for communities having families needing these. Experts find that ECCS can additionally improve child and family health services by supporting various early childhood service settings in employing nonprofessional/community health workers. Moreover, ECCS can help further equality and consistency of health care across varied demographic groups by applying research evidence-based guidelines regarding health care, family support, early learning, and related services and programs.

Benefits of Leveling Inequalities in Care, Health, and Education

Eliminating unequal treatment in early childhood has significant benefits, including lowering overall national rates of poverty; improving overall health and education measures; saving long-term health care costs; decreasing disabilities; and lengthening lives by decreasing mortality rates. The effects of low income and racism on young children and their families are complex, and these influences interact with one another. Therefore it is impossible or extremely difficult to solve problems generated by one of these social factors without including the other associated influencing factors. Because of the interrelationships of variables, strategies on a system level have the most potential for effectiveness. For example, job training and placement programs that could help parents economically are limited in effectiveness if quality child care is not also available to those parents. Enhancing educational programs could improve academic performance, but not if young students are too hungry to benefit from instruction. And the measurement and monitoring of developmental, health, and educational outcomes will not change their disparity unless treatment inequities are resolved.

Involving Families in Their Children's Education

Flexibility and variety are key elements for involving diverse families, with changing situations and needs, in ECE. Adaptable approaches include these: Educators include families in designing children's Individual Family Service Plans (IFSPs) for preschoolers. They ask families to develop their own goals for educational participation. They create volunteer calendars, encouraging parents to collaborate when able. They communicate with families regularly, using speech if written/printed language presents barriers. They establish media libraries for parents/families to browse and check out resources. They facilitate parental meeting attendance and school visits by providing transportation and child care. They adapt to parental work schedules by convening meetings at alternative times of day. They often send families communications about both their children and class content, including information regarding important developmental milestones and methods for nurturing growth and development. They offer families individualized, specific strategies for home use. They recruit interested family members to help in preschool. They also function as clearinghouses to facilitate family access to community supports like local health care agencies, businesses, and universities.

Causes of Intellectual Disabilities in Babies and Young Children

Infections

Congenital cytomegalovirus (CMV) is passed to fetuses from mothers, who may be asymptomatic. About 90% of newborns are also asymptomatic; 5% to 10% of these have later problems. Of the 10% born with symptoms, 90% will have later neurological abnormalities, including intellectual disabilities. Congenital rubella, or German measles, is also passed to fetuses from unvaccinated and exposed mothers, causing neurological damage including blindness or other eye disorders, deafness, heart defects, and intellectual disabilities. Congenital toxoplasmosis is passed to fetuses by infected mothers, who can be asymptomatic, with a parasite from raw or undercooked meat that causes intellectual disabilities, vision or hearing loss, and other conditions. Encephalitis is brain inflammation caused by infection, most often viral. Meningitis is inflammation of the meninges, or membranes, covering the brain and is caused by viral or bacterial infection; the bacterial form is more serious. Both encephalitis and meningitis can cause intellectual disabilities. Maternal human immunodeficiency virus (HIV) and acquired immunodeficiency syndrome (AIDS) can be passed to fetuses, destroying immunity to infections, which can cause intellectual disabilities. Maternal listeriosis, a bacterial infection from contaminated food, animals, soil, or water, can cause meningitis and intellectual disabilities in surviving fetuses and infants.

Environmental, Nutritional, and Metabolic Influences

Environmental deprivation syndrome results when developing children are deprived of necessary environmental elements—physical, including adequate nourishment (malnutrition); climate or temperature control (extremes of heat or cold); hygiene, like changing and bathing; and so on. It also includes lack of adequate cognitive stimulation, which can stunt a child's intellectual development, and neglect in general. Malnutrition results from starvation; vitamin, mineral, or nutrient deficiency; deficiencies in digesting or absorbing foods; and some other medical conditions. Environmental radiation, depending on dosage and time of exposure, can cause intellectual disabilities. Congenital hypothyroidism (underactive thyroid) can cause intellectual disabilities, as can hypoglycemia (low blood sugar) from inadequately controlled diabetes or occurring independently and infant hyperbilirubinemia. Bilirubin, a waste product of old red blood cells, is found in bile made by the liver and is normally removed by the liver; excessive bilirubin buildup in babies can cause intellectual disabilities. Reye syndrome, caused by aspirin given children with flu or chicken pox, or following these viruses or other upper respiratory infections, or from unknown causes, produces sudden liver and brain damage and can result in intellectual disabilities.

Genetic Abnormalities and Syndromes Affecting the Nervous System

Rett syndrome is a nervous system disorder causing developmental regression, particularly severe in expressive language and hand function. It is associated with a defective protein gene on an X chromosome. Having two X chromosomes, females with the defect on one of them can survive; with only one X chromosome, males are either miscarried, stillborn, or die early in infancy. Rett syndrome produces many symptoms, including intellectual disabilities. Tay-Sachs disease, an autosomal recessive disorder, is a nervous system disease caused by a defective gene on chromosome 15 resulting in a missing protein for breaking down gangliosides, chemicals in nerve tissues that build up in cells, particularly brain neurons, causing damage. Tay-Sachs is more prevalent in Ashkenazi Jews. The adult form is rare; the infantile form is commonest, with nerve damage starting in utero. Many symptoms, including intellectual disabilities, appear at 3 to 6 months and death occurs by 4 to 5 years. Tuberous sclerosis, caused by genetic mutations, produces tumors damaging the kidneys, heart, skin, brain, and central nervous system. Symptoms include intellectual disabilities, seizures, and developmental delays.

Genetic or Inherited Metabolic Disorders

Adrenoleukodystrophy is an X-linked genetic trait. Some female carriers have mild forms, but it affects more males more seriously. It impairs metabolism of very long-chain fatty acids, which build up in the nervous system (as well as adrenal glands and male testes). The childhood cerebral form, manifesting at ages 4 to 8, causes seizures, visual and hearing impairments, receptive aphasia, dysgraphia, dysphagia, intellectual disabilities, and other effects. Galactosemia is an inability to process galactose, a simple sugar in lactose, or milk sugar. By-product buildup damages the liver, kidneys, eyes, and brain. Hunter syndrome, Hurler syndrome, and Sanfilippo syndrome each cause the lack of different enzymes; all cause an inability to process mucopolysaccharides or glycosaminoglycans (long sugar-molecule chains). Hurler and Sanfilippo (but not Hunter) syndromes are autosomal recessive traits, meaning both parents must pass on the defect. All cause progressive intellectual disabilities. Lesch-Nyhan syndrome, affecting males, is a metabolic deficiency in processing purines. It causes hemiplegia, varying degrees of intellectual disabilities, and self-injurious behaviors. Phenylketonuria (PKU), an autosomal recessive trait, causes lack of the enzyme to process dietary phenylalanine, resulting in intellectual disabilities.

Prescription Drugs, Substances of Abuse, Social Drugs, and Diseases

Warfarin, a prescription anticoagulant drug to thin the blood and prevent excessive clotting, can cause microcephaly (undersized head) and intellectual disabilities in an infant when the mother has taken it during pregnancy. The prescription antiseizure drug Trimethadione can cause developmental delays in babies when it has been taken by pregnant mothers. Maternal abuse of solvent chemicals during pregnancy can also cause microcephaly and intellectual disabilities. Maternal crack cocaine abuse during pregnancy can cause severe and profound intellectual disabilities and many other developmental defects in fetuses, which become evident when they are newborns. Maternal alcohol abuse can cause fetal alcohol syndrome, which often includes intellectual disabilities, among many other symptoms. Maternal rubella (German measles) virus can cause intellectual disabilities as well as visual and hearing impairments and heart defects. Maternal herpes simplex virus can cause microcephaly, intellectual disabilities, and microophthalmia (small or no eyes). The varicella (chicken pox) virus in pregnant mothers can also cause intellectual disabilities as well as muscle atrophy in babies.

Characteristics of Infants and Young Children with Intellectual Disabilities

Newborns with intellectual disabilities, especially of greater severity, may not demonstrate normal reflexes, such as rooting and sucking reflexes, necessary for nursing. They may not show other temporary infant reflexes such as the Moro, Babinski, swimming, stepping, or labyrinthine reflexes, or they may demonstrate weaker versions of some of these. In some babies, these reflexes will exist but persist past the age when they normally disappear. Babies with intellectual disabilities are likely to display developmental milestones at later-than-typical ages. The ages when they do display milestones vary according to the severity of the disability and by individual. Young children with intellectual disabilities are likely to walk, self-feed, and speak later than normally developing children. Those who learn to read and write do so at later ages. Children with mild intellectual disabilities may lack curiosity and have quiet demeanors; those with profound intellectual disabilities are likely to remain infantile in abilities and behaviors throughout life. Intellectually disabled children will score below normal on standardized IQ tests and adaptive behavior rating scales.

Potential Variables Causing Learning Disabilities

LDs are basically neurological disorders. Though they are more specific to particular areas of learning than global disorders like intellectual disabilities, scientific research has found correlations between LDs and many of the same factors that cause intellectual disabilities, including prenatal influences like excessive alcohol or other drug consumption, diseases, and so on. Once babies are born, glandular disorders, brain injuries, exposure to secondhand smoke or other toxins, infections of the central nervous system, physical trauma, or malnutrition can cause neurological damage resulting in LDs. Hypoxia and anoxia (oxygen loss) before, during, or after birth is a cause, as are radiation and chemotherapy. These same influences often cause behavioral disorders as well as LDs. Another factor is genetic: Both LDs and behavior disorders have been observed to run in families. While research has not yet identified specific genetic factors, heritability does appear to be a component in influencing learning and behavioral disorders.

Types of Neurological Damage Found in Children with LDs and ADHD

Various neurological research studies have revealed that children diagnosed with LDs and ADHD have at least one of several kinds of structural damage to their brains. Scientists have found smaller numbers of cells in certain important regions of the brains of some children with learning and behavioral disorders. Some of these children are found to have brain cells of smaller than normal size. In some cases, dysplasia is discovered; that is, some brain cells migrate into the wrong area of the brain. In some children with learning and behavioral disorders, blood flow is found to be lower than normal to certain regions in the brain. Also, the brain cells of some children with learning and behavioral disabilities show lower levels of glucose metabolism; glucose (blood sugar) is the brain's main source of fuel, so inadequate utilization of glucose can affect the brain's ability to perform some functions related to cognitive processing, as in LDs, and to attention and impulse control, as in ADHD.

Attachment Styles Identified in Toddlers by Mary Ainsworth

Mary Ainsworth worked with John Bowlby, discovering the first empirical evidence supporting his attachment theory. From her Strange Situation experiments, she identified secure, insecure and avoidant, insecure and resistant, and insecure and disorganized attachment styles. Securely attached children show normal separation anxiety when mother leaves and happiness when she returns, avoid strangers when alone but are friendly with mother present, and use mother as a safe base for environmental exploring. Insecure and resistant children show exaggerated separation anxiety, ambivalence and resistance to mother upon reuniting, fear strangers, cry more, and explore less than secure or avoidant babies. Insecure and avoidant children show no separation anxiety or stranger anxiety and little interest on reunions with mother and are comforted equally by mother or strangers. Insecure and disorganized types seem dazed and confused, respond inconsistently, and may mix resistant and ambivalent and avoidant behaviors. Secure styles are associated with sensitive, responsive caregiving and children's positive self-images and other images, resistant and ambivalent styles with inconsistent caregiving, and avoidant with unresponsive caregivers. Avoidant, resistant, and disorganized styles, associated with negative self-images and low self-esteem, are most predictive of emotional disturbances.

Emotional Disturbances in Young Children Classified as Anxiety Disorders

Anxiety disorders include generalized anxiety disorder (GAD), obsessive-compulsive disorder (OCD), posttraumatic stress disorder (PTSD), panic disorder, social phobia, and specific phobias. All share a common characteristic of overwhelming, irrational, and unrealistic fears. GAD involves excessive worrying about anything or everything and free-floating anxiety. Anxiety may be about real issues but is nonetheless exaggerated and spreads, overtaking the child's life. OCD involves obsessive and preoccupied thoughts and compulsive or irresistible actions, including often bizarre rituals. Germ phobia, constant hand washing, repeatedly checking whether tasks are done or undone, and collecting things excessively are common. PTSD follows traumatic experiences/events. Children have frequent, extreme nightmares, crying, flashbacks wherein they vividly perceive or believe they are experiencing the traumatic event again, insomnia, depression, anxiety, and social withdrawal. Symptoms of panic disorder are panic attacks involving extreme fear and physical symptoms like a racing heart, cold hands and feet, pallor, hyperventilation, and feeling unable to move. Children with social phobia develop fear and avoidance of day care, preschool, or other social settings. Specific phobias are associated with specific objects, animals, or persons and are often triggered by traumatic experiences involving these.

Types and Characteristics of Learning Disabilities

Dyslexia, the most common LD, means deficiency or inability in reading. It primarily affects reading but can also interfere with writing and speaking. Characteristics include reversing letters and words, for example, confusing b and d in reading and writing; reading won as now, confusing similar speech sounds like /p/ and /b/, and perceiving spaces between words in the wrong places when reading. Dyscalculia is difficulty doing mathematical calculations; it can also affect using money and telling time. Dysgraphia means difficulties specifically with writing, including omitting words in writing sentences or leaving sentences unfinished, difficulty putting one's thoughts into writing, and poor handwriting. Central auditory processing disorder causes difficulty perceiving small differences in words despite normal hearing acuity; for example, couch and chair may be perceived as cow and hair. Background noise and information overloads exacerbate the effects. Visual processing disorders affect visual perception despite normal visual acuity, causing difficulty finding information in printed text or from maps, charts, pictures, graphs, and so on; synthesizing information from various sources into one place; and remembering directions to locations.

Factors Contributing to Emotional Disturbances

Researchers have investigated emotional disturbances but have not yet established known causes for any. Some disturbances, for example the major mental illness schizophrenia, seem to run in families and hence include a genetic component; childhood schizophrenia exists as a specific diagnosis. Factors contributing to emotional disturbances can be biological or environmental but more often are likely a combination of both. Dysfunctional family dynamics can often contribute to child emotional disorders. Physical and psychological stressors on children can also contribute to the development of emotional problems. Some people have attributed emotional disturbances to diet, and scientists have also researched this but have not discovered proof of cause and effect. Bipolar disorder is often successfully treated with the chemical lithium, which affects sodium flow through nerve cells, so chemical imbalance may be implicated as an etiology. Pediatric bipolar disorder, which has different symptoms than adult bipolar disorder, correlates highly with histories of bipolar and other mood disorders or alcoholism in both parents.

Symptoms of Pediatric Bipolar Disorder

Bipolar, formerly called manic-depressive disorder, has similar depressive symptoms in children as adults. However, children's mood swings often occur much faster, and children show more symptoms of anger and irritability than other adult manic symptoms. Bipolar children's most common symptoms include frequent mood swings; extreme irritability; protracted (up to several hours) tantrums or rages; separation anxiety; oppositional behavior; hyperactivity, impulsivity, and distractibility; restlessness and fidgetiness; silly, giddy, or goofy behavior; aggression; racing thoughts; grandiose beliefs or behaviors; risk-taking; depressed moods; lethargy; low self-esteem; social anxiety; hypersensitivity to environmental or emotional triggers; carbohydrate (sugar or starch) cravings; and trouble getting up in the morning. Other common symptoms include bed-wetting (especially in boys), night terrors, pressured or fast speech, obsessive or compulsive behaviors, motor and vocal tics, excessive daydreaming, poor short-term memory, poor organization, learning disabilities, morbid fascinations, hypersexuality, bossiness and manipulative behavior, lying, property destruction, paranoia, hallucinations, delusions, and suicidal ideations. Less common symptoms include migraines, bingeing, self-injurious behaviors, and animal cruelty.

Conduct Disorder in Children

Factors contributing to conduct disorders in children include genetic predispositions, neurological damage, child abuse, and other traumatic experiences. Children with conduct disorders display characteristic emotional and behavioral patterns. These include aggression: They bully or intimidate others, often start physical fights, will use dangerous objects as weapons, exhibit physical cruelty to animals or humans, and assault and steal from others. Deliberate property destruction is another characteristic—breaking things or setting fires. Young children are limited in some of these activities by their smaller size, lesser strength, and lack of access; however, they show the same types of behaviors against smaller, younger, weaker, or more vulnerable children and animals, along with oppositional and defiant behaviors against adults. Also, while truancy is impossible or unlikely in preschoolers, and running away from home is less likely, young children with conduct disorders are likely to demonstrate some forms of seriously violating rules, another symptom of this disorder.

Symptoms of Childhood-Onset Schizophrenia

The incidence of childhood-onset schizophrenia is rare, but it does exist. One example of differential diagnosis involves distinguishing qualitatively between true auditory hallucinations and young children's "hearing voices" otherwise: In the latter case, a child hears his or her own or a familiar adult's voice in his or her head and does not seem upset by it, while in the former, a child may hear other voices, seemingly in his or her ears, and is frightened and confused by them. Tantrums, defiance, aggression, and other acting-out, externalized behaviors are less frequent in childhood-onset schizophrenia than internalized developmental differences, for example, isolation, shyness, awkwardness, fickleness, strange facial expressions, mistrust, paranoia, anxiety, and depression. Children demonstrate nonpsychotic symptoms earlier than psychotic ones. However, it is difficult to use prepsychotic symptoms as predictors due to variance among developmental peculiarities. While psychiatrists find the course of childhood-onset schizophrenia somewhat more variable than in adults, child symptoms resemble adult symptoms. Childhood-onset schizophrenia is typically chronic and severe, responds less to medication, and has a more guarded prognosis than adolescent- or adult-onset schizophrenia.

Diagnosing the Emotional Disturbances in Children Classified as Psychotic Disorders

Psychosis is a general psychiatric category referring to thought disturbances or disorders. The most common symptoms are delusions that is, believing things that are not true, and hallucinations, that is, seeing, hearing, feeling, tasting, or smelling things that are not there. While early childhood psychosis is rarer than at later ages, psychiatrists confirm it does occur. Moreover, prognosis is poorer for psychosis with onset in early childhood than in adolescence or adulthood. Causes can be from known metabolic or brain disorders or unknown. Younger children are more vulnerable to environmental stressors. Also, in young children, thoughts distorted by fantasy can be from normal cognitive immaturity, due to lack of experience and a larger range of normal functioning, or pathology; where they lie on this continuum must be determined by clinicians. Believing one is a superhero who can fly can be vivid imagination or delusional; having imaginary friends can be pretend play or hallucinatory. Other developmental disorders can also cloud differential diagnosis.

Visual Impairments

Developmental Characteristics of Infants and Young Children with Visual Impairments

Historically, it was thought that VI children developed more slowly than normal; however, it is now known that ages for reaching developmental milestones are equally variable in VI babies as in others and that they acquire milestones within equal age ranges. One developmental difference is in sequence: VI children tend to utter their first words or subject-verb 2-word sentences earlier than other children. Some VI children also demonstrate higher levels of language development at younger-than-typical ages. For example, they may sing songs from memory or recall events from the past at earlier ages than other children. This is a logical development in children who must rely more on input to their hearing and other senses than to their vision when the latter is impaired. Totally blind babies reach for objects later, hence explore the environment later; hand use, eye-hand coordination, and gross and fine motor skills are delayed. Blind infants' posture control develops normally (rolling, sitting, all-fours, and standing), but mobility (raising on arms, pulling up, and walking) are delayed.

Causes of Visual Impairments in Babies and Young Children

Syndrome-related and other malformations like cleft iris or lens dislocation causing VI can have prenatal origins. Cataracts clouding the eye's lens can be congenital, traumatic, or due to maternal rubella. Eyes can be normal, but impairment in the brain's visual cortex can cause VI. Infantile glaucoma, like adult glaucoma, causes intraocular fluid buildup pressure and VI. Conjunctivitis and other infections cause VI. Strabismus and nystagmus are ocular-muscle conditions, respectively causing eye misalignments and involuntary eye movements. Trauma damaging the eyeball(s) is another VI cause. The optic nerve can suffer from atrophy (dysfunction) or hypoplasia, that is, developmental regression, usually prenatally due to neurological trauma; acuity cannot be corrected. Refractive errors like nearsightedness, farsightedness, and astigmatism are correctable. Retinoblastoma, or behind-the-eye tumors, can cause blindness and fatality; surgical or chemotherapeutic treatment is usually required before age 2. Premature infants can have retinopathy of prematurity or retrolental fibroplasia. Cryotherapeutic treatment seems to stop disease progression. Its effects range from none to severe VI (approximately 25% of children) to complete blindness.

Impacts of Blindness Upon Cognitive Development

Blind children have more difficulty determining and confirming characteristics of things, hence defining concepts and organizing them into more abstract levels; their problem-solving is active but harder, and they construct different realities than sighted children. Blind babies typically acquire object permanence (the understanding that unseen objects still exists) a year later than normal; they learn to reach for objects only by hearing. Understanding cause-and-effect relationships is difficult without visual evidence. Blind babies and toddlers take longer to understand and object's constancy regardless of their orientation in space, affecting their ability to orient toys and their own hands. Blind children can identify object size differences and similarities, but classifying object differences and similarities in other attributes requires longer times and more exposures to various similar objects. Blind children's development of the abilities to conserve object properties like material or substance, weight, amount and volume, length, and liquid volume is later than normal.

61

Effects of Blindness on Emotional and Social Development

Blind babies and children are more dependent than others on adults, affecting development. With control of their inner realities but not of their outer environments, blind children may withdraw, seeking and responding less to social interaction. They may not readily develop concepts of the external world or self-concepts as beings separate from the world and the understanding that they can be both agents and recipients of actions relative to the environment. Mother-infant smiling initiates recognition, attachment, and communication in sighted babies; blind infants smile on hearing mother's voice at 2 months. Only tactile stimuli like tickling and nuzzling evoke regular smiling in blind babies. Missing facial expressions and other visual cues, blind children have more complicated social interactions. They often do not understand the basics of playing with others and seem emotionally ambivalent or uninterested and uncommunicative. Peers may reject or avoid them; adults often overprotect them. Self-help skills like chewing, scooping, self-feeding, teeth brushing, grooming, and toilet training are delayed in blind children.

Hearing Impairments

Prevalence and Etiologies of Hearing Impairments

Half or more (50% to 60%) of infant hearing losses have genetic origins—Down and other genetically based syndromes or the existence of parental hearing loss. About 25% or more of infant hearing losses are caused by maternal infections during pregnancy, such as cytomegalovirus (CMV), postnatal complications like blood transfusions or infection with meningitis, or traumatic head injuries. Included in this 25% or more are babies having nongenetic neurological disorders or conditions that affect their hearing. Malformations of the ears, head, or face can cause hearing loss in babies. Babies spending 5 days or longer in neonatal intensive care units (NICUs) or having complications while in the NICU are also more likely to suffer hearing loss. Around 25% of babies are diagnosed with hearing loss whose etiology is unknown.

Signs of Hearing Impairments

If an infant does not display a startle response at loud noises, this is a potential sign of hearing loss. This can also indicate other developmental disabilities, but because hearing loss is the most prevalent disability among newborns, hearing screening is a priority. Between birth and 3 or 4 months old, babies should turn toward the source of a sound; if they do not, it could indicate hearing loss. A child who does not utter first words like mama or dada by age 1 could have hearing impairment. When babies or young children do not turn their heads when their names are called, adults may mistake this for inattention or ignoring; however, children turning upon seeing adults, but not upon hearing their names, can indicate hearing loss. Babies and children who seem to hear certain sounds but not others may have partial hearing losses. Delayed speech-language development or unclear speech, not following directions, saying "Huh?" often, and wanting higher TV or music volumes can indicate hearing loss in children.

Speech and Language Impairments

Factors Contributing to Speech and Language Impairments

Some speech and language disorders in children have unknown causes. Others have known causes such as hearing loss: Speech and language are normally acquired primarily through the auditory sense, so children with impaired hearing have delayed and impaired development of speech and language. Brain injuries, neurological disorders, viral diseases, and some medications can also cause problems with developing language or speech. Children with intellectual disabilities are more likely to have delayed language development, and their speech is also more likely to develop more slowly and to be distorted. Cerebral palsy causes neuromuscular weakness and incoordination of

62

speech. When severe, it can cause inability to produce recognizable speech sounds; some children without speech can still vocalize, and some cannot. A cleft palate or lip and other physical impairments affect speech. Inadequate speech-language modeling at home inhibits speech-language development. Vocal abuse in children (screaming, coughing, throat clearing, or excessive talking) can cause vocal nodules or polyps, causing voice disorders. Stuttering can be related to maturation, anxiety or stress, auditory feedback defects, or unknown causes.

Characteristics

In speech, most phonological disorders are articulatory; that is, children fail to pronounce specific speech sounds or phonemes correctly beyond the normal developmental age for achieving accuracy. Stuttering, disfluency, and rate and rhythm disorders cause children to repeat phonemes, especially initial word sounds; to repeat words; to prolong vowels or consonants; or to block, that is, straining so hard to produce a sound that, pressure builds, but no sound issues. Their speech rates may also speed and slow irregularly. Children with voice disorders can have voices that sound hoarse, raspy, overly nasal, higher- or lower-pitched than normal, overly weak or strident, and whispery or harsh. Hoarseness is common with vocal nodules and polyps. Cleft palate commonly causes hypernasality. In language, one of the most common impairments is delayed language development due to environmental deprivation, intellectual disabilities, neurological damage or defects, hearing loss, visual impairment, and so on. Children with neurological damage or disorders may exhibit aphasias, language disorders characterized by receptive difficulty with understanding spoken or written language, or expressive difficulty constructing spoken or written language.

Physical and Health Impairments

Examples of Physical and Health Impairments

In the special education field of early childhood education, other health impairment is a term referring to health and physical conditions that rob a child of strength, vitality, or alertness or that cause excessive alertness to environmental stimuli, all having the end result of impeding the child's ability to attend or respond to the educational environment. Health problems can be acute, that is short-term or temporary but serious, or chronic, that is, long-term, persistent, or recurrent. Some examples of such health and physical impairments include: cerebral palsy, spina bifida, amputations or missing limbs, muscular dystrophy, cystic fibrosis, asthma, rheumatic fever, sickle-cell anemia, nephritis or kidney disease, leukemia, Tourette syndrome, hemophilia, diabetes, heart disease, AIDS, and lead poisoning. All these conditions and others can interfere with a child's development and ability to attend and learn. In addition to seizure disorders, which often cause neurological damage, seizure-controlling medications also frequently cause drowsiness, interfering with attention and cognition. Attention deficit and attention deficit hyperactivity disorders (ADD and ADHD) limit attention span, focus, and concentration and thus are sometimes classified as health impairments requiring special education services.

Characteristics of Babies and Children with Physical and Health Impairments

The characteristics of children having various physical or health impairments can range from having no limitations to severe limitations in their activities. Children with cerebral palsy, for example, usually have deficiencies in gross and fine motor development and deficits in speech-language development. Physical and health conditions causing severe debilitation in some children not only seriously limit their daily activities but also cause multiple primary disabilities and impair their intellectual functioning. Other children with physical or health impairments function at average, above-average, or gifted intellectual and academic levels. An important consideration when working with babies and young children having physical or health impairments is handling and positioning them physically. Correctly picking up, holding, carrying, giving assistance, and

63

physically supporting younger children and arranging play materials for them based on their impairment is not only important for preventing injury, pain, and discomfort; it also enables them to receive instruction better and to manipulate materials and perform most efficiently. Preschoolers with physical impairments also tend to have difficulty with communication skills, so educators should give particular attention to facilitating and developing these.

Developmental Delays

Factors Leading to Developmental Delays

Developmental delays can come from genetic or environmental causes or both. Infants and young children with intellectual disabilities are most likely to exhibit developmental delays. Their development generally proceeds similarly to that of normal children but at slower rates; milestones are manifested at later-than-typical ages. Sensory impairments such as with hearing and vision can also delay many aspects of children's development. Children with physical and health impairments are likely to exhibit delays in their motor development and performance of physical activities. Another factor is environmental: Children deprived of adequate environmental stimulation commonly show delays in cognitive, speech-language, and emotional and social development. Children with autism spectrum disorders often have markedly delayed language and speech development; many are nonverbal. Autistic children also typically have impaired social development, caused by and inability or difficulty with understanding others' emotional and social nonverbal communications. When they cannot interpret these, they do not know how to respond and also cannot imitate them; however, they can often learn these skills with special instruction.

Characteristics Indicating Developmental Delays

Developmental delays mean that a child does not reach developmental milestones at the expected ages. For example, if most babies normally learn to walk between 12 and 15 months of age, a 20-month-old who is not beginning to walk is considered as having a developmental delay. Delays can occur in cognitive, speech-language, social-emotional, gross motor skill, or fine motor skill development. Signs of delayed motor development include stiff or rigid limbs, floppy or limp body posture for the child's age, using one side of the body more than the other, and clumsiness unusual for the child's age. Behavioral signs of children's developmental delays include inattention, or shorter than normal attention span for the age; avoiding or infrequent eye contact; focusing on unusual objects for long times or preferring objects over social interaction; excessive frustration when attempting tasks normally simple for children their age; unusual stubbornness; aggressive and acting-out behaviors; daily violent behaviors; rocking; excessive talking to oneself; and not soliciting love or approval from parents.

Traumatic Brain Injury (TBI)

IDEA's Legal Definition of Traumatic Brain Injury

TBI is defined by the IDEA law (the Individuals with Disabilities Education Act) as "an acquired injury to the brain from external physical force, resulting in total or partial functional disability or psychosocial impairment, or both, that adversely affect a child's educational performance." This definition excludes injuries from birth trauma, congenital injuries, and degenerative conditions. TBI is the foremost cause of death and disability in children (and teens) in the USA. The most common causes of TBI in children include falls, motor vehicle accidents, and physical abuse. In spite of the IDEA's definition, aneurysms and strokes are three examples of internal traumas that can also cause TBI in babies and young children. External head injuries that can result in TBI include both open and closed head injuries. Shaken baby syndrome is caused by forcibly shaking an infant. This causes the brain literally to bounce against the insides of the skull, causing rebound injuries, resulting in TBI and even death.

Characteristics

TBI can impair a child's cognitive development and processing. It can impede the language development of children, which is dependent upon cognitive development. Children who have sustained TBI often have difficulties with attention, retention and memory; reasoning, judgment, understanding abstract concepts and thinking abstractly, and problem-solving abilities. TBIs can also impair a child's motor functions and physical abilities. The sensory and perceptual functions of children with TBI can be abnormal. Their ability to process information is often compromised. Their speech can also be affected. In addition, TBIs can impair a child's psychosocial behaviors. Memory deficits are commonest, tend to be more long lasting, and are often area specific; for example, a child may recall personal experiences but not factual information. Other common characteristics of TBI include cognitive inflexibility or rigidity, damaged conceptualization and reasoning, language loss or poor verbal fluency, problems with paying attention and concentrating, inadequate problem solving, and problems with reading and writing.

Etiologies and Characteristics of Multiple Disabilities

The term multiple disabilities refers to any combination of more than one disabling condition. For example, a child may be both blind and deaf due to causes such as having rheumatic fever in infancy or early childhood. Anything causing neurological damage before, during, or shortly after birth can result in multiple disabilities, particularly if it is widespread rather than localized. For example, infants deprived of oxygen or suffering traumatic brain injuries in utero, during labor or delivery, or postnatally can sustain severe brain damage. So can babies having encephalitis or meningitis and those whose mothers abused drugs prenatally. Infants with this type of extensive damage can often present with multiple disabilities, including intellectual disabilities, cerebral palsy, physical paralysis, mobility impairment, visual impairment, hearing impairment, and speech-language disorders. They may have any combination of or all of these disabilities as well as others. In addition to a difficulty or inability with normal physical performance, multiply disabled children often have difficulty acquiring and retaining cognitive skills and transferring or generalizing skills among settings and situations.

Prematurity or Preterm Birth

Babies born before 37 weeks' gestation are classified as premature or preterm. Premature infants can have difficulty with breathing, as their lungs are not fully developed, and with regulating their body temperatures. Premature infants may be born with pneumonia, respiratory distress, extra air or bleeding in the lungs, jaundice, sepsis or infection, hypoglycemia (low blood sugar), severe intestinal inflammation, bleeding into the brain or white-matter brain damage, or anemia. They have lower-than-normal birth weights, body fat, muscle tone, and activity. Additional typical characteristics of premature infants include apnea (interrupted breathing); lanugo (a coating of body hair that full-term infants no longer have); thin, smooth, shiny, translucent skin through which veins are visible; soft, flexible ear cartilage; cryptorchidism (undescended testicles) and small, non-ridged scrotums in males; enlarged clitorises in females; and feeding difficulties caused by weak or defective sucking reflexes or incoordination of swallowing with breathing.

Disabling Conditions Resulting from Premature Births

Physicians find it impossible to predict the long-term results of prematurity for any individual baby based on an infant's gestational age and birth weight. However, some related immediate and long-term effects can be identified. Generally, the lower the birth weight and the more prematurely a

65

child is born, the greater the risk is for complications. Infants born at less than 34 weeks of gestation typically cannot coordinate their sucking and swallowing and may temporarily need feeding or breathing tubes or oxygen. They also need special nursery care until able to maintain their body temperatures and weights. Long-term complications of prematurity can include bronchopulmonary dysplasia, a chronic lung condition; delayed physical growth and development; delayed cognitive development; mental or physical delays or disabilities; and blindness, vision loss, or retinopathy of prematurity (formerly called retrolental fibroplasia). While some premature infants sustain long-term disabilities, some severe, other babies born prematurely grow up to show no effects at all; and any results within this range can also occur.

Required and Recommended Information in Screening for Developmental Disorders

If a young child has been screened for developmental disorders or delays within the past 6 months and no changes have been observed or reported, repeat screening may be waived. Initial screenings are required. Hearing and vision screenings are mandatory in screening young children. Formal developmental measures are also required, which may include screening tests of motor skills development, cognitive development, social-emotional development, and self-help skills development. Formal screening tests of speech-language development are also required. Additional tests recommended during screening include informal measures. For example, checklists, rating scales, and inventories may be used to screen a child's behavior, mood, and performance of motor skills, cognitive skills, self-help skills, and social and emotional skills. On checklists, parents or caregivers check whether the child does or does not demonstrate listed behaviors, or assessors may complete them via parent or caregiver interviews or interviewing and observing the child. Rating scales ask parents, caregivers, and assessors to rate a child's behaviors, affect, mood, and so on, within a range of numbered and labeled descriptions. Inventories list demonstrated skills and needs. Behavioral observations and existing records and information are also used.

Features of Developmental Screenings and Evaluations

If a child's development is suspected of being delayed—for example, the child is not reaching developmental milestones during expected age ranges—a developmental screening may be administered. Screening tests are quickly performed and yield more general results. The hospital or doctor's office may give a questionnaire to the parent or caregiver to complete for a screening. Alternatively, a health or education professional may administer a screening test to the child. Screening tests are not intended to diagnose specific conditions or give details; they are meant to identify children who may have some problem. Screenings can overidentify or under-identify developmental delays in children. Hence, if the screening identifies a child as having developmental delay(s), the child is then referred for a developmental evaluation—a much longer, more thorough, comprehensive, in-depth assessment using multiple tests, administered by a psychologist or other highly-trained professional. Evaluation provides a profile of a child's strengths and weaknesses in all developmental domains. Determination of needs for early intervention services or treatment plans is based on evaluation results.

Developmental Evaluation Data Types

The child's social history should be obtained. This is typically done by a social worker. Details of the child's developmental progress heretofore; the family's composition, socioeconomic status, and situation; and the child's and family's health and medical histories and status should be emphasized. A physician's or nurse's medical assessment is required, including a physical examination, and if indicated, a specialist's examination. A psychologist typically assesses intellectual and cognitive development; at least one such test is generally required. At least one test of adaptive behavior is also required to assess emotional-social development. Self-help skills are evaluated; this may be included within cognitive, adaptive behavior, or programming assessments. Communication skills are typically evaluated by a speech-language pathologist. Both receptive and expressive language must be tested and comprehensively rather than simply by single-word vocabulary tests. As indicated, speech articulation is also tested. At least one test of motor skills, typically administered by a physical or occupational therapist, is required. Programming evaluation requires at least one criterion-referenced or curriculum-based measure, typically administered by an educator.

Behavioral Variations and Characteristics of ADHD

While the chief symptoms associated with ADHD are inattentiveness, impulsive behavior, distractibility, and excessive physical activity, there is considerable variation among individual children having ADHD. For example, the degree of severity of this condition can vary widely from one child to the next. In addition, each child can vary in how much he or she exhibits each of these primary characteristics. Some children might not appear to behave very impulsively but show severe deficits in attention. Some may focus better, but only for short periods, and are very easily distracted. Some display very disruptive behavior, while others do not but may daydream excessively, not attending to programming. In general, children who have ADHD can show deficits in following rules and directions. Also, when their developmental skills are evaluated or observed, they are likely to demonstrate inconsistencies in performance over time. To identify or select specific intervention methods and strategies, professionals should use a comprehensive evaluation to obtain information about the child's specific behaviors in his or her natural environment that need remediation.

Child Find

Child Find is an ongoing process with the aim of locating, identifying, and referring young children with disabilities and their families as early as possible for service programs. This process consists of activities designed to raise public awareness and screenings and evaluations to identify and diagnose disabilities. The federal IDEA law mandates under Part B that disabled children are guaranteed early childhood special education services and under Part C that infants and toddlers at risk for developmental delays are guaranteed early intervention programs. (Eligibility guidelines vary by U.S. states.) The IDEA requires school districts to find, identify, and evaluate children with disabilities in their attendance areas. School districts have facilitated this Child Find process by establishing community informed referral networks whose members refer children who may have exceptional educational needs (EENs). Network members typically include parents, doctors, birth-to-3 programs, child care programs, Head Start programs, public health agencies, social service agencies, and any other community members with whom the young children come into contact.

Current Collaborative Approaches and Models of Screening

Historically, the tradition was to conduct kindergarten screenings of children entering schools around age 5. However, in recent years, school districts have developed community referral networks to assist in the processes of Child Find, screening, evaluation, and referral for early intervention and early childhood special education and related services. Current models are more informal, proactive, and collaborative. Cooperative educational interagency service efforts give parents information about normal early childhood development and available community resources and offer opportunities for developmental screenings of their young children. Specific procedures are governed by individual U.S. state laws. Generally, district networks implementing current models send developmental review forms to parents to complete in advance, and then they attend a developmental screening at a community site. Parents discuss normal early childhood growth and development with program staff, while in the same room, trained professionals observe their children as they play. Children's vision and hearing are also screened. Parents can discuss their children's current development with psychologists, early childhood educators, or counselors. Thereafter, they can learn about community resources.

Defining Developmental Delays in Infants and Toddlers

The IDEA Part C specifies the areas of development that states must include in defining developmental delays. However, individual states must identify the criteria they use to determine eligibility, including pertinent diagnostic instruments, procedures, and functional levels. States currently use quantitative and qualitative measures. Quantitative criteria for developmental delay include: difference between chronological age and performance level, expressed as a percentage of chronological age; performance at a given number of months below chronological age; or number of standard deviations (SDs) below mean of performance on a norm-referenced test. Qualitative criteria include: development considered atypical or delayed for established norms or observed behaviors considered atypical. At least one state differentially defines delay according to a child's age in months, with the rationale that a 25% delay, for example, is very different for a 1-year-old than a 3-year-old. Quantitative criteria for defining delay and determining eligibility vary widely among states. A 25% or 20% delay; 2 SDs below mean in 1+ areas or 1.5 SD below mean in 2+ areas are some common state criteria.

Single and Multiple Risk Factors in Infants and Toddlers for Developmental Delays

Scientists find that developmental outcomes for children are not reliably predicted by any one risk factor or event. Developmental risk increases with increased biological, medical, or environmental risk factors. However, researchers have found some variables that afford resiliency in children to offset risk factors. These can include the child's basic temperament, the child having high self-esteem, the child having a good emotional relationship with at least one parent; and the child having experiences of successful learning. These findings indicate that assessments should include criteria for multiple biological and environmental risk factors, for cumulative biological and environmental risk factors, and for protective or resilience factors, considering all of these in the context of change occurring over time. Under the IDEA (the Individuals with Disabilities Education Act), U.S. states have the option to provide early intervention services to children considered at risk for adverse developmental outcomes as well as those already identified with them. Some states apply multiple-risk models, requiring three to five risk factors for service eligibility. Some states also determine eligibility with less DD when biological, medical, or environmental risk factors also exist.

Information Sources on Early Intervention and Preschool Special Education Services

Military families stationed both in the United States and overseas who have young special needs children can seek information and assistance from the federally funded organization Specialized Training of Military Families (STOMP). The staff of STOMP is composed of parents having special needs children themselves, who also have been trained to work with other parents of special needs children. STOMP staff members are spouses of military personnel who thus understand the unique, specialized circumstances and needs of military families. Another government agency, the U.S. Department of Defense, includes the office of the Department of Defense Education Activity (DoDEA) and provides comprehensive guidance to military families with special needs children who are eligible to receive, or are receiving, free appropriate public education (FAPE) as mandated by the IDEA law (the Individuals with Disabilities Education Act), whether that education is located in the United States or in other countries.

Providing Special Education Services for Preschoolers

If parents observe that their preschooler is not attaining developmental milestones within the expected age ranges or does not seem to be developing in the same way as most other children, they should seek evaluation for possible developmental delay or disability. Although 3- to-5-year-olds are likely not in elementary school yet, the elementary school in a family's school district is still the best first contact because the IDEA law (the Individuals with Disabilities Education Act) specifies that school districts must provide special education services at no family cost to eligible children, including preschoolers. Another excellent source of more information about special education is the National Dissemination Center for Children with Disabilities (NICHCY) of the U.S. Department of Education's Office of Special Education Programs. They partner with nonprofit organizations like the Academy for Educational Development (AED) to produce useful documents for families with special needs children. NICHCY supplies state resource sheets listing main contacts regarding special education services in each U.S. state. Families can obtain these sheets at NICHCY's website or by telephone.

Information Sources for Evaluation to Determine Developmental Disability

Under the IDEA (the Individuals with Disabilities Education Act), evaluation information sources include: physicians' reports, the child's medical history, developmental test results, current classroom observations and assessments (when applicable), completed developmental and behavioral checklists, feedback and observations from parents and all other members of the evaluation team, and any other significant records, reports, and observations regarding the child. Under the IDEA, involved in the evaluation are parents, at least one regular education teacher and special education teacher if the child has these, and any special education service provider working with the child—for children receiving early intervention services from birth through age 2 and transitioning to preschool special education, it may be an early intervention service provider; a school administrator knowledgeable about children with disabilities, special education policies, regular education curriculum, and resources available; a psychologist or educator who can interpret evaluation results and discuss indicated instruction; individuals with special expertise or knowledge regarding the child (recruited by school or parents); when appropriate, the child; and other professionals, for example, physical or occupational therapists, speech therapists, medical specialists, and so on.

Special Education Services for Preschool Children

Special education for preschoolers is education specifically designed to meet the individual needs of a child aged 3 to 5 years with a disability or developmental delay. The specialized design of this instruction can include adaptations to the content, to the teaching methods, and the way instruction is delivered to meet a disabled child's unique needs. Special education for preschoolers includes various settings, such as in the home, in classrooms, hospitals, institutions, and others. It also includes a range of related services, such as speech-language pathology services, specialized physical education instruction, early vocational training, and training in travel skills. The school district's special education system provides evaluation and services to eligible preschoolers free of charge. Evaluation's purposes are to determine whether a child has a disability under the IDEA's (the Individuals with Disabilities Education Act) definitions and determine that child's present educational needs.

Post-Evaluation and the Individualized Education Program

After a preschool child is evaluated, the parents and involved school personnel meet to discuss the evaluation results. Parents are included in the group that decides whether the child is eligible for special education services based on those results. For eligible children, the parents and school personnel will develop an IEP. Every child who will receive special education services must have an IEP. The main purposes of the IEP are (1) to establish reasonable educational goals for the individual child and (2) to indicate what services the school district will provide to the child. The IEP includes a statement of the child's present levels of functioning and performance. It also includes a list of more general instructional goals for the child to achieve through school and parental support along with more specific learning objectives reflecting those goals and specifying exactly what the child will be able to demonstrate, under what circumstances, how much of the time—for example, a percentage of recorded instances—and within what time period (e.g., 1 year).

Individualized Education Program Goals and Objectives

In an IEP, the goals are more global, describing a skill for the child to acquire or a task to master. The objectives are more specific articulations of achievements that will demonstrate the child's mastery of the goal. For example, if a goal is for the child to increase his or her functional communicative vocabulary, a related objective might be for the child to acquire X number of new words in X length of time; another related objective could be for the child to use the words acquired in 90% of recorded relevant situations. If the goal is for the child to demonstrate knowledge and discrimination of colors, one objective might be for the child to identify correctly a red, yellow, and blue block 95% of the time when asked to point out each color within a group of blocks. Progress toward or achievement of some objectives may be measured via formal tests; with preschoolers, many others are measured via observational data collection.

Progress Monitoring, Updating, and Revising IEPs

Once a child has been identified with a disability, determined eligible for special education and related services under the IDEA (the Individuals with Disabilities Education Act), and had an IEP developed and implemented, the child's progress must be monitored. Monitoring methods may be related to evaluation methods. For example, if a child identified with problem behaviors was initially evaluated using a behavioral checklist, school personnel can use the same checklist periodically, comparing its results to the baseline levels of frequency and severity originally obtained. If an affective disorder or disturbance was identified and instruments like the Beck Depression Inventory or Anxiety Inventory were used, these can be used again periodically; reduced symptoms would indicate progress. If progress with IEP goals and objectives is less or greater than expected, the IEP team meets and may revise the program. This can include specifying shorter or longer times to achieve some goals and objectives; lowering or raising requirements proving too difficult or easy; resetting successive objective criteria in smaller or larger increments; changing teaching methods, content, or materials used, and so on.

Informal Assessment Instruments

EC teachers assess pre-K children's performance in individual, small-group, and whole-class activities throughout the day using informal tools that are teacher-made, school/program/district-furnished, or procured by school systems from commercial educational resources. For classroom observations, teachers might complete a form based on their observations during class story or circle time, organized using three themes per day, each targeting different skills—social-emotional, math, alphabet knowledge, oral language, or emergent writing. They note the names of children demonstrating the specified skill and those who might need follow-up, and provide needed one on one interventions daily. For individual observations, teachers might fill out a chart divided into domains like physical development; oral language development; math; emergent reading; emergent writing; science and health; fine arts; technology and media; social studies; social-emotional development; and approaches to learning, noting one child's strengths and needs in each area per chart. In addition to guided observation records, teachers complete checklists; keep anecdotal and running records; and assemble portfolio assessments of children's work. Tracking children's progress informs responsive instructional planning.

Screening Versus Assessment Instruments

A variety of screening and assessment instruments exist for EC measurement. Some key areas where they differ include which developmental domains are measured by an instrument; for which applications an instrument is meant to be used; to which age ranges an instrument applies; the methods by which a test or tool is administered; the requirements for scoring and interpreting a test, scale, or checklist; whether an instrument is appropriate for use with ethnically diverse populations; and whether a tool is statistically found to have good validity and reliability. EC program administrators should choose instruments that can measure the developmental areas pertinent to their program; support their program's established goals; and include all EC ages served in their program. Instruments' administration, scoring, and interpretation methods should be congruent with program personnel's skills. Test/measure administration should involve realistic time durations. Instruments/tools should be appropriate to use with ethnically diverse and non-English-speaking children and families. Tests should also be proven psychometrically accurate and dependable enough.

Typical Applications of Screening and Assessment Instruments

The ways in which screening and assessment instruments applicable to ECE are used include a wide range of variations. For example, ECE programs typically need to identify children who might have developmental disorders or delays. Screening instruments are used to identify those children showing signs of possible problems who need assessments, not to diagnose problems. Assessment instruments are used to develop and/or confirm diagnoses of developmental disorders or delays. Assessment tools are also used to help educators and therapists plan curricular and treatment programs. Another important function of assessment instruments is to determine a child's eligibility for a given program. In addition, once children are placed in ECE programs, assessment tools can be used to monitor their progress and other changes occurring through time. Moreover, program administrators can use assessment instruments to evaluate children's achievement of the learning outcomes that define their program goals—and by extension, the teachers' effectiveness in furthering children's achievement of those outcomes.

Formal Assessment Instruments

Formal assessment instruments are typically standardized tests, administered to groups. They give norms for age groups/developmental levels for comparison. They are designed to avoid administrator bias and capture children's responses only. Their data can be scaled and be reported in aggregate to school/program administrators and policymakers. The Scholastic Early Childhood Inventory (SECI) is a formal one on one instrument to assess children's progress in four domains found to predict kindergarten readiness: phonological awareness, oral language development, alphabet knowledge, and mathematics. Other instruments measuring multiple developmental domains include the Assessment, Evaluation and Programming System (0–6 years) for planning intervention; the Bayley Scale for Infant Development (1–42 months) for assessing developmental delays; the Brigance Diagnostic Inventory of Early Development (0–7 years) for planning instruction; the Developmental Profile II (0–6 years) to assess special needs and support IEP development; the Early Coping Inventory (4–36 months) and Early Learning Accomplishment Profile (0–36 months), both for planning interventions; and the Infant-Toddler Developmental Assessment (0–42 months) to screen for developmental delays.

Screening and Assessment Instruments Measuring Development

The available screening and assessment instruments for EC development cover a wide range in scope and areas of focus. Some measures are comprehensive, assessing young children's progress in many developmental domains including sensory, motor, physical, cognitive, linguistic, emotional, and social. Some other instruments focus exclusively on only one domain, such as language development or emotional-social development. Some instruments even focus within a domain upon only one of its facets, e.g. upon attachment or temperament within the domain of emotional-social development. In addition, some tools measure risk and resiliency factors influencing developmental delays and disorders. Programs like Head Start that promote general EC development should select comprehensive assessment instruments. Outreach programs targeting better identification of children having untreated and/or undetected mental health problems should choose instruments assessing social-emotional development. Clinics treating children with regulatory disorders might select an instrument measuring temperament. Prevention programs helping multiple-needs families access supports and services could use a measure for risk and resiliency factors. Multifaceted EC programs often benefit most from using several instruments in combination.

Age Ranges Included in Various Screening and Assessment Instruments

An important consideration for screening and assessment in early childhood is that EC development is very dynamic and occurs rapidly. Hence screening and assessment instruments must be sensitive to such frequent and pronounced developmental changes. Some instruments target specific age ranges like 0–36 months. Others cover wider ranges, e.g. children aged 2–16 years. The latter may have internal means of application to smaller age ranges; for example, sections respectively for 3–6-month-old babies, 7–12-month-olds, and 12–18-month-olds. Or they indicate different scoring and interpretation criteria by age; for example, some screening tools specify different numbers of test items depending on the child's age to indicate a need for assessment. Choosing screening and assessment instruments covering the entire age range served in an ECE program is advantageous—not only because they can be used with all child ages in the program, but also because they can be administered and readministered at the beginning and end of programs and/or in between, to compare and monitor changes, which is difficult with separate, age-specific tests.

Features of Paper-and-Pencil Reports

The most common form of paper-and-pencil report about infants and young children are questionnaires. Parents, caregivers, and teachers read printed questions or statements and respond by selecting Yes or No to a question or a number/level on a Likert-type scale showing the degree to which they agree with a statement. For self-administration, instruments must contain questions/statements written on reading levels accessible to the respondents and in their native languages. Alternatively, some questionnaires or surveys can be read to the respondent by an interviewer trained in or familiar with administration of the chosen instrument. Such self-reporting instruments usually take fewer than 20 minutes to finish, and ECE program personnel need comparatively little training to administer them. However, employees may need further training to score and/or interpret responses, or already-trained specialists may score and interpret them in some cases. ECE schools/programs/agencies can obtain some self-reporting instruments free of charge; other tools' publishers charge for response forms; and others charge only for initially obtaining their materials, allowing purchasers to reproduce them thereafter.

Features of Formal and Informal Observations

Some instruments require EC staff to watch a child's behavior and/or interactions with parents/caregivers and/or peers. Formal observations involve watching activities structured for the screening/assessment instrument. Informal observations involve watching a child's activities in natural settings like at home or in preschool during play times. Formal observation tools typically require staff to be trained to administer them. The trained observers' findings can include records of which developmentally normal behaviors a child has attained, incidences of problem behaviors noted, descriptions and evaluations of the quality of a child's social interactions with other people, and other observations of the child's behaviors that can inform screening and assessment. Observational screening and assessment instruments usually take more than 20 minutes for administration. Publishers of observational tests typically charge EC programs to order single-use recording forms; some allow them to purchase templates and then reproduce the forms.

Scoring and Interpretation of Various Screening and Assessment Instruments

Some instruments are fairly simple to score and interpret, needing little training of EC personnel. For example, paper-and-pencil questionnaires/surveys often only need the numbers/points for each item response added up for a total score; or a group of scores is obtained by summing values within sections. Interpreting some screening scores can be as simple as noting whether a child's score surpasses a designated cut-off value that signals assessment is needed. Such screenings can be scored and interpreted right after administration, and readily shared with parents and other stakeholders. Assessment instruments using more complicated scoring and interpretation include such procedures as weighting item values; reversing point values for certain items; converting raw scores into standardized scores or percentages; and referring to tables giving national norms for comparison. Standardized tests, including preschool IQ scales, commonly involve such methods. Assessors often need considerable training; advanced psychometric education and experience; thorough knowledge of EC development; and additional time to score and interpret these tests. Results may be discussed in separately scheduled meetings.

Interview Features

In EC programs conducting assessments, personnel usually conduct interviews with a child's parents, teachers, and/or caregivers. Interviews can be made in structured formats, i.e. the administrator reads prescribed questions as written to the interviewee, or semi-structured formats, wherein the administrator uses his/her judgment to add more questions to the written ones until s/he determines that the information provided is complete enough. Interview questions vary, covering subjects of parental concern, the child's identified areas of strengths and accomplishments, the child's identified areas of deficits or needs, the interactions between parents and child, and the child's behavior. Interviews can be brief, but usually they are longer than paper-and-pencil self-reporting questionnaires, surveys, or checklists. EC personnel frequently need to be trained to administer published interview-based instruments. Publishers typically charge schools/programs/agencies for ordering multiple, single-use response forms, or they may require a one-time order and allow them to reproduce the forms from their initial purchase to use for multiple administrations.

Features of Screening and Assessment Tools Using Structured Tasks

Screening and assessment instruments that use structured tasks involve a list of behaviors and/or skills that a child is expected to attain by a certain age range or developmental level. The administrators must present various activities or tasks to a child, and then record the details of the child's performance of each activity or task. Instruments using structured tasks require EC staff training for administration. They take over 20 minutes to complete. EC programs/schools/agencies must buy testing equipment/materials and single-use recording forms. Because paper-and-pencil questionnaires/surveys are easy to administer; apply across various settings, e.g. preschools, pediatricians' waiting rooms, homes, etc.; cost comparatively little; require minimal administrator training; and are frequently short, they are appropriate for screening use. While formal/informal observational tools, structured/semistructured interview tools, and structured-task tools take more training, time, and expense, they also provide more detailed information, making them useful for determining diagnoses and/or developing individualized care/instruction plans. Instruments using multiple methods, e.g. collecting data from various settings and respondents, yield the most comprehensive information.

Test-Retest Reliability

Test-retest reliability is how consistent/stable an instrument's results are across administrations. An instrument with good test-retest reliability yields the same results when administered twice or more to the same child within a short time. For example, the same assessor gives a child the same test twice within a few days or weeks, comparing the results. The more similar the results between/among administrations, the higher the test-retest reliability. This implies the instrument measures an attribute/construct that is stable over a short time. Due to the inherent rapidity and dynamism of EC development, we expect significant developmental changes over years and months; but over only weeks or days, we expect little or no substantial change. Therefore, instruments whose results are not stable over a short time are less utile for EC screening/assessment. For example, a child's scoring with "typical development" on one administration but "possible delay/disorder" a week later means the instrument does not define the child's developmental needs, and thus is not reliable.

Inter-Rater Reliability of Screening and Assessment Instruments

Inter-rater reliability is how consistent/stable an instrument's results are across different individual administrators/raters. Good inter-rater reliability means the instrument will give the same/similar results for the same child, at the same time, in the same setting, when administered by different people. This shows that the instrument measures a quality/construct that remains stable regardless of who administers the test. Significant differences among different raters' results present problems, especially with instruments using unstructured interviews, observations, or structured tasks. For example, if one rater scores a child as possibly having a developmental delay or disorder while another rater using the same test scores the same child as within the range of normal development, the instrument does not identify the child's true developmental needs and is unreliable. When different assessors (like parent vs. teacher) observe a child in different settings, though, like home vs. preschool, and/or at different times, varying results are expected and not necessarily indicative of inter-rater unreliability because children's behaviors can vary by setting.

Internal Consistency Regarding Test Instruments

A testing instrument is said to have internal consistency when its individual items correlate strongly with each other and with the total test score. This means that all of the individual items

74

(questions, stimuli, tasks, etc.) measure parts of the same construct that the test is intended to measure. A test with low internal consistency could be measuring additional attributes that the authors did not define or mean for the test to measure. Children with disparate developmental needs could thus receive similar scores, based on different test items. With comprehensive screening and assessment instruments that cover multiple domains of development, EC educators should look for internal consistency within each subscale of the test or within each domain tested. However, they should not necessarily expect internal consistency among the different domains or at the level of the test's full-scale/overall score. For example, they should not expect high correlation between a test's subscale measuring a child's language skills development and its subscale measuring a child's gross motor skills development.

Internal Consistency and Screening and Assessment Instruments

Whether a test's individual items contribute to measuring the construct the test is supposed to measure is internal consistency. It is determined by how much the test's individual items correlate with one another and with the overall score. A test with high internal consistency more accurately measures the specific content area/developmental domain/construct it means to measure. A test with low internal consistency poses problems when children who might have very different needs get the same score. For example, if a test meant to measure aggression has low internal consistency, its individual items are not correlated with one another or the overall score, implying it tests more than one construct. Two children given this test could score beyond the cutoff level indicating diagnosis or assessment need, but their scores could be due to completely different individual test items. Since individual test items do not correlate, the two children might have markedly different needs. Furthermore, those needs may not be related to aggression, since the test probably unintentionally measures additional constructs.

Concurrent Validity Regarding Screening and Assessment Instruments

When a screening or assessment instrument yields results comparable to those of another instrument whose validity has been previously established, it has good concurrent validity. Since the test used for comparison was already found valid, users have confidence in its results. Therefore, their confidence is warranted in another test showing high concurrent validity with the established test. For example, the Stanford-Binet Intelligence Scales and the Wechsler Preschool and Primary Scales of Intelligence (WPPSI) are both well-established IQ tests with demonstrated statistical validity and reliability. So if EC educators have found or been given a new instrument for measuring intelligence, they are likely to find that its authors have compared the test's results to the results obtained by the Stanford-Binet and/or WPPSI. Educators who have confidence in the Stanford-Binet and/or the WPPSI are then justified in having comparable confidence in the new test if its results were found similar to those of the established tests, indicating its high concurrent validity.

Content Validity Regarding Screening and Assessment Instruments

Whether a test instrument measures the entire content area it purports to measure is known as content validity. It determines whether a test can yield accurate and fair measures of the totality of the construct that the assessor wants to test. For example, if a screening instrument is intended to measure social-emotional development in a young child, it should include individual test items covering the range of this domain's important components. A screening test that covers a child's interactions with caregivers but not with peers; screens attention but not initiation of play; or screens for social skills but not communication skills would not address all elements of social-emotional development and thus not have good content validity. EC educators can use instruments with high content validity to generalize with more confidence about how a child's test performance predicts his/her levels of functioning in real life. By contrast, if a test has low content validity, generalizations about the tested child's development can exceed the test's scope and be inaccurate and/or unrealistic.

Predictive Validity in Screening and Assessment Instruments

A screening/assessment instrument's prediction of a child's behavior in real life is predictive validity. For example, an instrument screening for social-emotional disorders in preschool children might predict tantrum and/or oppositional behaviors in kindergarten. In another example, you would expect a screening instrument for social-emotional disorders to differentiate between children with normal/typical social-emotional development and those with mental health disorders. If a screening tool identifies a child with a potential mental health disorder and has high predictive validity, a complete clinical diagnostic evaluation of the screened child would diagnose a mental health disorder. Sensitivity is the instrument's accuracy—here, in identifying developmental disorders/delays, if it correctly identifies 9 of 10 children really having disorders/delays, it has 90 percent sensitivity. Specificity conversely would be accuracy in identifying children without disorders/delays. Despite high sensitivity and specificity, screeners yield some errors. False-positives over-identify delays/disorders where none exist; false-negatives under-identify existing delays/disorders. Unnecessary concern is a consequence of false-positives; lack of prevention/early intervention/treatment is a more serious consequence of false-negatives.

Norm-Referenced Versus Criterion-Referenced Tests

Norm-referenced tests compare a child's test results to those of a comparison group of other children in the same age group, grade, or developmental level. This comparison group is called a normative or standardization sample. Norm-referenced tests show how an individual child's performance compares to that of the general population of children. Criterion-referenced tests compare a child's test results to a predetermined standard of performance for the child's age group/grade/level. They show how an individual child's performance compares to standards established by educational experts. Norm-referenced tests are useful for determining whether a child is similar to the "average" child and identifying children performing significantly above or below average. Criterion-referenced tests are good for measuring the extent to which an individual child has mastered areas or domains of development and for monitoring changes over time in the child's levels of mastery.

Establishing and Maintaining Good Communication with Parents

When teachers send home a letter to parents explaining classroom practices and giving contact information at the beginning of the school year, parents perceive them as approachable and available. When a teacher calls each parent/guardian during school's first two weeks, parents appreciate and enjoy conversations. Calls also make it easier for teachers to contact parents later in the year regarding child issues if needed. Experts find it effective to mail postcards home, addressed to children or parents. Establishing simple class websites including teacher contact information facilitates parental access. Teachers' printing business cards and attaching them to their first parent letters conveys professionalism. Teachers using Internet/e-mail/print to publish weekly/monthly class newsletters informally keep parents apprised of children's instruction and teach parents to expect communication. Teachers can send parents invitations to visit prior to school/program Open Houses: teachers are perceived as more approachable when more parents are comfortable in classrooms. Having children write appreciation letters to parents for Open Houses encourages children to invite parents; parents also perceive teacher appreciation by association.

Applying Assessment Results to Planning Instruction for Individuals and Groups

ECE settings should provide organized outlines of developmentally appropriate guidelines for their children, including when and how to introduce and reinforce guidelines at each learning stage. These outlines are foundations for anecdotal observations and authentic assessments tracking developmental progress. ECE programs supply opportunities and activities to develop each discrete skill, including copious review and practice young children require for retention. Teachers should plan learning experiences meaningfully promoting developing identified guidelines and addressing children's interests. ECE settings should have organized progress-tracking systems following developmental sequences. These help teachers determine whether a child can move to the next level or prior skills that need additional reinforcement. Tracking systems should be easy to maintain and immediately give teachers basic information regarding each child's level of functioning for planning activities and discussions. Teachers should then create "ready reference" charts/graphs of assessment and monitoring results, giving an idea of the class/group's general functioning level, to inform activity/lesson planning and additional support needed for individual children—one on one for those below class/group level, enriched for those above it.

Knowledge of Children's Literature and the Writing Process

Communication Development Normally Occurring Within a Child's First Five Years of Life

Language and communication development depend strongly on the language a child develops within the first five years of life. During this time, three developmental periods are observed. At birth, the first period begins. This period is characterized by infant crying and gazing. Babies communicate their sensations and emotions through these behaviors, so they are expressive; however, they are not yet intentional. They indirectly indicate their needs through expressing how they feel, and when these needs are met, these communicative behaviors are reinforced. These expressions and reinforcement are the foundations for the later development of intentional communication. This becomes possible in the second developmental period, between 6 and 18 months. At this time, infants become able to coordinate their attention visually with other people relative to things and events, enabling purposeful communication with adults. During the third developmental period, from 18 months on, children come to use language as their main way of communicating and learning. Preschoolers can carry on conversations, exercise self-control through language use, and conduct verbal negotiations.

Milestones of Normal Language Development by the 2 Years Old

By the time most children reach the age of 2 years, they have acquired a vocabulary of about 150 to 300 words. They can name various familiar objects found in their environments. They are able to use at least two prepositions in their speech, for example in, on, and/or under. 2-year-olds typically combine the words they know into short sentences. These sentences tend to be mostly noun-verb or verb-noun combinations (e.g. "Daddy work," "Watch this"). They may also include verb-preposition combinations (e.g. "Go out," "Come in"). By the age of 2 years, children use pronouns, such as I, me, and you. They typically can use at least two such pronouns correctly. A normally developing 2-year-old will respond to some commands, directions, or questions, such as "Show me your eyes" or "Where are your ears?"

Salient General Aspects of Human Language Abilities from Before Birth to 5 Years of Age

Language and communication abilities are integral parts of human life that are central to learning, successful school performance, successful social interactions, and successful living. Human language ability begins before birth: the developing fetus can hear not only internal maternal sounds, but also the mother's voice, others' voices, and other sounds outside the womb. Humans have a natural sensitivity to human sounds and languages from before they are born until they are about 4½ years old. These years are critical for developing language and communication. Babies and young children are predisposed to greater sensitivity to human sounds than other sounds, orienting them toward the language spoken around them. Children absorb their environmental language completely, including vocal tones, syntax, usage, and emphasis. This linguistic absorption occurs very rapidly. Children's first 2½ years particularly involve amazing abilities to learn language including grammatical expression.

6 Months, 12 Months, and 18 Months

Individual differences dictate a broad range of language development that is still normal. However, parents observing noticeably delayed language development in their children should consult professionals. Typically, babies respond to hearing their names by 6 months of age; turn their heads

78

and eyes toward the sources of human voices they hear; and respond accordingly to friendly and angry tones of voice. By the age of 12 months, toddlers can usually understand and follow simple directions, especially when these are accompanied by physical and/or vocal cues. They can intentionally use one or more words with the correct meaning. By the age of 18 months, a normally developing child usually has acquired a vocabulary of roughly 5 to 20 words. 18-month-old children use nouns in their speech most of the time. They are very likely to repeat certain words and/or phrases over and over. At this age, children typically are able to follow simple verbal commands without needing as many visual or auditory cues as at 12 months.

Three Years

By the time they are 3 years old, most normally developing children have acquired vocabularies of between 900 and 1,000 words. Typically they correctly use the pronouns I, me, and you. They use more verbs more frequently. They apply past tenses to some verbs and plurals to some nouns. 3-year-olds usually can use at least three prepositions; the most common are in, on, and under. The normally developing 3-year-old knows the major body parts and can name them. 3-year-olds typically use 3-word sentences with ease. Normally, parents should find approximately 75 to 100 percent of what a 3-year-old says to be intelligible, while strangers should find between 50 and 75 percent of a 3-year-old's speech intelligible. Children this age comprehend most simple questions about their activities and environments and can answer questions about what they should do when they are thirsty, hungry, sleepy, hot, or cold. They can tell about their experiences in ways that adults can generally follow. By the age of 3 years, children should also be able to tell others their name, age, and sex.

Four Years

When normally developing children are 4 years old, most know the names of animals familiar to them. They can use at least four prepositions in their speech (e.g. in, on, under, to, from, etc.). They can name familiar objects in pictures, and they know and can identify one color or more. Usually they are able to repeat four-syllable words they hear. They verbalize as they engage in their activities, which Vygotsky dubbed "private speech." Private speech helps young children think through what they are doing, solve problems, make decisions, and reinforce the correct sequences in multistep activities. When presented with contrasting items, 4-year-olds can understand comparative concepts like bigger and smaller. At this age, they are able to comply with simple commands without the target stimuli being in their sight (e.g. "Put those clothes in the hamper" [upstairs]). 4-year-old children will also frequently repeat speech sounds, syllables, words, and phrases, similar to 18-month-olds' repetitions but at higher linguistic and developmental levels.

Five Years

Once most children have reached the age of 5 years, their speech has expanded from the emphasis of younger children on nouns, verbs, and a few prepositions, and is now characterized by many more descriptive words, including adjectives and adverbs. 5-year-olds understand common antonyms, e.g. big/little, heavy/light, long/short, hot/cold. They can now repeat longer sentences they hear, up to about nine words. When given three consecutive, uninterrupted commands, the typical 5-year-old can follow these without forgetting one or two. At age 5 most children have learned simple concepts of time like today, yesterday, tomorrow; day, morning, afternoon, night; and before, after, and later. 5-year-olds typically speak in relatively long sentences, and normally should be incorporating some compound sentences (with more than one independent clause) and complex sentences (with one or more independent and dependent clauses). 5-year-old children's speech is also grammatically correct most of the time.

Personal Narratives

Personal narratives are the way that young children relate their experiences to others by telling the stories of what happened. The narrative structure incorporates reporting components such as: who was involved; where the events took place; and what happened. Understanding and using this structure is crucial to young children for their communication; however, many young children cannot follow or apply this sequence without scaffolding (temporary support as needed) from adults. Adults can ask young children guiding questions to facilitate and advance narratives. They can also provide learning tools that engage children's visual, tactile (touch), and kinesthetic (body position and movement) senses. This reinforces narrative use, increases the depth of scaffolding, and motivates children's participation. Children learn to play the main character; describe the setting; sequence plot actions; and use words and body language to express emotions. Topic-related action sequences or "social stories" are important for preschoolers to comprehend and express to promote daily transitions and self-regulation. Such conversational skills attainment achieves milestones in both linguistic and emotional-social development.

Achievements or Processes Enabled by Oral Language Skills Development

Crucial oral language development skills enable children to (1) communicate by listening and responding to others' speech; (2) comprehend meanings of numerous words and concepts encountered in their listening and reading; (3) acquire information on subjects they are interested in learning about; and (4) use specific language to express their own thoughts and ideas. Research finds young children's ability to listen to, understand, and use spoken and written language is associated with their later reading, spelling, and writing literacy achievement. Infants typically begin developing oral language skills, which continue developing through life. Babies develop awareness of and attend to adult speech, and soon begin communicating their needs via gestures and speech sounds. Toddlers express emotions and ideas and solicit information via language. They start uttering simple sentences, asking questions, and giving opinions regarding their likes and dislikes. Young preschoolers expand their vocabularies from hearing others' speech and from books. They describe past and possible future events and unseen objects; tell fictional/"make-believe" stories; and use complete sentences and more complex language.

Benefits of Play-Based Activities

When young children play, they often enact scenarios. Play scenarios tell stories that include who is involved, where they are, what happens, why it happens, and how the "actors" feel about it. Children engage in planning when they decide first what their playing will be about; which children are playing which roles; and who is doing what. This planning and the thought processes involved reflect narrative thinking and structure. Children who experience difficulties with planning play are more likely to avoid participating or to participate only marginally. Since playing actually requires these thought and planning processes, children who do not play spontaneously can be supported in playing by enabling them to talk about potential narratives/stories as foundations for play scenarios. When conflicts emerge during play, conversation is necessary to effect needed change. Narrative development constitutes gradual plot development; play conflicts are akin to fictional/personal narrative problems and result in changed feelings. Adults can help young children discuss problems, identify the changed feeling they cause, and discuss plans/actions for resolution.

Conversation of Adults with Young Children

Adults should converse with young children so the children get practice with: hearing and using rich and abstract vocabulary and increasingly complex sentences; using language to express ideas and ask questions for understanding; and using language to answer questions about past, future, and absent things rather than only about "here-and-now" things. To ensure they incorporate these elements in their conversations, adults can consider the following: in the home, care setting, or classroom, whose voices are heard most often and who does the most talking; the child, not the adult, should be talking at least half of the time. Adults should be using rich language with complex structures when conversing with young children. Adults should be talking with, not at children; the conversation should be shared equally rather than adults doing all the talking while children listen to them. Adults should also ask young children questions, rather than just telling them things. Additionally, adult questions should require that children use language to formulate and communicate abstract ideas.

Natural vs. Intentional

Children enjoy conversing with significant adults, including parents, caregivers, and teachers; and they require practice with doing so. Caregivers tend to talk with young children naturally, sometimes even automatically, throughout the day, which helps children develop significant language skills. However, caregivers can enhance young children's oral language development further through intentional conversations. One element of doing this is establishing an environment that gives the children many things to talk about and many reasons to talk. Another element of intentionally promoting oral language skills development is by engaging in shared conversations. When parents and caregivers share storybook reading with young children, this affords a particularly good springboard for shared conversations. Reading and conversing together are linguistic interactions supplying foundations for children's developing comprehension of numerous word meanings. Researchers find such abundant early word comprehension is a critical basis for later reading comprehension. Asking questions, explaining, requesting what they need, communicating feelings, and learning to listen to others talk are some important ways whereby children build listening, understanding, and speaking skills.

1:1 Conversations with Children

When parents, caregivers, or teachers converse 1:1 with individual children, children reap benefits not as available in group conversations. Caregivers should therefore try to have such individual conversations with each child daily. In daycare and preschool settings, some good times for caregivers to do this include when children arrive and leave; during shared reading activities with one or two children; and during center time. 1:1 talk allows the adult to repeat what the child says for reinforcement. It allows the adult to extend what the child said by adding more information to it, like new vocabulary words, synonyms, meanings, or omitted details. It allows the adult to revise what the child said by restating or recasting it. It allows the child to hear his or her own ideas and thoughts reflected back to them when the adult restates them. Moreover, 1:1 conversation allows adults to contextualize the discussion accordingly with an individual child's understanding. It also allows adults to elicit children's comprehension of abstract concepts.

Extended Conversations and Turn-Taking

When adults engage young children in extended conversations including taking many "back-and-forth" turns, these create the richest dialogues for building oral language skills. Adults make connections with and build upon children's declarations and questions. Adults model richer descriptive language by modifying/adding to children's original words with new vocabulary, adjectives, adverbs, and varying sentences with questions and statements. For example, a child

81

shows an adult his/her new drawing, saying: "This is me and Gran in the garden," the adult can build on this/invite the child to continue: "What is your gran holding?" The child identifies what they planted: "Carrot seeds. Gran said to put them in the dirt so they don't touch." The adult can then encourage the child's use of language to express abstract thoughts: "What could happen if the seeds were touching?" The adult can then extend the conversation through discussion with the child about how plants grow or tending gardens. This introduces new concepts, builds children's linguistic knowledge, and helps them learn to verbalize their ideas.

In-Depth Comprehension of Word Meanings

To support deeper word-meaning comprehension, teachers can give multiple definitions and examples for the same word and connect new vocabulary with children's existing knowledge. For example, a teacher conducting a preschool classroom science experiment incorporates new scientific concepts with new vocabulary words and conversational practice: pouring water on a paper towel, the teacher asks children what is happening to the water. A child answers, "It's going into the paper." The teacher asks how. Another child says, "The paper's soaking it up." The teacher confirms this, teaches the word "absorb," compares the paper to a sponge, and asks how much more water will be absorbed. A child responds probably no more since water is already dripping out. The teacher pours water on a plastic lid, asking if it absorbs. Children respond, "No, it slides off." Confirming, the teacher teaches the word "repel." This teacher has introduced new science concepts and new vocabulary words; engaged the children in conversation; related new concepts and words to existing knowledge; and added information to deepen comprehension.

Adults' Narration of Child Activities and Actions

One oral language development technique adults can use is to narrate, i.e. describe what a child is doing as s/he does it. For example, a caregiver can say, "I see you're spreading paste on the back of your paper flower—not too much so it's lumpy, but not too little so it doesn't stick. Now you're pressing the flower onto your poster board. It sticks—good work!" Hence narration can be incorporated as prelude and segue to verbal positive reinforcement. This promotes oral language development by introducing and illustrating syntaxes. Communicating locations and directionality employs verbs and prepositions. Describing intensity and manner employs adverbs. Labeling objects/actions that are currently present/taking place with new vocabulary words serves immediately to place those words into natural contexts, facilitating more authentic comprehension of word meanings and better memory retention. Caregivers/teachers can narrate children's activities during formal instructional activities and informal situations like outdoor playtime, snack time, and cleanup time, and subsequently converse with them about what they did.

Topics That Young Children Enjoy Talking About

Personal content is important with young children, who enjoy talking about themselves; e.g., what their favorite color is or where they got their new shirt; about their activities, like what they are constructing with Legos or shaping with Play-Doh; or about familiar events and things that access their knowledge, like their family activities and experiences with neighbors and friends. Here is an example of how a teacher can make use of children's conversation to reinforce it, expand it, and teach new vocabulary and grammar. The teacher asks a child what s/he is building and the child answers, "A place for sick animals." The teacher asks, "You mean an animal hospital [or vet clinic]?" and the child confirms. When a child says someone was taken to a hospital "in the siren," the teacher corrects the usage: "They took him to the hospital in the ambulance with the siren was sounding?" This recasts "siren" with the correct word choice, "ambulance." It incorporates "siren" correctly and extends the statement to a complete sentence.

Storytelling

Young children like to communicate about their personal life experiences. When they can do this through narrative structure, it helps them use new words they are learning, organize their thoughts to express them coherently, and engage their imaginative powers. Teachers/caregivers can supply new words they need; model correct syntax for sentences by elaborating on or extending child utterances and asking them questions; and build further upon children's ideas. For example, a teacher asks a child what they did at her sister's birthday party. When the child describes the cake and makes gestures for a word she doesn't know, the teacher supplies "candles," which the child confirms and repeats. When the child then offers, "Mom says be careful with candles," the teacher asks what could happen if you're not careful, the child replies that candles can start a fire. In this way, teachers give young children models of sentence structure, teach vocabulary, and guide children in expressing their thoughts in organized sequences that listeners can follow.

Shared Book Reading

When teachers share books with preschoolers, they can ask questions and discuss the content, giving great opportunities for building oral language through conversation. Books with simple text and numerous, engaging illustrations best invite preschoolers to talk about the characters and events in the pictures, and the plotlines they hear. Children's listening and speaking skills develop; they learn new information and concepts; their vocabularies increase; and their ability to define words and explain their meanings is enhanced through shared reading. Many children's books include rich varieties of words that may not occur in daily conversation, used in complete-sentence contexts. Teachers should provide preschoolers with fictional and nonfictional books; poetry and storybooks; children's reference books like picture dictionaries/encyclopedias; and "information books" covering single topics like weather, birds, reptiles, butterflies, or transportation whereby children can get answers to questions or learn topical information. Detailed illustrations, engaging content, and rich vocabulary are strong elements motivating children to develop oral language and understand how to form sentences, how to use punctuation, and how language works.

Abstract thought is stimulated by asking young children to think about things not observed and/or current. During/after sharing books, teachers can ask children what else might happen in the story; what they imagine the story's characters could be feeling or thinking—which also engages their imaginations; and ask them the meaning of the story's events using questions necessitating children's use of language to analyze this meaning. Teachers can ask younger children vocabulary words: "What did we call this animal?" and encourage them to use language by asking them to describe story details, like "How do the firemen reach people up high in the building?" Once younger children are familiar with a story, teachers can activate and monitor their retention and recall: "Do you remember what happened to Arthur the day before that?" Teachers can ask older children to predict what they think will happen next in a story; to imagine extensions beyond the story ("What would you do if...?"); and make conclusions regarding why characters feel/behave as they do.

Enhancing the Effects of Shared Reading

According to researchers' findings, the effectiveness of shared reading experiences is related to the ways that adults read with young children. Rather than merely labeling objects or events with vocabulary words, teachers should ask young children to recall the shared reading, which monitors their listening comprehension and retention abilities. They should ask children to predict what will happen next based on what already happened in a book; speculate about what could possibly happen; describe characters, actions, events, and information from the shared reading; and ask their own questions about it. Shared reading with small groups of 1–3 children permits teachers to involve each child in the book by questioning and conversing with them about the pictures and plots. To teach vocabulary, teachers can tell children word meanings; point to illustrations featuring new words; relate new words to words the children already know; give multiple, varied examples of new words; and encourage children to use new words they learn in their conversations.

Repeating Shared Reading

Young children develop preferences for favorite books. Once they know a story's plot, they enjoy discussing their knowledge. Teachers can use this for extended conversations. They can ask children who the characters are; where the story takes place; and why characters do things and events occur. They can ask specific questions requiring children to answer how much/how many/how far a distance/how long a time, etc. Teachers can also help children via prompting to relate stories to their own real-life experiences. In a thematic approach, teachers can select several books on the same theme, like rain forests or undersea life. This affords richer extended conversations about the theme. It also allows teachers to "recycle" vocabulary by modeling and encouraging use of thematically related words, which enhances memory and in-depth comprehension of meanings. Teachers can plan activities based on book themes, like painting pictures/murals, sculpting, making collages, or constructing models, which gives children additional motivation to use the new language they learn from shared readings of books.

Reading Aloud

Just before reading a story aloud to young students, the teacher should identify vocabulary words in the story that s/he will need to go over with the children. The teacher can write these words on the board or on strips of paper. Discussing these words before the reading will give the children definitions for new/unfamiliar words, and help them understand word meanings within the story's context. Teachers can also give young children some open-ended questions to consider when listening to the story. They will then repeat these questions during and after the reading. Questions should NOT be ones children can answer with yes/no. When discussing vocabulary words, the teacher can also ask the children to relate words to personal life experiences. For example, with the word fish, some children may want to talk about going fishing with parents. Teachers can encourage children to tell brief personal stories, which will help them relate the story they are about to hear to their own real-life experience, making the story more meaningful.

Before reading a story aloud, adults should tell young children its title and the author's name. Then they can ask the children what an author does (children should respond "write stories" or something similar). Giving the illustrator's name, the adult also can then ask the children what illustrators do (children should respond "draw pictures" or something similar). Holding up the book, an adult can identify the front, spine, and back and ask the children if we start reading at the front or back (children should respond "at the front"). Adults can show young children the illustration on the front cover of the book and ask them, "From this picture, what do you think is going to happen in this story?" and remind them to answer this question in complete sentences. These exchanges before reading a story aloud activate children's fundamental knowledge regarding print and books, as well as the last example's exercising their imagination and language use.

When a teacher is reading a story aloud to young children, after reading each page aloud, s/he should have the children briefly discuss the picture illustrations on each page and how they relate to what the teacher just read aloud. After they read aloud each plot point, action, event, or page, they should ask the children open-ended (non yes/no) questions about what they just heard. This monitors and supports listening comprehension and memory retention/recall and stimulates expressive language use. When children associate something in the story with their own life experiences, teachers should have them explain the connection. As they read, teachers should stop periodically and ask the children to predict or guess what will happen next before continuing. This promotes abstract thinking, understanding of logical sequences, and also exercises the imagination. After reading the story, teachers should ask children whether they liked it and why/why not, prompting them to answer using complete sentences. This helps children to organize their thoughts and opinions and to develop clear, grammatical, complete verbal expression.

Environmental Print

Street signs, traffic signs, store and restaurant names, candy wrappers, food labels, product logos, etc.—all the print we see in everyday life—are environmental print. Just as parents often play alphabetic games with children in the car ("Find something starting with A...with B..." etc.), adults can use environmental print to enhance print awareness and develop reading skills. They can ask children to find letters from their names on colorful cereal boxes. They can select one sign type, e.g. stop, one-way, or pedestrian crossing, and ask children to count how many they see during a car trip. They can have children practice reading each sign and talk about the phonemes (speech sounds) each letter represents. Adults can take photos of different signs and compile them into a little book for children to "read." By cutting familiar words from food labels, they can teach capitalized and lowercase letters; associate letters with phonemes; have children read the words; and sort words by their initial letters and by categories (signs, foods, etc.).

Alphabetic Principle

The alphabetic principle is the concept that letters and letter combinations represent speech sounds. Children's eventual reading fluency requires knowing these predictable relationships of letters to sounds, which they can then apply to both familiar and unfamiliar words. Young children's knowing the shapes and names of letters predicts their later reading success: knowing letter names is highly correlated with the ability to view words as letter sequences and to remember written/printed words' forms. Children must first be able to recognize and name letters to understand and apply the alphabetic principle. Young children learn letter names first, via singing the alphabet song and reciting rhymes and alphabetical jump-rope chants ("A my name is Alice, I come from Alabama, and I sell Apples; B my name is Betty..." etc.). They learn letter shapes after names, through playing with lettered blocks, plastic/wood/cardboard letters, and alphabet books. Once they can recognize and name letters, children learn letter sounds after names and shapes and spellings after sounds.

To help young children understand that written or printed letters represent corresponding speech sounds, teachers should teach relationships between letters and sounds separately, in isolation, and should teach these directly and explicitly. They should give young children daily opportunities during lessons to practice with letter-sound relationships. These opportunities for practice should include cumulative reviews of sound-letter relationships they have already learned and new letter-sound relationships as well. Adults should begin early in providing frequent opportunities to young children for applying their increasing knowledge and understanding of sound-letter relationships to early experiences with reading. They can do this by providing English words that are spelled phonetically (i.e. spelled the same way that they sound) and have meanings that are already familiar to the young learners.

Print Awareness

Even before they have learned how to read, young children develop print awareness, which constitutes children's first preparation for literacy. Children with print awareness realize that spoken language is represented by the markings on paper (or computer screens). They understand that the information in printed books adults read comes from the words, not the pictures. Children who have print awareness furthermore realize that print serves different functions within different contexts. They know that restaurant menus give information about the foods available; books tell stories or provide information; some signs show the names of stores, hotels, or restaurants, and other signs give traffic directions or danger warnings. Moreover, print awareness includes knowledge of how print is organized, e.g. that words are combinations of letters and have spaces in between them. Children with print awareness also know that [English] print is read from left to right and top to bottom; book pages are numbered; words convey ideas and meaning; and reading's purpose is to understand those ideas and acquire that meaning.

One way in which a teacher can get an idea of whether or to what extent a young child has developed print awareness is to provide the child with a storybook. Then the teacher can ask the child the following: "Show me the front of the book. Show me the back of the book. Show me the spine of the book. Where is the book's title? Where in the book are you supposed to start reading it? Show me a letter in the book. Now show me a word. Show me the first word of a sentence. Can you show me the last word of a sentence? Now will you show me the first word on a page? Please show me the last word on a page. Can you show me a punctuation mark? Can you show me a capital letter? Can you find a small letter/lowercase letter?" The teacher should also praise each correct response, supply the correct answers for incorrect responses, and review corrected answers.

Teachers should show young children the organization of books and the purpose of reading. When they read to them, they should use books with large print, which are more accessible for young children to view and begin to learn reading. Storybook text should use words familiar/predictable to young children. While reading together, teachers should point out high-frequency words like the, a, is, was, you; and specific letters, words, and punctuation marks in a story. Teachers can use index cards to label objects, areas, and centers in the classroom, pairing pictorial labels with word labels, and direct children's attention to them. They can invite preschoolers to play with printed words by making greeting cards, signs, or "writing" shopping lists and personal letters. They should point out print in calendars, posters, and signs. Also, teachers can have children narrate a story using a wordless picture book; write down their narrative on a poster; and reinforce the activity with a reward related to the story (e.g. eating pancakes after narrating the book Pancakes).

Self-Concept

Self-concept development begins during early childhood. Children come to identify characteristics, abilities, values, and attitudes that they feel define them. From 18–36 months, children develop the Categorical Self. This is a concrete view of oneself, usually related to observably opposite characteristics, e.g. child versus adult, girl versus boy, short versus tall, and good versus bad. A four-year-old might say, "I'm shorter than Daddy. I have blue eyes. I can help Mommy clean house!" Young children can also describe emotional and attitudinal aspects of self-concept, e.g. "I like playing with Joshua. I'm happy today." Preschoolers do not usually integrate these aspects into a unified self-portrait, however. Also, many preschoolers do not yet realize one person can incorporate opposite qualities; a person is either good or bad to them, rather than having both good and bad qualities. The Remembered Self develops with long-term memory, including autobiographical memories and things adults have told them, to comprise one's life story. The Inner Self is the child's private feelings, desires, and thoughts.

Phonics Instruction

Because children display individual differences in their speeds of learning sound-to-letter relationships, instruction should consider this; there is no set rate. Generally, a reasonable pace ranges from two to four sound-letter relationship per week. Relationships vary in utility: many words contain the sounds/letters m, a, t, s, p, and h, which are high-utility; but x as in box, gh as in through, ey as in they, and the sound of a as in want are lower-utility. High-utility sound-letter relationships should be taught first. Teachers should first introduce consonant relationships using f, m, n, r, and s, which are continuous sounds children can produce in isolation with less distortion than word-initial or word-medial stops like p, b, t, d, k, and g. Teachers should also introduce similar-sounding letters like b and v or i and e, and similar-looking letters like b and d or p and g, separately to prevent confusion. Single consonants versus clusters/blends should be introduced in separate lessons. Blends should incorporate sound-letter relationships children already know.

Language Experience Approach (LEA)

The LEA teaches beginning reading by connecting students' personal life experiences with written/printed words. A unique benefit is students using their own language and words, enabling them to interact with texts on multiple levels simultaneously. They thus realize they acquire knowledge and understanding through not just instruction, but also their own experiences. Four steps for implementing the LEA with EC groups: (1) Children and teacher choose a topic, like an exciting trip, game, or recent TV show, to discuss with teacher guidance. (2) Each child takes a turn saying a sentence using his/her own words that advances the discussion/story. The teacher writes the children's words verbatim without corrections, visibly and clearly. (3) Every few sentences or several words, the teacher stops and reads the record aloud for children to confirm accuracy. (4) Record review: the teacher points to each word, they read aloud together, or children repeat after the teacher. The teacher gives children copies of the record for independent review and possible compilation into books of LEA stories.

Whole Language Approach

The whole language approach concentrates on children's seeking, finding, and constructing meaning in language. As such, young children's early technical correctness is not the priority. Whole language teachers do not ignore children's errors. However, they do not make correction more important than overall engagement, understanding, and appreciation of reading, writing, and literature. Instead, teachers make formative assessments taking into account the errors each child makes. Then they design learning experiences for children that give them opportunities and assistance in acquiring mechanically correct linguistic forms and structures. While this holistic approach finds analytical techniques that break language down into components like phonemes and alphabet letters less useful, children with language processing/reading problems need to learn phonemic awareness, phonics, and other decoding skills to develop reading fluency. The National Reading Panel conducted a study (1997–2000) to resolve controversy over phonics vs. whole language as the best teaching method, finding that any effective reading instruction program must teach phonemic awareness, phonics, reading fluency, vocabulary development, and reading comprehension.

The whole language approach is based on constructivist philosophy and psychology: children construct their own knowledge through their interactions with their environments. In contrast to analytical approaches like phonics and alphabetic learning, constructivism views learning as an individual's unique cognitive experience of acquiring new knowledge, shaped by the individual's existing knowledge and personal perspective. Whole language instruction emphasizes helping children create meaning from their reading and express meaning in their writing. The whole-language philosophy emphasizes cultural diversity, integrating literacy instruction across subject domains, reading high-quality literature, and giving children many opportunities for independent reading, small-group guided reading, and being read to aloud by teachers. Whole language believes children learn to read by writing and vice versa. Realistically purposeful reading and writing are encouraged, as is using texts that motivate children to develop a love for literature. Early grammatical/spelling/technical correctness is not stressed, which can be problematic for children with reading/language processing disorders, who need explicit instruction in decoding skills and strategies.

Addressing Early Mechanical Errors in Learning Reading and Writing

The basal reader is America's commonest approach, used in an estimated 75–85 percent of K–8th-grade classrooms. The number of publishers offering basal reading series has decreased to about one-fourth of that in the 20th century, decreasing teacher responsibility for investigating/piloting readers for district approval. Using basal readers is a skills-based/bottom-up approach. Teaching smaller-to-larger reading subskills in systematic, rigid sequence assists students' transition from part to whole. Texts graded by reading level contain narration and exposition organized thematically by unit, including children's literature and diverse other genres. Phonics and other specific instructional strands with practice assignments develop skills, which are assessed with end-of-unit tests. For young children, text decoding is enabled through exact control of vocabulary items and word analysis skills, "big [enlarged] books," and word and picture cards. 20th-century and older series sacrificed comprehension and enjoyment for vocabulary control and skill acquisition, but 21st-century series vary methods more (like multiple story versions or book excerpts enabling selection sharing), affording children more motivation to read.

Directed Reading Activity (DRA) and the Directed Reading-Thinking Activity (DR-TA)

Using basal readers, the DRA comprises: (1) The teacher prepares children for reading by stimulating their motivation and introducing new concepts and/or vocabulary. (2) Students read silently, guided by teacher questions and statements. (3) The teacher develops student comprehension and students discuss characters, plots, or concepts to further comprehension. (4) After silent reading, students read aloud and read answers to teacher questions, known as "purposeful rereading." (5) Students' follow-up workbook activities/practice review comprehension and vocabulary. Some selections may include enrichment activities relating them to writing, art, drama, or music. The DR-TA approach is designed to develop critical readers through instruction in group comprehension. It requires children's active engagement in reading by processing information, asking questions, and receiving feedback as they read. The first phase of DR-TA is the teacher's direction of student thought processes throughout reading. The second phase involves developing student skills according to their needs as identified in phase 1, and additional extension or follow-up activities.

<u>Differences Between DRA and DR-TA Approaches</u>

(1) One main difference is that the DR-TA approach gives teachers all the responsibility and greater flexibility for developing lessons. As such it contains fewer directions than the DRA approach, which contains specific materials and questions to use, specific guidelines, and is more teacher-manual-oriented and materials-oriented. Therefore DR-TA can be used for not only basal readers, but also planning lessons in other curriculum areas involving reading; the DRA approach applies more directly to basal reader programs. (2) DRA manuals use mostly literal, factual questions, requiring only convergent thinking for student responses. However, in DR-TA, questions also demand divergent (creative) thinking of students, stimulating higher-level reading comprehension and interpretation. (3) New vocabulary is pretaught in the DRA approach before children read. The DR-TA approach excludes preteaching, realistically requiring student decoding of new vocabulary words during reading. (4) DRA manuals specify when to teach which skills for reading

comprehension. DR-TA approaches do not, requiring more questioning expertise and acceptance of some alternative student responses by teachers.

Phonological Awareness, Phonemic Awareness, and Phonics

Phonological awareness refers to the awareness of the sounds that make up a spoken language. This includes being aware of the fact that certain speech sounds rhyme with one another, and that it is possible to break down spoken sentences into individual words, words into individual syllables, and syllables into individual phonemes or speech sounds. Phonological awareness also includes the abilities to talk about speech sounds; to think about them; and to manipulate them into various combinations, sequences, and patterns. The latter includes changing one word into another by inserting, deleting, or exchanging an individual phoneme. Moreover, phonological awareness is an understanding of the relationship between spoken and written language. Typically, children's phonological awareness skills develop continuously and gradually throughout the later preschool years. Children develop phonological awareness through their exposure to language and through direct training, both of which are provided by the adults around them and in their lives.

Phonological awareness focuses on the awareness of speech sounds, which young children typically develop and learn before they learn to read. Phonemic awareness refers to awareness of the individual phonemes or speech sounds used in the child's native language, which the child hears in the language spoken by the adults and older children around them in their environment. Phonological awareness instruction teaches children to recognize the speech sounds they hear, to identify and differentiate these sounds, to produce them accurately, and to manipulate them. Good phonological awareness facilitates children's ability to make connections between sounds and alphabet letters, hence facilitating phonics. Phonics is the instructional method used to establish the Alphabetic Principle (i.e. the concept of sound-to-letter correspondence) and teach skills for decoding (breaking words down to their component sounds/letters) and encoding (blending/combining individual sounds/letters to form words).

Importance of Developing Phonological and Phonemic Awareness Skills

By developing phonological and phonemic awareness skills, young children develop awareness of the sounds used in their native language. Significantly, they also learn to make the association between the speech sounds (phonemes) they hear and the written/printed letter symbols that represent them. Understanding this connection gives young children the foundation they need for the development of future skills, including word recognition skills and the decoding skills needed to read printed/written language. When young children develop phonological and phonemic awareness, they are less likely to experience deficits or delays in learning to read, and are more likely to achieve success in reading and spelling. The consensus of a great deal of educational research is that strong phonological and phonemic awareness in children is often a predictor of future long-term success in spelling, reading, and overall literacy performance. Research has also found that this awareness is a more accurate predictor of future success than vocabulary knowledge, intelligence, socioeconomic status, and other related factors.

Examples of Phonological Awareness Skills

Young children who have developed phonological awareness can typically recognize the sounds of alliteration in spoken language, which is the repeated use of the same or similar consonants (e.g., "She sells seashells by the seashore"); the sounds of rhyming words; the sounds of words with the same initial sounds (e.g., "Wee Willie Winkie"); and final sounds. They can typically divide words into smaller parts, such as syllables and phonemes (speech sounds). They can usually also count these smaller parts. When given isolated speech sounds, they are typically able to blend these separate phonemes together to form familiar words. Children with good phonemic awareness realize that words are composed of phonemes, and that these individual sounds are symbolically represented by written/printed letters. Hence, they understand the relationship between speech and writing/print. Phonologically aware preschool children can typically also manipulate spoken language by adding, removing, or substituting specific speech sounds to create different words.

<u>Benefits of Phonological and Phonemic Awareness Instruction</u>

Phonological and phonemic awareness (PPA) instruction benefits all children learning to read, which includes preschoolers, kindergarteners, and first-graders. In addition, PPA instruction is important for children who are at risk for reading problems. Such children typically have fewer alphabetic skills due to less exposure to and less experience with using the alphabet. This can be because their families have less access to books and/or libraries; their parents have different expectations of reading, or they prioritize reading differently; or their parents do not realize the importance of reading aloud to children to literacy development. Preschoolers with delayed language development, who are more likely to be diagnosed with reading disorders by the time they reach school age, also benefit from PPA instruction. Enhanced PPA enables enhanced awareness of correct speech, so children with articulation disorders also benefit. According to research, children with spelling disorders perform poorly when given PPA tasks. Phonemic instruction improves their understanding of sound-to-letter relationships and their ability to recognize common spelling units found in words, thereby strengthening their spelling skills.

Oral Language Development

Because of the amount of variation among individual children in the process of normal oral language development, it is neither easy nor accurate to pin down any linguistic developmental milestone to a specific age. Therefore, ranges rather than ages are identified. For example, most normally developing children will utter their first recognizable words sometime between the ages of 12 months and 18 months. However, the progress of normal language acquisition is unpredictable in the individual child, a statement which holds true for other areas of normal growth and development. For example, one child may say his/her first word at the age of 10 months, while another child may begin using words at 20 months. The majority of typically developing children tend to begin speaking in complex sentences around the ages of four to four-and-a-half years. But again, because the pace of normal language development can vary, some children might use complex sentences by three years old, while others only develop this ability by five-and-a-half years old.

<u>Considerations for Adults</u>

The vast majority of children's oral language develops with great natural efficiency. Adults need not try to force it, but can nurture it by providing language-rich environments. Practices that may help include talking to children regularly starting at birth; reading regularly to babies, toddlers, and preschoolers; naming objects, actions, and events children encounter for them; and playing games with speech sounds, words, rhymes, etc. Adults need not be concerned when younger children distort or substitute more difficult phonemes like /r/ and /s/ with easier ones; this is normal. However, if a child still mispronounces such sounds beyond the age of about eight or nine, hearing and speech testing and therapy are indicated. Newborn hearing screenings are vital, as hearing loss is the most common disability in infants. If a child seems not to hear others' speech, a child's closest family/friends have trouble understanding the child's speech, or a child's communication is obviously different from that of same-age peers, adults should consult hearing and speech language specialists.

Genetic and Environmental Influences

As with so many other aspects of human growth and development, oral language development is a product of the combined influences of nature and nurture, and of the interactions between the two. Humans have inborn inclinations to seek out social interaction with other people. Babies communicate their needs and wants through crying and gesturing before acquiring spoken language, and they frequently understand adult communication. Researchers have pointed out that social interactions and oral language development do not take place for the purpose of learning rules, but for connecting with others and making sense of the reality we experience. Children have inherent abilities to decipher linguistic rules through their environmental exposure to spoken language. They can do this without formal instruction. This is evidence of the influence of nature on oral language development, as is over-regularization. An example of the latter includes applying regular verb rules to irregular exceptions (e.g., "tooths," "freezed," "goed," etc.) until exceptions are learned. Adults' constant corrections during this learning stage are typically futile. In addition to natural and environmental influences, children's language development is also influenced by their own cognitive abilities.

Phonology, Morphology, Semantics, Syntax, and Pragmatics

Phonology is concerned with the rules for the combinations of speech sounds within a given language. For example, while some African languages include words beginning with the –ng/[ŋ] phoneme, in English this sound is only word-medial or word-final, never word-initial. Most speakers follow such rules unconsciously. Morphology focuses on the smallest structural/grammatical units that convey or affect meaning. For example, in books, the noun book and the plural –s ending are each morphemes. Semantics focuses on the meanings of morphemes, words, and sentences. Syntax refers to sentence structure and word order, and is related to a language's rules for correctly combining morphemes and words into suffixes/inflections, sentences, questions, imperatives, etc. For example, features like participial modifiers and the verbs they modify are placed in a different order in German and English. The verb-containing phrase "I walked" would follow modifiers like "happily," "down the street," and "on a sunny day" in German, but would precede most if not all modifiers in English. Pragmatics focuses on rules for using language appropriately in various situations. An example of pragmatics would be how to speak at home versus how to speak at school or work.

Supporting Natural Development

Teachers should realize that whatever language and/or dialect a child speaks is a reflection of that child's family's and community's values, identity, and experiences. As such, it is a valid communication system that deserves respect. Adults should treat babies and young children as conversationalists even before they begin talking, because they learn conversational rules very early (e.g., attentive gazing, facial expressions, and turn-taking). A significant component of language development is peer learning, particularly in mixed-age child groups. Adults should encourage child interaction by providing activities conducive to talking and using a broad range of materials. Individual and collaborative activities should be balanced. Sharing books, building with blocks, engaging in dramatic play, and taking part in "shop"/carpentry-related activities all stimulate interaction and discussion. While peer learning is important, adults are children's main resources for initiating conversations, questioning, listening, responding, and maintaining language development. Adults should always keep this in mind. Continued interaction into the elementary grades and written language comprehension also support oral language development in children. Language informs all curriculum areas, so active learners in classrooms are always communicating.

Approaches to Communicating with Young Children

Researchers have found that a common practice among teachers when they are using language in their classrooms is to use linear or one-way questions requiring linear/one-way responses. However, experts recommend using reciprocal instructional approaches (e.g., asking open-ended questions that enable two-way/three-way responses). Studies also reveal that teachers are likely to dominate the classroom verbally. Experts believe a better approach would be to encourage and elicit children's conversational language and higher order cognitive skills by deliberately incorporating these into children's play activities. Experts state that teachers should have someone record a video of them during children's play time so they can monitor their own verbal behavior. Teachers should note how many times they verbally describe what the children do, how many times they repeat what a child says and then add some further information to it, how often they comment on and describe the properties of objects, and how often they ask open-ended questions. They should reflect not only on the number and duration of verbal interactions, but also on the quality of each conversation.

"Following the CAR" Teaching Strategy

Some researchers recommend using a teaching strategy called "Following the CAR" to engage in conversations with two- to five-year-old children. The C in CAR stands for Comment. In this step, the adult should comment on what a child is looking at, handling, or talking about. The adult should then wait five seconds. Experts find that this interval is important because it gives the young child time to hear and cognitively process the adult's comment, experience a response, formulate that response into verbal form, and then express it orally. The A stands for Ask. To continue the conversation the adult has begun and/or to start a new one, the adult should then ask the child questions about something the child is looking at, handling, or talking about. The adult should again wait five seconds to give the child time to respond. The R stands for Respond. Once the child gives an oral response, the adult should respond to what the child says by repeating the child's response and then adding a bit more information to extend the child's knowledge.

"Real" Conversations

Experts define "real" conversations as those that interest the child and consist of three to four exchanges/"turns" between the child and the adult. Having at least one real conversation with each child on a daily basis is a highly effective way to improve vocabulary development and develop listening comprehension beyond the level of individual words. Teaching strategies that support children's active participation in real conversations include the following: attentively listening to what the children say; inviting the children to join extended conversations with adults and peers; demonstrating genuine interest in and affection for the children; sending verbal and non-verbal messages that are consistent; avoiding making judgmental comments about children or anybody else to or in front of the children; addressing the children with courtesy; availing oneself of spontaneously occurring opportunities for informal conversations with each child, and/or even planning some opportunities; basing conversations on children's specific interests; and using children's experiences, as well as songs, stories, and books, as topics for conversation.

Using Stage-Appropriate Prompts with Children Learning English as a Second Language

Children in the preproduction stage of ESL acquisition comprehend little English. They do not speak English, but can nod, point, and draw. Teachers can give prompts like "Where is…?" "Who has…?" "Show me the…" or "Circle the…." In the early production stage, children's comprehension is limited. They can give one- or two-word answers, use some important words and familiar phrases, and use verbs in present tense. Teachers can ask "Yes/No" and "Either/Or" questions and questions requiring short answers consisting of one or two words. They can also use lists and labels to access and expand vocabulary knowledge. In the speech emergence stage, comprehension improves and simple sentences emerge, albeit with grammatical and pronunciation errors. Teachers can now ask children "Why...?" "How...?" and "Explain..." questions, and can expect answers in the form of phrases or short sentences. In the intermediate fluency stage, when students have excellent comprehension and can use correct grammar more often, teachers can ask children more abstract questions like "What would happen if...?" or "Why do you think...?" During the advanced fluency stage, when students approach native proficiency, teachers can instruct students to retell stories and make decisions.

Stages of Second Language Acquisition

For ESL children, the first stage of second language acquisition is preproduction, which takes place during roughly the first six months of learning. Listening comprehension is minimal. The child does not speak in English, but can nod/shake the head "yes/no," draw pictures, and point at things. In the second, early production stage, which lasts from roughly six months to one year into learning, children have limited English comprehension. They can utter one- to two-word answers, essential words, familiar phrases, and present tense verbs. In the third, speech emergence stage, which lasts from about one to three years into learning, children comprehend English well. They can speak in simple sentences, but still make mistakes in pronunciation and grammar. They often misunderstand jokes in English. The fourth stage is intermediate fluency, which begins about three years into the language acquisition process and extends to about the fifth year. By this stage, children have attained excellent English listening comprehension, and do not make many grammatical errors. In the fifth, final stage of advanced fluency, children's English language proficiency is similar to that of a native English speaker. Children typically reach this stage between five and seven years after they start learning English.

Improving (ESL) Instruction

Research in the early 1990s found that regardless of the type of bilingual education language programs used (e.g., early-exit, late-exit transitional, or immersion), teachers tended to ask ESL students questions requiring low levels of English language proficiency and lower-order cognitive skills. Teacher knowledge of what stages of second language acquisition students are in, as well as an awareness of the kinds of prompts and questions that are appropriate for each stage both enable teachers to approach children using suitable levels of discourse. Another advantage of knowing the stages is that teachers can assess students' content knowledge as well as their English language proficiency. A third benefit is that knowing language acquisition levels enables teachers to use what Vygotsky termed the zone of proximal development (ZPD), the gap between a learner's current capability and the next level of ability. Vygotsky found that the ZPD can be utilized by providing necessary temporary support—which Bruner called scaffolding—that is gradually withdrawn as students progress.

Using Scaffolding and the Zone of Proximal Development (ZPD)

Scaffolding, a term coined by Jerome Bruner, involves temporarily providing the support a learner needs to accomplish tasks just above his/her current performance level (i.e. things s/he cannot do independently, but can achieve with assistance). Lev Vygotsky identified the ZPD as the gap between a learner's current ability and the next level. He found that providing scaffolding enables teachers to exploit the ZPD to enhance learning. Teachers can apply this concept to ESL language development through direct instruction, by asking challenging questions, and/or by modeling correct English pronunciation and grammar. For example, a student in the first, preproduction stage of second language acquisition is able to find things, point at objects, and circle pictures, and such tasks are stage appropriate. However, a teacher can promote higher development by providing scaffolding to support students in answering Yes/No questions and/or giving one-word answers. These are tasks associated with the second, early production stage. With teacher support, the student can move to a higher stage of ESL acquisition.

Conversational Versus Academic English for ESL Learners

Conversational English requires basic skills that are used in interpersonal communication in everyday life, including basic vocabulary, grammar, and pronunciation. Conversational English enables ESL students to comprehend and participate in informal conversations with adults and peers. ESL children generally develop it after living in English-speaking locations for about two years. Conversational English is not particularly difficult cognitively. Children with conversational English skills sound fluent to most people. They converse in English, understand teacher questions, and may even translate for parents. However, their conversational fluency is often not reflected in school homework and tests. Teachers and parents may wrongly assume a child is unmotivated/learning disabled/lazy, when the true reason for the child's academic underachievement is that he or she lacks a knowledge of more cognitively demanding academic English (such as content specific vocabulary in math, science, etc.) and complex-compound sentence syntax. ESL students take at least five to seven years to become fluent in academic English, and take even longer when they lack native language literacy at the time they enroll in an English language school. To understand textbooks, solve word problems, write reports/papers, and develop the problem solving and critical thinking skills needed to comprehend and communicate abstract and novel concepts, students must master academic English.

Using Word Walls to Enhance Vocabulary Building for ESL Children

Young ESL children learn English vocabulary words by repeatedly singing the same familiar songs and chants, and by hearing the same stories many times. Such repetition is also favored by young children. While ESL children are involved in activities featuring repeated story readings, rhyme recitations, and/or singing, teachers can supplement these activities to enhance further vocabulary building by providing word walls. A word wall uses visuals to illustrate concepts represented by vocabulary words, as well as by related words. Key characteristics of vocabulary words and related words may also be shown. A word wall can also illustrate concepts like synonyms and subcategories. For example, a word wall for "Chicken Little," "The Little Red Hen," or another poultry-related story could have a picture of a chicken at the top labeled Chicken. Below it on the left might be several related pictures labeled with their names: Rooster, Hen, and Chick. Under the main chicken picture on the right could be several labeled pictures showing chicken characteristics (e.g., Feathers, Beak, and the Eggs that hens lay).

Input Hypothesis

Krashen and Terrell, who identified the stages of second language acquisition, posited the input hypothesis. This states that when an ESL learner in one stage of acquisition is given instructional input that includes some structures characteristic of the next stage of acquisition, and is also encouraged to use language reflective of that next, higher stage, the learner will advance to that next stage in listening and speaking. The input hypothesis is expressed as i + 1, where i represents the speaker's actual or current level (or stage) of second language acquisition, and i + 1 represents the speaker's potential second language development level. Teachers who know the stages of second language acquisition and the appropriate types of prompts to use for each stage can adapt their prompting so that students respond commensurately with their current stage of English language development and with the next higher stage at the same time.

Application of the Word-MES Formula to ESL Instruction

Jane Hill's "Word-MES" stands for "Word selection," "Modeling," "Expanding," and "Sounding like a book," respectively. Include examples in your response. "Word-MES" is a mnemonic for the key steps in applying the stages of second language development to ESL instruction. Students in the preproduction stage need to learn English vocabulary Words. Teachers should focus on helping students learn and correctly apply basic vocabulary. For example, using the story of "Goldilocks and the Three Bears," teachers can teach words like house, bed, cereal, oatmeal, too, hot, cold, hard, and soft. When working with students in the early production stage, teachers should Model correct English usage. For example, if a child says "Goldie runned," the teacher can respond, "Yes, Goldilocks ran and ran." Teachers should not make explicit corrections. When working with children in the speech emergence stage, teachers can focus on Expanding spoken/written sentences. For example, if a child says, "Bed was too soft," the teacher can expand on this by saying, "Yes, the second bed was too soft," adding the correct article and specifying adjective. Teachers can help students in intermediate and advanced fluency stages to Sound like books by exposing them to words outside their repertoires, repeatedly reading familiar books and singing songs, and using supplementary word walls.

Causes and Signs of Articulation Disorders

Articulation refers to the pronunciation of specific speech sounds and phonemes. Some phonemes are harder to produce than others. Therefore, it is normal for young children not to produce some sounds correctly until they reach a certain level of maturity. For example, children are around seven or eight on average before they can pronounce difficult phonemes like /r/ and /s/. Some children continue to distort, omit, or substitute a certain sound beyond the age norm. Speech therapy can help address these types of issues. If a child mispronounces multiple phonemes beyond the typical age ranges, testing is needed to determine the cause. Multiple factors can affect articulation, including hearing loss, misaligned teeth/jaws, missing teeth, a tongue that is shorter or longer than normal, velopharyngeal insufficiency interfering with complete vocal tract closure, breathing problems, mild cerebral palsy causing neuromuscular weakness and incoordination of the speech mechanisms, mild to moderate intellectual disabilities, and others. Some children's speech is difficult to understand due to multiple misarticulations, which may also be caused by any combination of the factors outlined above.

Causes and Signs of Delayed Language Development

Some children develop skills for understanding and using spoken and written language significantly later than normal, even when individual variations are taken into account. This can be due to a number of causes. Children with mild or moderate intellectual disabilities are likely to show delayed language development as well as delayed cognitive development, as these are closely related. Some children do not test with obvious cognitive deficits, but may have minimal neurological damage, which can delay language development. Other children may have no organic basis for the delay, but have been born into environments where they are deprived of adequate environmental stimulation. For example, if a child's parents and/or caregivers/teachers do not routinely talk to them, have limited daily interactions with them, and never read to them, young children are likely to exhibit delayed language development. Some parents who do interact with and talk to their children may still be linguistically, educationally, and culturally deprived themselves. Their children may feel loved and have good self-esteem, but may have a level of language development that is below average for their age.

Alphabetic Principle and Its Predictive Value for Future Literacy

The concept that written/printed letters and their patterns correspond to speech sounds is called the alphabetic principle. Children's future success with reading is strongly predicted by their early knowledge of the shapes and names of written/printed letters. Children's development of the abilities to view words as series of letters and to remember printed/written word forms is closely associated with their knowledge of letter names. Children cannot learn letter sounds or recognize words without knowing letter names. Being able to recognize and name multiple letters is a prerequisite for comprehending the alphabetic principle, which explains that spoken sounds and printed letters have predictable, systematic relationships. Children follow a sequence of first learning letter names, then learning letter shapes, and finally learning letter sounds. Singing the "ABC" song and reciting rhymes help children learn letter names. Playing with lettered blocks, large 3-D letters, and alphabet books helps them learn letter shapes. Teachers can plan informal instruction so that children are given multiple, varied opportunities to view, compare, and manipulate letters. Relevant activities may include identifying, naming, and writing upper-case and lower-case letters.

Instruction Principles in Teaching the Alphabetic Principle

Not all children begin preschool or school with good alphabetic knowledge, which refers to an awareness that written letters represent spoken sounds. For those who have not developed this prerequisite skill, educators must provide well-organized instruction to enable students to identify, name, and write the letters of the alphabet. Once they master these skills, they will have the foundation necessary to learn letter sounds and word spellings. A general instructional plan revolving around the alphabetic principle includes several elements. First, teachers should give children explicit instruction in isolated letter-sound correspondences. Second, during each day's lessons and activities, teachers should give children opportunities to practice their developing knowledge of letter-sound relationships. Teachers should both review children's cumulative learning of letter-sound correspondences already taught and create opportunities for children to practice new letter-sound relationships they are just learning. Finally, to give students opportunities to apply their expanding knowledge of the alphabetic principle early and frequently, teachers can supply phonetic spellings of words with meanings familiar to children for them to read.

Pace and Order of Lessons in Teaching the Alphabetic Principle

There is no expert consensus regarding the speed or sequence that should be used to teach young children letter-to-sound relationships. However, educators generally agree that phonemes and letters with the highest utility—those used most often—should be taught earliest. These include m, a, t, s, p, and h. Conversely, x as in "box," gh as in "through," ey as in "they," and a as in "want" are letter-phoneme relationships that are used less frequently. The letter-sound relationships of consonants least subject to distorted articulation when pronounced in isolation should be taught first. These include f, m, and n. Word-initial or word-medial stops (p, b, t, d, k, and g) are more difficult for young children to combine with other sounds than continuous (fricative/affricate) phonemes are. Sounds that are easily confused (like /b/ and /v/) or letters that look similar (like b and d, or p and g) should be introduced to young children in separate lessons.

96

Sound-to-Alphabet Letter Relationships Instruction

When a teacher is instructing preschoolers on the relationships between spoken sounds and written letters (known as the alphabetic principle), s/he might begin by introducing a few (e.g., two, three, or four) single consonant sounds and one or two short vowel sounds. Once the children have mastered these, the teacher can present some additional new single consonant sounds, present some additional new short vowel sounds, and introduce one long vowel sound in a subsequent lesson. Then, the teacher could introduce consonant blends like st-, cl-, etc. in a separate lesson. Another lesson after the one on consonant blends could focus on digraphs (e.g., ch, sh, and th), which would enable children to read frequently used words like "chair," "she," and "the." A later lesson could introduce consonant clusters such as str-, spl-, etc. Teachers should always teach young children single consonants and consonant blends/clusters in separate lessons to avoid confusion.

Pacing and Order of Lessons on Sound-Letter Correspondences

Early childhood alphabetic principle instruction should be logical and consistent with the rates at which young children are able to learn. Teachers should introduce sound-to-letter relationships that will enable children to work with words as early as possible. According to research findings, direct and explicit instruction controlled by the teacher is more effective for teaching children the alphabetic principle than indirect and implicit methods are. Many teachers also use eclectic approaches, combining multiple teaching methods. Educators should remember that individual children normally learn sound-letter relationships at varying rates. A reasonable rate for introducing sound-letter relationships ranges from two to four relationships weekly. The earliest relationships teachers should introduce are high-utility ones. When introducing consonants and vowels, teachers should present them in an order that facilitates children's reading words readily. Teachers should avoid presenting similar-sounding phonemes and/or similar-looking letters together. They should use separate sessions/lessons to introduce single consonant sounds and consonant blends/clusters. Instruction in blending letters/sounds should use words with letter-sound relationships children have already learned.

English Literacy Development in ESL Students

To teach ESL students to read English, teachers must know the essential elements of literacy development, the principles of second language acquisition, and the differing conventions of both the students' first (L1) and second (L2) languages. Second language acquisition is an ongoing, lifelong process. In many ways, the process of second language acquisition parallels that of first language acquisition. Regardless of their L1 or their formal L2 instruction, students demonstrate predictable error patterns in learning. Acquiring language is not a linear process. While formal instruction can expand knowledge and inform and ease the process of language acquisition, it cannot accelerate it. Therefore, it is also detrimental to require sequential mastery of each curriculum element before proceeding onto the next element. Activities using language that are meaningful to students within a relevant context and teacher guidance help develop L2 acquisition. Varying language conventions must be kept in mind during instruction. For example, letter-sound correspondences are more consistent in Spanish than in English. Spanish letters are pronounced the same way they are spelled, so Spanish-speaking children can find the multiple pronunciations of the same phoneme in English confusing.

Phonological Differences Between Spanish and English Affecting the ELL Process

Because letter-sound correspondences are more consistent in Spanish than in English, Spanish vowels have fewer possible pronunciations than English vowels. Spanish has fewer total vowel sounds than English, regardless of spelling. This makes learning English more complicated for Spanish-speaking children. In modern Spanish, the pronunciation for the consonants v and b is the same, but these letters have different pronunciations in English. Spanish and English both contain the phoneme /ð/. In Spanish, it is represented by the letter d; in English, it is represented by the letters th. In English, the consonant clusters /sk/, /sp/, and /st/ are word-initial, as in school, special, and star. In Spanish, they are always preceded by /e/, as in escuela (school), especial (special), and estrella (star). Spanish speakers thus have difficulty pronouncing such initial clusters, and often end up using Spanish conventions, saying "estart" for start, "espeak" for speak, etc. Some sounds exist in L2 but not in L1; some L1 sounds transfer to L2; and letter-sound correspondences may differ between languages. Therefore, phonological and phonemic awareness and oral language development are crucial for ELLs.

English Literacy Development Versus Spanish Literacy Development

In English literacy instruction with native English-speaking children, educators teach individual phonemes/speech sounds and their corresponding alphabetic letters (phonics instruction). Spanish, however, is a syllabic language, and Spanish reading is taught using syllables rather than single phonemes. Spanish instruction uses syllables to teach word spellings, word divisions, stressed/accented parts of a word, word reading, and simple sentence construction. English-speaking children are taught to "sound out" a new word they encounter while reading by separating it into individual letters representing individual sounds. Spanish-speaking children are taught to "sound out" words by separating them into their component syllables. For example, in English, children sound out "man" as /m/, /æ/, and /n/. In Spanish, children sound out manzana (apple) as man, za, and na. Teachers must realize that ELLs encounter many phonological, syntactic, and semantic differences between their first and second languages, and that children with less English proficiency depend more on L1 cues. ELLs also expend double the cognitive effort of native English speakers through their attention to new language sounds, meanings, and structures, as well as their attempts to learn new literacy concepts and skills.

Writing Systems of Different Languages

Not only do different languages have phonological and orthographic differences, but they also use different writing systems. For example, although Spanish is syllabic in phonology and Spanish literacy instruction is syllabic, the Spanish writing system and letter-sound correspondences are (like English) alphabetic. The Chinese writing system is logographic. Rather than using alphabet letters to symbolize speech sounds, Chinese uses ideographs, or characters depicting concepts, to symbolize words. The Japanese language has a combined logographic and syllabic writing system. Directionality can differ, too. In English, Spanish, and other European-based languages, lines of writing/print go from left to right. In Hebrew, they go from right to left; in Chinese, they go from top to bottom. Therefore, children's ESL progress relies on their phonological awareness, their oral language knowledge, their grasp of the alphabetic principle, and their print awareness and book knowledge. These are best developed in purposeful contexts that are relevant to children.

Helping ELL Students Develop English Language Literacy

When teaching children learning English as a second language, teachers should make their instruction understandable to them. They can do this by providing visual aids, graphic organizers, and concrete examples of what they are teaching. They should consistently monitor children's language for development levels and use. They can paraphrase to clarify unfamiliar words and the concepts they describe. Teachers should take advantage of every opportunity to establish connections between children's L1 and English. They must repeat things frequently. They can also help ELLs by establishing a safe atmosphere where children receive ongoing support and feel comfortable taking risks. Teachers should adopt and communicate high learning expectations. They should enable children to develop necessary language and literacy skills that are consistent with their current levels of oral English proficiency. Literacy instruction should build upon children's comprehension, the alphabetic principle, and print concepts. Teachers should use language that children understand and find meaningful.

Teachers should assess their students' specific needs, and then design instructional programs that address those needs. They should also design instructional plans expressly for new students. They should design instruction so children can understand it. They should assess student progress often. Based on data they collect through assessment and monitoring, teachers should make instructional decisions, including adjusting schedules accordingly. They should create plenty of opportunities for children to participate in extended conversations in English. Teachers should also seek out others in their preschool's community who have expertise in one or more areas, and should use these assets when creating their curriculum. ESL teaching strategies should be integrated into instruction in all content areas. Teachers should activate and access children's background knowledge and connect instructional content to children's real lives. They should give children opportunities to discuss learning materials, topics, and early texts. Teachers must also acknowledge and value diverse cultural patterns of speech and discourse.

Print Awareness

Print awareness, also called print literacy, emerges gradually during the preschool years in normally developing children. Print awareness is the understanding that print conveys meaning, and the understanding of print's form and function. Research has found that children typically tend to develop print awareness between three and five years of age. Some researchers have observed that at this age, children go through a significant metamorphosis, wherein they demonstrate exponential increases in self-motivated, independent interactions with print. Such interactions include reciting the alphabet, identifying printed letters, recognizing printed words, and using print as a communicative mechanism. Many studies have concluded that the development of these print literacy skills by preschool-aged children is a strong predictor of their future achievement in reading. Studies have also shown that while four-year-olds have not mastered either word concepts or print concepts, they may acquire many print concepts sooner than word concepts.

Instructional Strategies for Promoting Literacy Development and Reading Comprehension

Instructional strategies designed to promote early literacy development and reading comprehension that are used in many ECE programs (like the EC component of the Partners for Literacy [PfL] Curriculum) include interactive book reading, the 3N strategy, extended teaching, problem solving, and curriculum-embedded assessments. These are also suitable for teaching ESL children. Interactive book reading is a teaching method that should be used at least once per day with each child. Children participate either individually or in pairs. This interactive reading is done in addition to (not instead of) reading in large and small groups. The purpose of interactive book reading is to stimulate responsive, reciprocal instructional conversations between each child and the teacher. Interactive book reading employs three main component strategies: the 3S strategy (3S stands for see, show, and say), wh- questions, and expanded book reading.

Using 3S Strategy and Wh- Questions in Interactive Book Reading

Interactive book reading is a strategy aimed at generating responsive instructional conversations between the child and teacher. In the 3S strategy, the 3 S's are see, show, and say. First, the teacher asks the child to see/look at a specific feature in a book, such as the main character. If the child succeeds, the teacher then asks him/her to locate an image or a word on a page. If the child does this correctly, the teacher then asks the child to say a word/answer a question. This requires multiple responses, promoting children's attending behavior and building upon each student's abilities. During the say part of 3S, the teacher asks the child questions beginning with who, what, where, when, and why. These wh- questions help teachers assess children's listening and/or reading comprehension levels, and also encourage ongoing conversations between each child and the teacher.

Using Interactive Activities in Expanded Book Reading

Expanded book reading is an instructional strategy that is part of the interactive book reading teaching format, which is used to promote early childhood literacy development. In expanded book reading, teachers can ask children to predict the possible subject matter of a book. They can give children an overview of a book. They can discuss setting, characters, and events in a book with children. They can help children relate the story in a book to their own lives, thereby making the book meaningful and relevant to children and helping them establish connections between literature and real life. Teachers can enhance the meaning of stories in books by acting them out using puppets and other props. To integrate literacy into all content areas across the curriculum, teachers can design math, science, art, and/or music activities that are related to a book students read. Teachers can ask children to retell the story they read together, which is an excellent way to informally assess their comprehension. This activity also assesses children's receptive and expressive language processing and speech-language production abilities.

Promoting Early Childhood Literacy Development with the 3N Strategy

In the 3N strategy, the 3 Ns are notice, nudge, and narrate. This teaching strategy involves providing scaffolding. Scaffolding is temporary support that helps a child advance from his or her current skill, knowledge, or competency level to a higher level. Scaffolding permits advancement that the child could not achieve on his or her own. The 3N teaching strategy can be employed to make any activity a learning experience for a young child, because it provides a structure for how teachers should interact with children. First, the teacher notices the level of an individual child's literacy skill(s). Second, the teacher verbally nudges the child to do things that are a step above his or her current skill level. Third, the teacher narrates what the child does, verbally describing and reflecting the child's activities. A number of literacy games designed for young children, including the Partners for Literacy curriculum's Literacy Games, utilize a 3N instructional strategy.

Incorporating Problem-Solving Strategies and Skills into Curriculum and Daily Instruction

During each preschool day, teachers can help young children recognize their emotions, identify their own needs and wants, develop empathy for and identify with the emotions of others, recognize situations involving problems, come up with simple solutions to problems, and think about the potential consequences of problem solutions. These activities help children develop age appropriate and developmentally appropriate competencies for solving problems and making decisions. Periods of both formal and informal instruction afford opportunities for children to develop these skills. Developing problem-solving and decision-making skills at an early age has a number of benefits. Young children learn to self-regulate their emotions and behaviors through this development. They develop social skills for interacting with others. Moreover, developing early problem-solving and decision-making skills prepares children for the further development of the higher order cognitive skills they will need to succeed in formal primary, secondary, and higher education settings, as well as in everyday life.

Strategies to Help Read New and/or Difficult Words

Phonics helps children read unknown/difficult words by teaching them how to sound out the phonemes represented by each printed letter. Teachers can help when children mispronounce words that have irregular spellings. They can also confirm children's correct pronunciations of words they have not heard or seen before. Context helps children deduce which of several possible words is most likely to be found in a particular sentence, paragraph, or book by examining its meaning in relation to the overall subject matter. Looking at a word's part of speech and how it fits into the sentence in question is also an example of using context. For example, reed and read have different spellings and meanings, but sound the same (homonyms). After reading the sentence "Reeds grow in marshes," a child knowing the meaning of "reads" can rule this word out even without knowing how it is spelled because it makes no sense in the context of the sentence. Children could also use their knowledge of language structure to analyze the sentence above. Children can ascertain whether a new word is a noun (person/place/thing) or a verb (action/state of being) by looking at its syntactic placement and its relation to the other words in the sentence that they are familiar with.

Children's Literature

Formats and Genres in Children's Literature

The picture book is both a genre and a format that encompasses various other genres. It includes wordless storybooks, which contain only pictures. Picture books integrate pictures and text to create a multimodal experience. Text is the most important feature of illustrated story books. Illustrations are secondary but complementary to the text. Poetry books contain poems rather than prose. Poems can use concrete verse, free verse, and rhymed and metered verse. Poetry emphasizes the sounds and meanings of words, and appeals to both readers' emotions and thoughts. Traditional literature is an adapted form of oral storytelling. It includes fairy tales, fables, folklore, epics, and proverbs. "Once upon a time..." introductions and happy endings are common features. Modern fantasy is based on traditional literature, but it is original. It includes modern fairy tales, such as those written by Lewis Carroll and Hans Christian Andersen. White's Charlotte's Web and Milne's Winnie the Pooh are also examples. Fantasy stories are imaginary, and often focus on good vs. evil conflicts, magic, and/or quests. Non-fiction informational books include narrative, how-to, question and answer, activity, life cycle, and concept texts.

Features Promoting Literacy Development

Books that some EC educational experts refer to as "predictable books" contain repetitive text throughout. A salient characteristic of young children is their behavior of repeating familiar rhymes/songs/chants/phrases and stories over and over. Children find such repetition enjoyable. They also ask adults to read them the same books repeatedly. In addition to being enjoyable, repetition provides young children with opportunities to practice words and language patterns, and also encourages retention. Children also like repetitive books because they can immediately participate in the reading of the story. Some examples of good "predictable" children's books include the traditional stories "The Three Little Pigs" and "The Little Red Hen." Other examples are Dr. Seuss's "Green Eggs and Ham" and his story "What Was I Scared Of?" found in the compilation Yertle the Turtle. Another feature of children's books promoting early literacy development is pictures. Picture books with equal, interrelated/interdependent pictures and text help young children learn to recognize and begin to read letters and words by relating them to familiar visual images. The pictures in illustrated storybooks inform text, supporting beginning readers' continuing literacy development.

Characteristics of Good Children's Literature

To select good children's literature, adults should determine whether a book tells an interesting story. The story should be age appropriate. It should also be appealing to a teacher's students. Books should be well-written, and should have original, believable, and well-constructed plots. Story characters should be credible and convincing, and they should grow and change as a result of their experiences. Dialogue should suit the characters, and should sound natural. Stories should have themes that are important to children. Adults should consider whether a book's theme is obviously moralistic. They should consider what the reader can expect based on a book's title and format. Illustrations should contribute to text, and vice versa. Good children's books avoid stereotypes based on race, gender, etc. They should afford pleasant reading/listening experiences. Adults can also read book reviews for guidance. Children's book authors should be knowledgeable about their subject matter, and they should write in a style suitable for the subject being discussed. Informational books should be accurate and well-organized.

Abilities Demonstrating Phonological and Phonemic Awareness

Young children with phonological awareness recognize rhymes they hear, can rhyme words, can "count" the number of syllables in a word by clapping, and can identify words with matching initial sounds (e.g., "mother" and "milk"). Children with phonemic awareness can manipulate individual phonemes in words. For example, they can separate the word "cat" into the sounds /k/, /æ/, and /t/. Children who have problems with phonemic awareness frequently experience reading problems without early intervention. There are several issues teachers may observe in the classroom that can indicate phonological and/or phonemic awareness deficits. Children may not correctly combine individual phonemes to make a word. For example, they may not be able to select and blend the phonemes /k/, /æ/, and /t/ to make "cat." A child may not correctly perform phoneme substitution tasks to make different words. For example, a child may not be able to change the /k/ in "cat" to /m/ to make "mat." A child may have difficulty determining how many syllables are in a word like "paper." A child may also have problems rhyming, syllabicating, or spelling new words based on how they sound.

Word Decoding and Phonics

Word decoding ability consists of being aware of letter-sound correspondences and letter patterns, and applying them to correctly pronounce the words we read. Phonics is a reading instruction approach that focuses on letter-sound correspondences, exceptions to general rules, and strategies for sounding out new words. In the classroom, if a teacher observes a child is having trouble matching up letters with sounds (or vice versa), this can signal decoding and phonics problems that can interfere with a child's ability to read and spell. Children who can decode words, but must use a great deal of effort to do so, may have decoding and phonics problems. Difficulties with spelling words phonetically and reading are also signs of possible problems. Children who struggle greatly with phonics activities and patterns may have decoding deficits. Children who try to guess words based on the first one or two letters may have problems with decoding and phonics. If after teaching several letter sounds/patterns to a class, a teacher finds that certain children cannot recognize them while reading words and do not include these sounds and patterns in their writing, the teacher should suspect that these children are having problems with decoding and phonics.

Types of Vocabulary

Educators frequently divide vocabulary into listening, speaking, reading, and writing vocabulary. These are not necessarily the same. Listening vocabulary refers to the words we must know to understand what we hear others say. Speaking vocabulary refers to the words we use when we talk.

Reading vocabulary refers to the words we must know to comprehend what we read. Writing vocabulary refers to the words we use when we write. To read print, children must understand the majority of the words they encounter in a text. Children learn the majority of word meanings indirectly through daily life experiences. Well-designed instruction teaches them additional vocabulary. If a teacher observes that a child has more questions than usual about what words mean in age appropriate/developmentally appropriate texts, the child may have vocabulary issues. A teacher may observe that a child does not use or recognize many words compared to his or her peers, which could also indicate vocabulary issues. A child who cannot see connections/relationships among words in different texts may have vocabulary deficits. If a child frequently cannot find the correct word to express a thought, idea, etc., this could also indicate vocabulary difficulties.

Reading Fluency

Reading fluency is the ability to read quickly, accurately, and smoothly both silently and aloud, and to read aloud with appropriate vocal intonations and expression. Children who do not read fluently sound awkward and choppy when they read aloud. Some students who read dysfluently have word decoding problems. Others simply need more reading practice to read quickly and smoothly. Reading fluency is important to children's reading motivation. When children find reading laborious or view it as a chore rather than an enjoyable experience, they dislike reading and avoid it. This exacerbates reading problems. Reading fluency becomes more important in upper elementary grades, when the volume of required reading increases exponentially for students. Therefore, younger children with poor reading fluency will also have difficulty meeting academic reading demands in the future. When teachers conduct correct words per minute assessments, children who do not meet the criteria for their grade level may have fluency issues. Struggling and becoming frustrated with speed and/or accuracy while reading aloud may indicate fluency problems. Reading aloud without expression is another sign of fluency issues, as are failing to pause at meaningful breaks in a sentence or a paragraph and failing to "chunk" words into meaningful units.

Abilities Necessary to Have Good Reading Comprehension

To have good reading comprehension, children must be able to (1) decode the words they read, (2) connect what they read to things they already know, and (3) think about what they have read in depth. Knowing enough word meanings (i.e. having enough vocabulary) plays a major role in reading comprehension. Children with good comprehension can make conclusions about what they read, including identifying factual elements, determining the causes of specific events, and identifying comedic characters. Therefore, comprehension involves a combination of reading, thinking, and reasoning. Teachers may observe a number of signs of reading comprehension problems. A child may focus on details/"trees" to the exclusion of the main point/"forest." This child can report how stories end, but cannot explain why. A child may not speculate about characters' motivations or upcoming events when reading a book. When trying to relate reading to his/her life, a child may choose irrelevant information. A child may not be able to recount logical event sequences in stories or isolate main facts in informational texts. A child may appear to have inadequate vocabulary to understand a text. Finally, a child may be unable to relate details of a story, such as the setting, what the characters look like, etc.

Basic Reading Components of Phonological and Phonemic Awareness

The five basic reading components of phonological and phonemic awareness are word decoding, phonics, fluency, vocabulary, and comprehension. A deficit in any of these components can lead to reading problems. In addition to deficits in one or more of these areas, about two to three percent of children have central auditory processing disorders (CAPDs). Our ears receive environmental sound waves and convert them to acoustic impulses that are carried by nerves to the brain, which interprets these signals as various sounds, including speech. This is auditory processing. Children with CAPD have problems attending to, listening to, and remembering spoken information, and often take longer to process auditory input. They frequently cannot differentiate among sounds in words that sound similar to other phonemes, despite being able to hear them clearly. This causes decoding difficulties, which interferes with reading. Some children with strong auditory (and language) processing skills have deficits in phonological processing (i.e. processing phonemes/speech sounds specifically). This also typically causes decoding and hence reading difficulties. Language processing problems are broader, including deficiencies in linguistic experiences, vocabulary, comprehension (despite being able to correctly decode words), reading, and writing.

Role of Memory in Children's Reading Development

For children to read, understand what they read, and switch efficiently between the printed language they see and the information they have stored in their memories, children must be able to store information and retrieve it as it is needed. There are three main types of memory. Short-term memory holds small pieces of information for short periods of time. For example, when we hold a phone number in our mind only long enough to dial it, but do not retain it after it is dialed, we use our short-term memory. Working memory holds interim information in the mind for use during calculations. For example, we use our working memory when mentally multiplying double digit numerals or doing long division. Processing new information so that it can be stored for a long period of time, searching for stored information, and retrieving information as it is needed are also functions of working memory. Phonological working memory is a component of phonological processing that is important in reading comprehension, spelling, written expression, and retention. We store enormous amounts of information for many years in our long-term memory. This information influences our differential attention to various environmental factors and our perceptions of the world.

Dyslexia

Difficulties Displayed When Speaking That May Be Signs of Dyslexia

Preschoolers/kindergarteners who have trouble learning alphabet letters are more likely to have trouble identifying sound-letter correspondences in first grade, and are more likely to have subsequent life-long difficulties with reading. Issues related to children's speech that can indicate dyslexia include mispronouncing unfamiliar, long, or complex words. This may include omitting word parts and/or arranging syllables or word parts in the wrong sequence. Other signs of dyslexia include speech that is not fluent (e.g., speech that is marked by frequent hesitations, "um's," and pauses); speech that uses vague or non-specific wording, such as "things" or "stuff," instead of correct nouns and names of specific objects; speech that suggests the child is having difficulty finding words while speaking, which is indicated when students confuse words that sound similar (e.g., substituting "volcano" for "tornado," substituting "humidity" for "humility," etc.); and speech that shows an inability to generate verbal responses to questions quickly and on demand. Students with dyslexia may also require more time than normal to respond orally to language stimuli; and may also have difficulties with rote memory (e.g., retaining and/or retrieving names, dates, phone numbers, random lists, and other isolated items contained in information presented verbally).

Observable Reading Problems

Dyslexic children typically show abnormally slow progress in their acquisition of reading skills. They often lack systematic strategies for reading new words (decoding, sounding out, etc.), and make wild guesses instead. Being unable to read short function words (e.g., "an," "on," and "that") is common, as is stumbling over multisyllabic words. Dyslexic children often miss parts of words when reading and/or fail to decode word parts, and may, for example, read a word aloud with its middle syllable missing (e.g., "imation" for "imagination"). Children with dyslexia tend to fear and hence avoid oral reading because they have made errors in the past and have an expectation that they will make additional errors if they attempt to read aloud again. When they do read aloud, they may omit appropriate inflections; sound like they are reading a foreign language; sound laborious and choppy, rather than fluent and smooth; mispronounce numerous words; and make numerous omissions and substitutions. While reading, they depend on the context to comprehend meaning, and have more difficulty understanding single/isolated words. Their performance on objective (e.g., multiple choice) tests is typically much poorer than their intelligence and knowledge would predict.

Children who consistently cannot complete written tests in the time allowed may have dyslexia. Children who cannot pronounce more difficult printed words and substitute easier ones for them instead (e.g., "car" for "automobile") may have dyslexia. In math, dyslexia causes difficulty reading word problems. Dyslexic children often misspell words. The spellings are not phonetic, but are often bizarre and wildly different from actual spellings and from native language conventions. Children with dyslexia read very slowly, finding it laborious and exhausting. Reading is such a chore to dyslexic children that they do not enjoy it, do not read for pleasure, and will avoid reading whenever possible. Such children have a lot of trouble learning foreign languages. Despite good fine motor skills and word processing abilities, they often have poor handwriting. Homework seems to take forever for dyslexics. Some students ask parents to read so they don't have to. Dyslexics' reading becomes more accurate with time and practice, but still remains labored and dysfluent. Dyslexic children often have family histories of problems with reading, spelling, and learning foreign languages. Dyslexia can cause low self-esteem. This is not always obvious, but can be detected by sensitive, skilled professionals.

Learning to Spell

Children must understand the alphabetic principle—the concept that words are comprised of individual phonemes/speech sounds, and that the letters of our alphabet represent those sounds in writing/print—in order to learn how to spell. They must also develop a knowledge of specific letter-to-sound correspondences. As children gain more experience hearing, understanding, and using words, they start to observe patterns in the ways in which letters are combined. They also notice repeated series of letters that create syllables, common roots for many related words, prefixes, suffixes, word endings, and other word features. When children know these basic patterns and have also learned their language's basic spelling principles and rules, they can usually figure out how to spell new words they hear. Moreover, children can usually read words that they can spell. Therefore, children's development of good spelling skills promotes the development of good reading and writing skills as well.

Salient Characteristics of the Stages of Spelling Development

(1) Precommunicative stage: Children use alphabet letters, but may not know the whole alphabet, may not differentiate between upper case and lower case letters, or may not know that English is written from left to right. They do not demonstrate knowledge of letter-to-sound correspondences. (2) Semiphonetic stage: Children begin to comprehend letter-to-sound correspondences. They frequently use simple logic to symbolize words with single letters. A good example is using "U" for

"you" (early texting potential!). (3) <u>Phonetic stage:</u> Children use letters to represent all speech sounds they hear in words. These representations may not always be correct, but are systematic and understandable (e.g., writing "kom" instead of "come"). (4) <u>Transitional stage:</u> Children begin the transition from phonetically spelling words according to their sounds to visually and structurally learning conventional word spellings. They still make errors as they assimilate this new knowledge (e.g., writing "highked" instead of "hiked"). (5) <u>Correct stage:</u> Children know fundamental English orthographic rules, including silent letters, irregular and alternative spellings, prefixes, suffixes, and other word features. They have learned many word spellings, and recognize misspellings. Their knowledge of exceptions to spelling rules and the generalizations they make about spelling are usually correct.

Invented Spelling and What It Reveals About Phonetic Awareness

When young children have not yet learned how to spell many (or any) words, they commonly "invent" spellings for spoken words they hear. They do this by identifying letters that correspond to the separate phonemes (speech sounds) they hear and arranging them in a sequence that matches the word's sounds. Linguistic researchers (e.g., Read, 1975) studying preschoolers have found that different children choose the same phonetic spellings. These children have developed phonemic and phonetic awareness, enabling them to invent spellings before they have actually learned to spell. This skill is a prerequisite to learning how to read, spell, and write. Researchers observe that neither adult influence nor chance could explain diverse children's high incidence of selecting the same phonetic spellings. Therefore, even at young ages, children can identify the phonetic properties of English words that are symbolized by their real spellings. Experts conclude from these observations that spelling is a developmental process rather than merely a word memorization process, and that it results in comprehension that goes beyond understanding simple sound-to-letter correspondences.

Writing

According to the National Institute for Literacy, writing is defined as "the ability to compose text effectively for various purposes and audiences." We use writing as a tool to help us collect detailed information, document it, and disseminate it to widespread audiences. We use writing to express our ideas, thoughts, and feelings, and to persuade our readers to believe or agree with what we write. Researchers have also found that the learning capacity of an individual increases when his or her writing skills improve. This aspect of writing skills mirrors that of reading skills in that the development of both improves learning ability. Students need instruction to learn to write well. Reading skills have been found both to be reinforced by and to reinforce important writing skills like spelling and grammar. Thus, when teachers help children improve their writing, they are contributing to the improvement of their reading abilities as well.

Stages of Writing Skills Development

(1) <u>Scribbling and drawing:</u> Young children grasp crayons/pencils with their fists, exploring form, space, and line. As their fine motor skills and cognitive understanding of symbolic representation develop concurrently, they progress to (2) <u>letter-like forms and shapes</u>. They comprehend that written symbols represent meanings. They start including shapes like circles and squares into their drawing and writing, but they are randomly located without much spatial orientation. Children in this stage commonly write figures and ask parents, "What does this say?" (3) <u>Letters:</u> Children can form letters, and start writing them randomly. They usually write consonants first. They do not initially possess a knowledge of symbol-to-sound correspondence; this develops gradually. Children tend to favor writing their own initials. (4) <u>Letters and spaces:</u> Children realize that printed/written

words are separated by spaces, develop an understanding of the concept of a word, use 1:1 word correspondence, and write correctly spaced words. They write initial and final word sounds and vowels, correct the spelling of some high frequency words, and experiment with sentence construction and punctuation. (5) <u>Conventional writing and spelling:</u> Children write, spell, and punctuate correctly most of the time. They view various forms of purposeful writing as more important.

POWER Strategy

One popular model of the writing process proposed by experts, the POWER strategy, has five steps. In (1) planning, student and teacher ask and select Yes/No on a checklist to decide whether the student selected a good topic, researched/read about the topic, considered what information readers would want to know, and wrote down all of his/her ideas. In (2) organization, the student and teacher ascertain if the student grouped similar ideas together, selected the best ideas for the composition, and arranged the ideas in a logical sequence. In (3) writing, the student and teacher decide whether the student wrote down his/her ideas in sentences. They also decide whether the student did his/her best to get help when it was required. To get the necessary information and assistance, the student may have consulted a text, asked a learning partner/classmate for assistance, and/or asked the teacher for help. In (4) editing, the student and teacher consider whether the student read his/her first draft to himself/herself, marked the parts s/he liked and those that might need changing, read the first draft to his/her partner/classmate, and listened to the other student's input. In (5) rewriting, the student and teacher look at whether the student made changes in his/her composition, edited it for correct mechanics, and wrote the final draft using his/her best handwriting.

Rating Early Writing Efforts

One easy rating scale (Clay, 1993) focuses on three areas: language level, message quality, and directional principles. Each category has six progressive levels. For <u>language level</u>, the categories are (1) alphabetical (writes letters), (2) word (writes any recognizable word), (3) word group (writes any two-word phrase), (4) sentence (writes any simple sentence), (5) punctuated story (writes two or more related sentences), and (6) paragraphed story (includes two themes). The levels for <u>message quality</u> are as follows: (1) Student has a concept of signs/symbols. (2) Student has a concept that a message is communicated. (3) Student copies a message. (4) Student repeats sentence patterns like "This is a..." (5) Student tries to record his/her own ideas in writing. (6) Student writes a successful composition. The levels for <u>directional principles</u> are as follows: (1) Student does not demonstrate knowledge of directionality. (2) Student exhibits partial directional knowledge (e.g., left to right or start at the top left or return from top right down to the left). (3) Student reverses the direction. (4) Student follows the correct directional pattern. (5) Student uses correct directionality and spacing between words. (6) The student writes extensively without problems related to arranging and spacing text.

Written English

Written English should meet the standard conventions of correct spelling, capitalization, punctuation, grammar, and handwriting. Traditionally, teachers have paid more attention to a composition's appearance, length, word usage, and spelling than to how well-organized it is or how appropriate its content is. This habit can cause a superficial focus on imperfect form, while essentially ignoring the fact that the function is effective and meaningful. Other readers also form negative first impressions of writing when its appearance and/or format are less than acceptable, even if it otherwise effectively conveys its message. One type of common spelling error is vowel combination reversals (e.g., writing "siad" instead of "said," writing "freind" instead of "friend," etc.). Capitalization errors include failing to capitalize words at the start of sentences, months of the year, and proper nouns/names. Another type of capitalization error is incorrectly capitalizing words/letters within words. Punctuation errors include omitting commas in dates, omitting commas before conjunctions in compound sentences, omitting/substituting semicolons in complex sentences, and adding extraneous punctuation marks. Grammatical errors include incorrect/conflicting verb tenses, subject-verb disagreement, missing articles, misplaced modifiers, and dangling participles. Handwriting errors/problems include illegible writing, poor alignment, and incorrect/poor spacing.

Techniques and Activities to Motivate Young Children to Write

Experts note that like adults, children prefer participating in activities they find exciting rather than ones they find unexciting/uninteresting. To motivate students to write, teachers can share personal journals and other samples of their own writing, post e-mailed/handwritten letters/notes in classrooms, display favorite magazines and books, and show children fun greeting cards/invitations. They should also invite children to bring writing samples from home. Teachers can create classroom "writing corners" that contain varied writing examples contributed by children and teachers. Diverse writing activities help children stay enthusiastic about writing. Children can take turns contributing a sentence for a daily class newsletter/journal/newspaper, and teachers can have students practice sounding out and spelling words as they dictate their sentences. Teachers can deliberately make some transcribing errors and have children correct them. Daily pages can be compiled into monthly class books. Connecting writing subjects to people/things that are familiar and exciting to children, and guiding students in how to write and ask classmates "interview" questions using modeling and other techniques both help motivate students. Encouraging/guiding children to evaluate and record their comments about authors, illustrators, and books can also be a motivational tool. Ultimately, children will learn to write their own critiques.

Core Knowledge in the Content Areas

Problem Solving Skills

Being able to solve problems is fundamental to all other components of mathematics. Children learn the concept that a question can have more than one answer and a problem can have more than one solution by participating in problem solving activities. To solve problems, a child must be able to explore a problem, a situation, or a subject; think through the problem, situation, or subject; and use logical reasoning. These abilities are needed to not only solve routine/everyday problems, but also novel/unusual ones. Using problem solving skills not only helps children think mathematically, but also promotes their language development and their social skills when they work together. Children are naturally curious about how to solve everyday problems. Adults can take advantage of this inherent curiosity by discussing everyday challenges, asking children to propose ways to solve them, and asking them to explain how they arrived at their solutions. Adults can also invite children to propose problems and ask questions about them. This helps them learn to analyze different types of problems and realize that many problems have multiple possible solutions.

Common Steps That Prepare Children to Learn Math

The process of solving problems often involves the following steps: understanding the problem; coming up with a plan to solve the problem; putting that plan into action; and, finally, observing the outcome and reflecting on whether the solution was effective, and whether the answer arrived at makes sense. Solving problems not only involves learning this series of steps, but also requires children to develop the qualities needed to solve problems. Children who are able to solve problems have a number of characteristics. For example, children who are effective problem solvers are able to focus their attention on the problem and its individual component parts. They can formulate hypotheses about the problem/situation, and then test them for veracity. They are willing to take risks within reason. They are persistent if they do not solve a problem right away, and do not give up if their first attempt at solving a problem is unsuccessful. They maintain flexibility, and experiment with alternate methods. They also demonstrate self-regulation skills.

Using Problem Solving Skills in Daily Life

Young children continually explore their environments to unravel mysteries about how things work. For example, preschoolers use math concepts to understand that they have three toys, to comprehend that three fingers equals three toys, or to understand that two cookies plus one more equals three cookies. To do abstract mathematics in the future, young children will need two major skills that are also used to solve problems: being able to visualize a scenario, and being able to apply common sense thinking. Thinking and planning to achieve goals within the constraints of the properties of the surrounding environment is a natural behavior for young children. They will persist in their efforts to get an older sibling to stop another activity to play with them, to repair broken toys with tape or chewing gum, to manipulate a puzzle or plastic building blocks to get one uncooperative piece to fit, etc. The great 20th century mathematician and teacher George Polya stated that problem solving is "the most characteristically human activity." He pointed out that problem solving is a skill learned by doing, and that developing this skill requires a great deal of practice.

Games/Activities That Encourage the Use of Problem Solving Skills

One method that has been found to enhance children's reasoning skills is using adult-child conversations to play mental mathematics games. For example, once children are able to count beyond five, adults can give them basic oral story problems to solve (e.g., "If you have two plums

109

and I give you two more, how many will you have?"). Using children's favorite foods in story problems, which takes advantage of their ready ability to envision these foods, is a good place to start. Thereafter, adults can add story problems involving pets, toys, cars, shopping, and other familiar objects/animals/activities. Experts advise adults not to restrict the types of problems presented to a child based solely on the child's grade level. Children can work with any situation if they can form mental imagery. Adults can sometimes insert harder tasks (e.g., problems involving larger numbers, problems involving division with remainders, or problems with negative number answers). Even toddlers can solve problems such as how to divide three cookies between two people. The division may not be fair, but it will likely be efficient. Adults should use the Socratic method, asking guiding questions to allow children to arrive at a solution to a problem themselves, rather than telling them a "right" answer.

Beneficial Practices of Playing Mental Math Games

Adults can use children's favorite foods and toys to pose story problems to children that involve addition and subtraction. For example, they can ask them questions like "If I give you [this many] more, how many will you have?" or "If we take away [this many], how many are left?" It is better to ask children questions than to give them answers. It is important to use turn taking. In this method, the adult poses a story problem to the child, and then the child gets to pose one to the adult. Adults must try to solve the problem, even if the child makes up numbers like "bazillion" or "eleventy." Games should be fun, not strictly factual like math tests. Adults can introduce age-appropriate story topics as children grow older. At the end of early childhood/around school age, children can handle the abstract algebraic concept of variables/unknown numbers (which some experts call "mystery numbers") and use this concept in games. Adults can pose riddles where "x" or "n" is the unknown number, and children must use an operation (e.g., $x + 4 = 7$) to solve the riddle.

> **Review Video:** **Addition and Subtraction**
> Visit mometrix.com/academy and enter code: 521157

Reasoning Skills

Communicating with Children to Promote Mathematical Reasoning Skills

Adults reciprocally talk to and listen to children during communication that is focused on using mathematical skills like problem solving, reasoning, making connections, etc. To promote young children's understanding, adults can express mathematical concepts using pictures, words, diagrams, and symbols. Encouraging children to talk with their peers and adults helps them clarify their own thoughts and think about what they are doing. Communicating with children about mathematical thinking problems also develops their vocabularies and promotes early literacy and reading skills. Adults should listen to what children want to say, and should have conversations with them. Communicating about math can also be accomplished through reading children's books that incorporate numbers and/or repetition or rhyme. In addition to talking, adults can communicate math concepts to children by drawing pictures or diagrams and using concrete objects (e.g., blocks, crayons, pieces of paper, fingers, etc.) to represent numbers and/or solve problems. Children also share their learning of math concepts through words, charts, drawings, tallies, etc. Even toddlers hold up fingers to tell others how old they are.

Using Reasoning Skills to Understand and Apply Early Mathematical and Scientific Concepts

A major component of problem solving is reasoning. Children reason when they think through questions and find usable answers. They use reasoning skills to make sense of mathematical and scientific subject matter. Children use several abilities during the reasoning process. For example, they use logic to classify objects or concepts into groups. They follow logical sequences to arrive at conclusions that make sense. They use their analytical abilities to explain their own thought processes. They apply what they have learned about relationships and patterns to help them find solutions to problems. They also use reasoning to justify their mental processes and problem solutions. To support children's reasoning, adults can ask children questions, give them time to think about their answers, and listen to their answers. This simple tactic helps children learn how to reason. Adults can also ask children why something is as it is—letting them think for themselves rather than looking for a particular answer—and listen to the ideas they produce.

Role of Representation Skills in Children's Learning

Young children develop an understanding of symbolic representation—the idea that objects, written letters, words, and other symbols are used to represent other objects or concepts—at an early age. This is evident in their make-believe/pretend play, and in their ability to learn written language and connect it to spoken language. As children develop early math skills, representing their ideas and information they acquire helps them organize, document, and share these ideas and facts with others. Children may count on their fingers; create tallies using check marks/tick marks and/or words; draw pictures or maps; and, as they grow older, make graphs. Teachers must help children apply mathematical process skills as they use learning center materials. For example, when a child enjoys sorting rocks by color, the teacher can state that the child is classifying them, bridging informal math activities with math vocabulary. Asking the child how s/he is categorizing the rocks emphasizes math vocabulary. Asking the child after s/he finishes what other ways s/he could classify the rocks encourages problem solving.

Making Connections and Helping Children Transition from Intuitive to Formal Math Thinking

Children informally learn intuitive mathematical thinking through their everyday life experiences. They naturally apply mathematical concepts and reasoning to solve problems they face in their environment. However, one frequent problem among children when they begin formal education is that they can come to see academic mathematics as a collection of procedures and rules, instead of viewing it as a means of finding solutions to everyday, real-life problems. This view will interfere with children's ability to apply the formal mathematics they learn to their lives in a practical and useful way. Teachers can help prevent this outcome by establishing the connection between children's natural intuitive math and formal mathematics. They can do this by teaching math through the use of manipulative materials familiar to children. They can use mathematics vocabulary words when describing children's activities, which enables children to develop an awareness of the natural mathematical operations they use in their daily lives. When a teacher introduces a new mathematical concept to children, s/he can give illustrative examples that draw upon the children's actual life experiences.

Relationship of Mathematics to Everyday Life and Other Academic Subjects

We use math throughout our lives during everyday activities. There are countless examples and combinations of various mathematical concepts in the real world. Additionally, math concepts inform other academic content areas, including music, art, and the sciences. Therefore, it is important for children not to view math as an isolated set of procedures and skills. Children comprehend math more easily when they can make connections, which involve applying common mathematical rules to multiple, varied functions, processes, and real-life activities. For example, adults can ask children to consider problems they encounter daily and solve them. When a parent asks a child to help put away groceries, the child practices sorting categories of foods and packages, and experiments with comparative package sizes and shapes. Parents need not be concerned with what specific mathematical processes are involved, but should simply look for examples of math in everyday life and expose children to these examples on a regular basis. For example, pouring liquid into containers of various sizes and speculating which one will hold the most is an easy, fun activity that incorporates a number of skills and concepts, including estimation, measurement, spatial sense, and conservation of liquid volume.

Patterns and Relationships

Patterns are generally defined as things that recur or are repeated regularly. Patterns can be found in images, sounds, numbers, events, actions, movements, etc. Relationships are generally defined as connections or associations between things that are identified and/or described using logic or reasoning. Being aware of patterns and relationships among aspects of the environment helps us comprehend the fundamental structure of these aspects. This awareness enables us to predict what will occur next in a series of events, even before it actually happens. This gives us more confidence in our environment and in our ability to interact with it. We find patterns and relationships in such areas of life as art, music, and clothing. Math-specific activities like counting numbers and working with geometrical shapes, lines, arcs, and curves also involve patterns and relationships. When children understand patterns and relationships, they can understand repetition; rhythm; categorization; and how to order things from smallest to biggest, from shortest to longest, etc.

Adults can help young children develop their understanding of patterns and relationships in life by looking at pictures and designs with them, encouraging and guiding them to identify patterns within drawings, paintings, and abstract designs such as prints on fabrics and other decorative designs. When children participate in movement activities, including dancing to music, running, skipping, hopping, playing simple musical instruments, etc., adults can help them identify patterns in their own and others' movements. Adults can encourage young children to participate in hands-on activities, such as stringing wood, plastic beads, or penne and other hollow dry pasta tubes onto pieces of string to make necklaces with simple patterns (e.g., blue-yellow-blue-yellow). As children grow older, adults can encourage them to create more complicated patterns. They can alternate a larger number of colors, and they can vary the numbers of each color in more complex ways (e.g., three blue, two yellow, one red, etc.).

Contribution of Number Sense and Number Operations to Math Comprehension

Counting is one of the earliest numeracy skills that young children develop. Even before they have learned the names of all the numbers, young children learn to count to three, then to five, etc. However, number sense involves a great deal more than just counting. Number sense includes understanding the various applications of numbers. For instance, we use numbers as tools for conveying and manipulating information, as tools for describing quantities, and as tools for characterizing relationships between or among things. Children who have developed number sense are able to count with accuracy and competence. Given a specific number, they can count upwards from that number. They can also count backwards. They are able to break down a number and then reassemble it. They are able to recognize relationships between or among different numbers. When children can count, are familiar with numbers, and have good number sense, they can also add and subtract numbers. Being familiar with numbers and being able to count easily helps young children understand all other areas of mathematics.

Activities to Help Develop Number Sense and Numeracy Skills

As children complete their daily activities, it is beneficial for adults to count real things with children and encourage them to count as well. This helps children understand numbers by using their own experiences with objects in the environment, and gives them practice counting and using numbers. To help children understand that we use numbers to describe quantities and relationships, adults can ask children to sort objects by size, shape, or color similarity. They can also ask children to sort objects according to their differences (e.g., which object is bigger/smaller). Adults can also discuss with children how numbers are used to find street addresses and apartment numbers, and to keep score during games. To help children count upwards and downwards with efficiency and accuracy, adults can point out that counting allows us to determine how many items are in a group. Adults should point to each object as they count it. They can count on their fingers and encourage young children to do the same. Adults should also help children count without repeating or skipping any numbers.

Spatial Sense and Geometry

Spatial sense is an individual's awareness of one's own body in space and in relation to the objects and other people around the individual. Spatial sense allows young children to navigate environmental spaces without colliding with objects and other people; to see and hear adequately, and to be aware of whether others can see and hear them; and to develop and observe a socially and culturally appropriate sense of their own and others' personal space. Geometry is the area of mathematics involving space, sizes, shapes, positions, movements, and directions. Geometry gives descriptions and classifications of our physical environment. By observing commonplace objects and spaces in their physical world, young children can learn about solid objects and substances, shapes, and angles. Adults can help young children learn geometry by identifying various shapes, angles, and three-dimensional figures for them; asking them to name these shapes, angles, and figures when they encounter them in the future; and asking them to describe different shapes, draw them in the air with their fingers, trace drawings of the shapes with their fingers, and then draw the shapes themselves.

Activities to Help Develop Spatial Sense and Geometry

Because it involves many physical properties like shape, line, and angle, as well as abstract concepts, young children learn geometry most effectively via hands-on activities. Learning experiences that allow them to touch and manipulate concrete objects, such as boxes, containers, puzzles, blocks, and shape sorters, usually work best. Everyday activities can also help children learn geometry concepts. For example, adults can cut children's sandwiches into various geometrical shapes and let children fit them together and/or rearrange them into new patterns. Children become better able to follow directions and navigate through space when they develop geometric knowledge and spatial sense. Adults can provide activities that promote the development of geometric knowledge and spatial sense. For example, they can let children get into and out of big appliance boxes; climb over furniture; and go into, on top of, out of, under, around, over, and through different objects and structures to allow children to experience the relationship between their bodies and space and solids. As they mature, children can play games in which they search for "hidden" shapes. Such shapes may be irregular, may lack flat bases, or may be turned in various directions.

Measurement

Measurement is the process of determining how long, wide, and tall something is physically and how much it weighs by using measuring units such as inches, feet, yards, square feet, ounces, and pounds. Measurement is also used to quantify time using units like seconds, minutes, hours, days, weeks, months, years, centuries, millennia, etc. Measurement is not just a formal means of quantifying size, area, and time. It is also an important method for young children to seek and identify relationships between and among things they encounter outside of school in everyday life.

113

When young children practice measuring things, they are able to understand not only the sizes of objects and beings, but also their comparative sizes (i.e. how large or small something is compared to another object used as a reference). Furthermore, they are able to figure out how big or little something is on their own.

While it is obviously important for children to eventually learn standardized measurement units like inches, feet, yards, etc., adults can facilitate early development of measurement skills by letting children choose their own measurement units. For example, they might use their favorite toy to describe a playmate or sibling as "three teddy bears tall"; or they might describe a room as "seven toy cars long." Similarly, when children are too young to know formal time measurements like minutes and hours, adults can support children's ability to quantify time using favorite TV shows. For example, four-year-olds can often relate to the idea of one episode of a show (whether it is 30 minutes or 60 minutes long) as a time measurement. Adults can apply this with statements like, "Daddy will be home in one episode." Numerous everyday activities, including grocery shopping, cooking, sewing, gardening, woodworking, and many others, involve measurement. Adults can ask children to help with these tasks, and then discuss measuring with children as they participate.

Measurement of Time

Younger children typically do not have an understanding of the abstract concept of time. However, adults can still help children understand that time elapses, and that we count/measure this process. For example, adults can ask younger children simple questions, such as "Who can stand on one foot longer?" This comparison strategy helps children figure out which of two or more actions/activities takes a longer/the longest period of time. Even when children do not yet understand what "five minutes" means, adults should still make such references (e.g., "You can play for five minutes longer, and then we must leave."). Repeating such references will eventually help children understand that time passes. Adults can time various everyday activities/events and tell children how long they took. They can also count the second hand's ticks on a watch/clock (e.g., "one second...two seconds...three seconds..."). This familiarizes children with counting, and with using counting to track the passage of time. Until children are old enough to understand abstractions like today/yesterday/tomorrow, adults can use concrete references like "after lunch" or "before bedtime."

Fractions

Fractions are parts or pieces of a whole. While adults understand this and do not remember ever not understanding it, very young children think differently in this regard. As Piaget showed, children in the preoperational stage of cognitive development cannot perform logical or mathematical mental operations. They focus on one property of an object rather than all of its properties, a practice he called centration. Hence, if you cut an apple into pieces, very young children see that there are more pieces than there were before, and they believe that several apple pieces are more than one apple. They cannot yet comprehend the logical sequence of dividing an apple into fractions. To comprehend fractions, children must know what a whole unit consists of, how many pieces the unit is divided into, and whether the pieces are of equal size. Adults can help children understand fractions through informal sharing activities, such as slicing up a pizza or a pan of brownies, and/or equally dividing household/preschool chores and play materials.

Estimation

Estimation is making an educated or informed guess about a measurement when no actual measurement is available. As adults, we often make estimates about the sizes of objects when we do not know their exact measurements, about the amounts of substances we have not actually

114

measured, and about the numbers of small objects in large collections when we have not actually counted the objects. However, young children are in the process of learning the concepts of sizes and numbers. Children must comprehend concepts of comparison and relativity (e.g., larger, smaller, more, less, etc.) before they will be able to make accurate estimates. When children start to develop the ability to estimate amounts or sizes, this process helps them learn related math vocabulary words, such as "about" or "around," and "more than" and "less than" [something else]. Through estimating, they also learn how to make appropriate predictions and arrive at realistic answers. It is important for young children to learn how to make estimates, to recognize when it is appropriate to apply the estimation method, and to recognize when their estimates are reasonable.

Activities to Help Develop Estimation

To accustom young children to the idea of estimating, adults should regularly use words related to estimation in their conversations with children (e.g., "around," "about," "approximately," "near," "more than [some other amount or number]," "less than [some other amount or number]," "between [two numbers or amounts]," etc.). During everyday activities like shopping or eating, adults can ask children to estimate amounts of foods, numbers of items, or lengths of time. Later, adults can help children compare the actual outcome with their original estimate. This process helps children learn to make realistic/reasonable estimates. Activities promoting estimation skills can be very simple. Adults can ask children, for example, to guess which of their friends is tallest, and then test the accuracy of the guess using real measurements. When children grow older, adults can write down estimates and real measurements, and can then repeat the exercise described above or present a similar one. With repetition, children will eventually begin making more accurate estimates. The goal is not for children to come up with exact measurements, but ones that are close to actual amounts/numbers. Giving children opportunities to practice improves their estimating skills.

Probabilities and Statistics

In general, when people work with statistics, they present them in graphs or charts to organize them, interpret them, and make it easier to see relationships among individual statistics. Graphs are a visual alternative that depict mathematical information and show relationships among individual statistics, especially changes over time. Graphs also allow for the comparison of different groups. Probabilities indicate the likelihood that something will happen. Adults use probabilities to predict things, such as people's risks of developing or dying from various diseases or medical conditions; the chances of accidents; children's risks of experiencing academic difficulties, dropping out, or developing emotional and behavioral disorders; and the chances that a certain area will receive rain or snow. Scientists use probabilities to predict the likelihood of various behaviors or outcomes they are studying. They use statistics to show the numbers and proportions of responses or results obtained in research studies. Calendars are one type of chart. Adults can help children use them to organize daily and weekly activities, and to understand how we organize information.

Charts and Graphs

According to experts, almost every daily activity can be charted in some way. For example, adults can help children peel the little stickers off of plums, bananas, etc. and stick them to a piece of paper/poster board divided into columns. After a week, they can count each column to determine how many pieces of each kind of fruit they ate. Similarly, adults can show children how to use removable stickers or color forms to document the number of times they performed any daily activity. For example, children could place a color form near the telephone every time it rings and/or every time somebody picks it up to make a call. They could also place a color form near the front door every time somebody comes in, goes out, and/or rings the doorbell/knocks. This enables children to count the number of times given events occur by recording them. Some children are better able to understand math by viewing and making graphs. This is because creating graphs involves representing quantities visually instead of just listing numbers.

Counting

Counting is considered a math skill milestone for young children. Typical four-year-olds enjoy counting aloud. Experts identify three levels of counting. The first is counting from 1 to 12, which requires memorization. The second level is counting from 13 to 19, which requires not only memorization, but also an understanding of the more unusual rules for "teen" numbers. The third level is counting from 20 on. This process is very consistent, and the numbers are ordered according to regular rules. Experts in math education believe that at this level of counting, children are discovering a regular mathematical pattern for the first time, which is base ten (i.e. 20, 30, 40, 50, etc. are 2 tens, 3 tens, 4 tens, 5 tens, etc., and after the base a number between 1 and 9 is added). Researchers and educators in early childhood mathematics programs recommend encouraging children as young as four years old to learn to count up to 100. They find that doing this helps young children learn about and explore patterns in depth.

Perceiving and Identifying Shapes

The three levels of perceiving shapes that children typically move through sequentially are seeing, naming, and analyzing. Very young children recognize simple shapes like circles, squares, and triangles. As their cognitive and language skills develop, they learn the names for these shapes, and use these names to identify single shapes. The third level is analyzing each shape to understand its properties. Whereas identifying shapes visually is intuitive and based on association, analyzing their properties is more abstract, since a shape can have a number of different appearances. For example, three-year-olds can differentiate a triangle from other shapes. However, if you show them a very tall, skinny/short, wide/lopsided/crooked triangle, they will have trouble identifying it as a triangle. At the analysis level, children realize that a triangle has three sides, which are not necessarily equal in length. An activity that young children enjoy is closing their eyes, reaching into a bag of assorted shapes, finding a triangle by touch, and explaining why it is a triangle. This involves both the second and third levels of naming and analysis.

Integrating Math into Everyday Activities and Using Early Childhood Math Curricula

Integrating math into the context of everyday activities has been the philosophy of early childhood math education until recently. For example, when teachers have children line up, they ask them who is first, second, third, etc. to practice counting. When children play with blocks, teachers ask them to identify their shapes and whether one block is larger/smaller than another. During snack times, teachers help children learn 1:1 correspondence by having them place one snack on each plate. These activities are quite valuable. However, some educators maintain that they are insufficient when used on their own, because in larger classes it is not always possible to take advantage of "teachable moments" with every child. Therefore, this educational approach cannot be applied systematically. These educators recommend that in addition to integration strategies, EC teachers should use a curriculum. The HighScope curriculum, the Creative Curriculum, and Big Math for Little Kids are just a few examples. Many teachers combine several curricula, selecting parts of different programs. Using a curriculum allows teachers to use a more planned approach to integrate math into all activities.

Clinical Interview

Background, Method, and Advantages

Clinical interviews have long been used by individual and family therapists, as well as by researchers. Piaget used them along with observations and case histories to understand young children's thinking as he formulated his cognitive developmental theory. Interviewers ask structured/semi-structured/open-ended questions and listen to the responses, often recording them for accuracy. This method gives the interviewer a way to find out what the respondent is thinking and feeling inside, which cannot be determined by observing outward behaviors alone. In educational settings, a teacher might ask a child questions like, "How did you do this?" "What is happening now?" "Can you tell me more about this?" "Why are you doing this?" "What are you thinking about now?" etc. Flexible questioning helps uncover the child's thought process, which is what is leading him/her to engage in specific behaviors. Just observing the behaviors alone does not allow the child to express his/her knowledge. While fully interviewing each child in a classroom is not practical, teachers can adapt this method by asking clinical interview-type questions as part of their instruction.

Using Questioning

Teachers can gain a lot of information and insight about how children are learning math concepts by observing their behaviors. For children to actually express their knowledge and thinking processes, however, teachers must ask them questions. For example, when a teacher introduces new shapes to young children, s/he can ask them the shapes' names, how they differ from one another, and why they think the shapes differ. Teachers can then use children's various responses to elicit further responses from them. This technique requires children to use language in significant ways during math activities. Therefore, these activities not only teach math skills, but also promote literacy development. Asking clinical interview-type questions promotes children's development of math communication skills, one of the essential components of math education. Additionally, being able to put one's knowledge and thoughts into words is a skill that is very important in all areas of education, not just math education. Using clinical interview-type questions helps children learn to use language to explain their thinking, share ideas, and express themselves, promoting and strengthening children's awareness of the functions of mathematical language.

Characteristics of Young Children's Thinking and Learning That Inform EC Math Curricula

Young children think in concrete ways and cannot understand abstract concepts, so effective EC math curricula typically use many concrete objects that children can see, feel, and manipulate to help them understand math concepts. Young children also naturally learn through exploring their environments, so good EC math curricula have many exploration and discovery activities that allow and encourage hands-on learning. In everyday life, young children start to observe relationships as they explore their surroundings. They match like objects, sort unlike objects, categorize objects, and arrange objects in simple patterns based on shared or contrasting properties. They start to understand words and phrases like "a little," "a lot," "more," "less," and "the same [as...]." Preschoolers use available materials such as sticks, pieces of string, their feet, their hands, their fingers, etc. as tools to measure objects. They also use rulers, measuring cups, and other conventional tools. They use their measurements to develop descriptions, sequences, and arrangements, and to compare various objects.

Activities That Help Children Develop Spatial Awareness

When preschool children build structures with blocks and put together pieces of puzzles during play, they are not only having fun, but are also developing spatial awareness. The relationships of objects to each other and within space are important concepts for children to learn, and serve as a foundation for the principles of geometry and physics that children will learn later. When they are moving around, preschoolers begin to notice how other people and objects are positioned in space, and how their own bodies move through space in relationship to objects and other people. This type of spatial awareness supports children's developing gross motor skills, coordination, and social skills. Young children can and should learn a number of math concepts and skills, such as the ones recommended by preschool math curricula like the High Scope program's "Numbers Plus" preschool mathematics curriculum. These concepts and skills include number symbols and names, counting, shapes, spatial awareness, relationships of parts to the whole, measurement, units, patterns, and analyzing data.

Rational Numbers and Irrational Numbers

In mathematics, rational numbers are numbers that can be written as ratios or fractions. In other words, a rational number can be expressed as a fraction that has a whole number as the numerator (the number on top) and the denominator (the number on the bottom). Therefore, all whole numbers are automatically rational numbers, because all whole numbers can be written as fractions with a denominator of 1 (e.g., 5 = 5/1, 68 = 68/1, 237 = 237/1, etc.). Even very large, unwieldy fractions (e.g., 9,731,245/42,754,021) are rational numbers, because they can be written as fractions. Irrational numbers can be written as decimal numbers, but not as fractions, because the numbers to the right of the decimal point that are less than 1 continue indefinitely without repeating. For example, the value of pi (π) begins as 3.141592..., and continues without end. The square root of 2 ($\sqrt{2}$) = 1.414213.... There are an infinite number of irrational numbers between 0 and 1. However, irrational numbers are not used as commonly in everyday life as rational numbers.

Cardinal, Ordinal, Nominal, and Real Numbers

Cardinal numbers are numbers that indicate quantity. For example, when we say "seven buttons" or "three kittens," we are using cardinal numbers. Ordinal numbers are numbers that indicate the order of items within a group or a set. For example, when we say "first, second, third, fourth, fifth, etc.," we are using ordinal numbers. Nominal numbers are numbers that name things. For example, we use area code numbers along with telephone numbers to identify geographical calling areas, and we use zip code numbers to identify geographical mailing areas. Nominal numbers, therefore, identify categories or serve as labels for things. However, they are not related to the actual mathematical values of numbers, and do not indicate numerical quantities or operations. Real numbers include all rational and irrational numbers. Rational numbers can always be written as fractions that have both numerators and denominators that are whole numbers. Irrational numbers cannot, as they contain non-repeating decimal digits. Real numbers may or may not be cardinal numbers.

Activities and Games That Make Learning Fun

Button Board

By gluing buttons of various sizes and colors to a piece of cardboard, teachers can initiate a number of activities that help preschoolers learn math concepts while having fun. Preschoolers are commonly learning shapes and how to draw them. Teachers can give children lengths of string/twine/yarn or long shoelaces and show them how to wrap them around different buttons to form shapes like rectangles, triangles, and squares. To practice counting and 1:1 correspondence, teachers can ask children to wrap their string around a given number of buttons. Preschoolers need to learn the concept that spoken number words like "five" can equate to a group of five concrete objects (such as buttons), and this activity promotes that learning. The button board is also useful for giving preschool children practice with sorting or classifying objects into groups based on a common characteristic. For example, the teacher can ask children to wrap their pieces of string around all the big buttons, all the little buttons, only the red buttons, only the blue buttons, etc.

Beanbags and Hopscotch

Teachers can encourage preschool children's counting and number development by creating a grid on the floor with the numbers 1 to 10 using masking tape, construction paper, and markers. Teachers could also draw the grid outdoors by drawing on pavement with chalk. The teacher arranges the numbers in ascending order within the grid of 10 squares/rectangles. S/he asks the children if they can name these numbers. The teacher provides beanbags. Each child gets a chance to throw a beanbag into any one of the numbered squares. Children can see how far they can throw and/or practice their aim. Each child names the number inside the square/rectangle where his/her beanbag lands. The children then play a version of hopscotch by hopping from numbered square to square, collecting their beanbags, and then hopping back. If desired, the teacher can write the number each child's beanbag lands on onto a "scoreboard" graph. Children will observe his/her writing the same numbers found on the floor/ground onto a "scoreboard." Teachers can review learning after the game to assess whether children can count using number words, name selected numbers, and throw accurately with consistency.

Reusing Sectioned Plastic Trays

A teacher can wash and reuse the compartmentalized plastic trays from the grocery store that are used for vegetable and fruit to create a preschool counting activity. The teacher supplies beads, pennies, erasers, or other small objects, as well as about a dozen sticky notes. S/he writes a number on each note. For older preschoolers, the teacher can write the numeral and the word (e.g., "7" and "seven"). For younger children, the teacher can write the numeric symbol ("7," for example) plus seven dots or other marks as a clue to that number symbol. The teacher puts one numbered note in each compartment and the supply of small objects in the central dip compartment. Then, s/he guides each child to transfer the correct number of each small object to the correct compartment. The child should count aloud while transferring each small object, and should repeat this process until all compartments with a numbered sticky note have the correct number of objects. Children can then repeat the process to practice and perfect their counting, or the teacher can place notes with different numbers in the tray's compartments.

Fishing for Numbers

Teachers can help preschoolers practice identifying numbers and counting by creating a fun "fishing for numbers" game. Teachers cut 10 fish shapes that are about 6 inches long from pieces of construction paper that are different colors. Teachers then write a single number between 1 and 10 on each "fish." Near each fish "mouth," the teacher punches a hole and inserts a paper clip through it. The teacher makes "fishing rods" by tying strings to dowels and gluing a magnet to each string. After spreading out the fish so the children can easily see the numbers, the teacher assigns each child a number and they "fish" for it, picking up the fish by bringing the magnet close to the paper clip. The children then "reel in" their catches. This gives children practice correctly identifying number names. The game can be adapted for more advanced math concepts as well. For example, the teacher can cut out fish shapes of various sizes and have children "fish" for larger/smaller fish. The activity can also be adapted to promote literacy development. The teacher can write letters instead of numbers on the fish to give students practice with alphabet recognition, or s/he can write a Dolch word/sight word on each fish to give students practice recognizing and identifying important vocabulary words.

Collages

Fundamental math skills that prepare preschoolers for kindergarten include shape recognition. To introduce children to an activity they will view as fun rather than as work, teachers can show children how to make a collage of a familiar figure. This will also give children the opportunity to experiment with an artistic process. For example, they can create a Santa Claus or an Easter Bunny as a holiday art project. They can make collages of other imaginary/real people for various events/seasons/topics. Teachers cut out paper templates, including circles for heads, triangles for hats, squares for bodies, and narrow rectangular strips for limbs. First, they help children name each shape. They have each child trace the template shapes onto paper and cut them out with child-safe scissors. The teacher then instructs children to arrange their cutout shapes on a piece of cardboard/construction paper. Once they are in the correct positions, the children glue the shapes in place. Teachers can subsequently teach additional shapes (octagons, ovals, etc.), challenging children to make new, different collages.

Grab Bag

Young children learn to name numbers in a way that is similar to how they learn to recite alphabet letters. However, learning to associate number symbols with concrete objects in the real world environment is a major advance in their cognitive development. The concept of 1:1 correspondence entails matching number symbols to the quantities they represent, an essential early math skill. Teachers can support the development of this math skill with a simple "grab bag" game youngsters enjoy. The teacher writes a number from 1 to 10 on each of ten cards, folding each card in half and putting them into a paper lunch bag. The teacher provides each child with a handful of pennies/play coins/buttons/little blocks to use as counting tokens. Each child takes a turn closing his/her eyes and pulling a card out of the bag. The child reads the number on the card, counts out the corresponding number of pennies/tokens, and puts them with the card. As children learn, teachers can place additional and/or different numbers (e.g., 11 to 20) in the grab bag. To promote the development of early literacy skills, teachers can also include the name of the number on each card.

Pattern Resist Art

A significant mark of progress in early math skills development is the ability to not only identify various shapes, but also to draw them. Once young children develop this ability, they typically want to practice it all the time. Teachers can encourage this by helping children make pattern resist paintings. The teacher tapes white paper to children's tables/trays, gives them crayons, and invites them to fill the paper with drawings of different shapes of various sizes and colors. Teachers can introduce young children to new shapes (e.g., ovals, stars, crescent moons, etc.) by drawing them on separate pieces of paper for children to look at and copy. Then, the teacher replaces the crayons with water, watercolor paints, and brushes; shows the children how to dip brushes into paint and water to dilute the colors; and allows them to paint over their crayoned shapes, covering all the white paper with color. The children see the shapes show through the paint, creating the pattern resist. Dipping brushes and diluting various colors also develop children's color recognition skills and their hand-eye coordination.

Ice Cube Necklaces

In hot weather, making ice cube necklaces is a fun activity that helps young children cool off while learning to sequence objects. The activity also helps children develop their manual motor skills and learn about liquid and solid states of matter. Regular ice cube trays are fine; those with "fun-shaped" compartments are even better. The teacher cuts plastic drinking straws so that they will fit into each ice cube compartment. The children participate, watching and/or helping pour water into trays and adding various food colorings/fruit juices. The teacher places one straw clipping into each

Copyright © Mometrix Media. You have been licensed one copy of this document for personal use only. Any other reproduction or redistribution is strictly prohibited. All rights reserved.

compartment. While putting the trays into the freezer, the teacher tells children that 32° Fahrenheit/0° Celsius is the temperature at which water freezes. Children practice making scientific observations by noting how long the water takes to freeze. They empty the cubes into a big bowl. The children put on bathing suits or other clothing that can get wet, and the class goes outdoors. The teacher provides strings that are knotted at one end, and calls out a color pattern (e.g., one blue cube, then a yellow cube, etc.). Children follow the teacher's instructions to create color-patterned necklaces they can tie, wear, and watch melt.

Red Rover

Red Rover is a good game for groups of children who are attending parties or playing outdoors at parks/playgrounds. Two teams take turns calling and roving. The child called runs to the other team and tries to fit into its line. If successful, s/he gets to call another player to bring back to his/her home team. If not, s/he joins the opposite team. The game continues until one team has no more members. Teachers can adapt this game to teach shape recognition by cutting out various shapes from construction paper of different colors and pinning a shape to each child's shirt. In large groups, more than one child can have the same shape or color. Instead of children's names, the teacher instructs players to use shapes and colors when calling (e.g., "Red Rover, Red Rover, blue circles come over!"). This supports the development of shape and color recognition skills. Teachers can vary action verbs (e.g., "....hop over/jump over/skip over") to support vocabulary development and comprehensive skills. When children perform such movements, they are also practicing and developing gross motor skills.

Counting on Fingers

A common practice among preschool children is counting on their fingers. Young children learn concretely before they develop abstract thought, so they must have concrete objects to work with to understand abstract mathematical concepts. They use their fingers to count because fingers are concrete. A simple activity that allows children to continue finger counting while removing additional visual support is "blind finger counting." Using eyesight to count objects we can see is relatively easy. However, when children cannot see objects, they must learn to count mentally instead. This allows them to take another step in their progress from concrete to abstract thinking. To count mentally without visual reinforcement takes practice. Teachers can tape a shoebox lid to the box and cut a small hole in it. Children can fit a hand through the hole, but cannot see inside. Children close their eyes; the teacher drops several small objects into the box; and each child reaches in, counting the objects using only touch. Varying objects and quantities maintains the fun of this activity.

Sorting and Categorization

One of the major learning accomplishments of young children is being able to identify similarities and differences among objects. Developing this ability enables children to sort like objects into groups, and to place objects into categories based on their differences. When preschoolers compare and contrast objects, they demonstrate an important early step in the development of critical thinking, analytical, and problem solving skills. For an easy, entertaining guessing game, adults can select assorted household items familiar to children and put them into a bag/pillowcase. They then give children various clues (e.g., "I stir lemonade with this...," "It's made of wood," "We keep it in the kitchen drawer...," etc.) and ask them to guess which items are in the bag. It is important to give young children one to two minutes to consider each clue before they make a guess. Adults repeat clues when children guess incorrectly. If children guess correctly, they are allowed to look inside the bag. Youngsters greatly enjoy seeing that the object they guessed is actually inside the bag. Adults can gradually make the game more challenging by beginning with very common objects, and then eventually progressing to more unusual ones.

Baking Cookies

Young children are typically curious about adult activities like baking. They usually want to know more about the process, and often ask many questions. They also love to be included and to participate, frequently offering/asking to help. Letting them help builds their self-esteem and self-efficacy (i.e. their confidence in their competence to accomplish a task). Adults can allow children to help while also providing instruction and practice with shape recognition, measurement, sorting, and categorization. The adult prepares a favorite cookie recipe. Some children can help measure ingredients, which helps develop the math skill of measurement. With the dough rolled out, children use cookie cutters of various shapes. Recognizing, naming, and selecting the shapes promote the development of shape recognition skills. Adults "shuffle"/mix the baked cookie shapes and have children separate cookies with like shapes into groups, which promotes sorting skills. Having children identify similar/different shapes, sizes, and colors promotes categorization skills. Arranging cookie shapes into patterns for children to identify promotes pattern recognition skills, which are necessary to the development of math skills and many other skills. Giving each child a cookie to eat afterward is naturally reinforcing.

Creative Crafts

Prerequisite abilities that young children need in order to develop early math skills include the ability to identify, copy, expand, and create patterns; as well as the ability to count. Adults can promote the development of these skills by giving children a craft project and introducing them to an interactive game they can play using their crafts. First, the children paint six ping pong balls red on one side to make red-and-white balls. Then, the children paint six ping pong balls blue on one side to make blue-and-white balls. Once the paint dries, the adult puts several balls into an egg carton so that one color is face up. The adult starts making a simple pattern (e.g., two white, then two red, then two blue), and asks each child to continue the pattern. Then, the adult allows each child to create his or her own original color patterns. Once a child masters creating patterns using solid colors, he or she can then use both the white and colored sides of the balls to create more complex patterns. Children can design an infinite number of patterns, which are often quite artistic.

Shape Matching Games

In one type of shape matching game, EC teachers help children make a game board out of construction paper that is shaped like a tree. Teachers first help the children cut a treetop and leaf shapes from green paper. They discuss children's preferences for tall/short and thick/thin trunks, giving them practice using descriptive vocabulary words, particularly ones related to size. This step builds both general and math concept vocabulary. Children cut trunks from brown paper and paste/glue them on the treetops. While out of the children's sight, the teacher cuts 5 to 10 (or more) pairs of shapes per child/tree from different colors of construction paper. Pairs should not match exactly (e.g., a blue square can be paired with a red square). The teacher glues one of each pair of shapes to each child's tree while the child is not looking. The teacher then gives each child the rest of the shapes, and invites children to see how quickly they can match each shape to its "partner" on the tree. The teacher can provide "warmer/cooler" distance clues, and should provide reinforcement each time a child correctly matches a pair of shapes. Teachers can make this activity more challenging by using more shapes and/or getting students to match shapes that are different sizes (e.g., children can be asked to match smaller diamonds to larger diamonds).

Homemade Beanbag Game

Young children enjoy tossing objects and practicing their aim. Adults can make a beanbag game that helps children learn numbers and identify sets, while also allowing them to construct their own game rules. First, the adult should cover five big, equally-sized coffee (or similar) cans with paper that is adhesive on one side. The adult should then use markers to write a number from 1 to 5 and draw the corresponding number of dots on each can. The next step is to fill 15 tube socks with beans and knot/tie/sew them shut. The following numerals and the corresponding number of dots should be written on each homemade beanbag using markers: the number 1 on five beanbags, the number 2 on four beanbags, the number 3 on three beanbags, the number 4 on two beanbags, and the number 5 on one beanbag. Next, the adult should attach the cans to the floor with tape or Velcro. Then, the adult should mark a line on the floor that children must stand behind, and should direct children ONLY to toss the beanbags into the cans. Children will devise various games/rules. First, they may simply toss the beanbags into the cans; then, some may try to toss beanbags into a can that has the same number as the one marked on the beanbag. Eventually, some may throw three beanbags into the "3" can. They may/may not keep score. Allowing children to determine the details and rules gives them an opportunity to develop their imagination and decision making skills, and to create their own games while learning number and set identification.

Guessing Game

Adults can adapt the format of "20 Questions," "I Spy," and other similar guessing games to focus on numbers and help children learn number concepts. For example, adults could say, "I'm thinking of a number from 1 to 10...." and then give children 10 guesses. Adults give children cues as they guess, such as "higher" and "lower," to help them narrow down the number of possible correct answers. As children improve, adults can increase the number range (e.g., from 0 to 50) or use larger numbers (e.g., from 20 to 40). As children's skills and self-confidence develop, adults can reverse roles, having children think of numbers and give clues while adults guess. Young children enjoy the fun of guessing, getting closer using clues, deducing correct answers, and fooling adults with their own clues. Concurrently, they learn to describe numbers, compare them, and sequence them. Adults can make the game more difficult by limiting the number of guesses allowed and/or setting time limits. They can make it easier by providing a written number line for children to reference. This game requires no materials (or just a basic number line), is a great way to pass time, and entertains children while helping to develop numeracy skills.

Arts and Crafts

According to the U.S. Department of Agriculture, preschoolers need three ½-cup servings of fruit and three ½-cup servings of vegetables daily. However, many young children are picky/resistant. Adults can motivate them to eat produce with a "food rainbow" project. Adults show children a picture of a rainbow, and discuss its colors and their sequence (teaching some earth science, optics, and color theory!). A fun art project is allowing students to color their own rainbows, which improves fine motor skills. Then, adults can have children cut out pictures from grocery circulars and name each food. The adult can help children find one healthy fruit/vegetable for each color, gluing each food to its corresponding stripe on the rainbow. Adults can then help children pull apart cotton balls and glue them to their rainbow pictures to represent clouds. Children can then post their food rainbows on refrigerators as artwork and as healthy eating reminders. At the bottom, children can draw and color one box (bottom-up) for each food they eat (e.g., blue = blueberries, orange = carrots, red = apples, etc.) to create a bar graph. Children should try to "eat" the entire rainbow every week. This activity gives children the opportunity to produce colorful art, eat better, track and document their diets, and develop graphing skills.

Review Video: Bar Graph
Visit mometrix.com/academy and enter code: 226729

Treasure Hunt

A treasure hunt is an ideal outdoor activity for young children, and can also be adapted for indoor fun. The treasure can be anything (e.g., a small toy/play money/chocolate "coins"/rocks spray painted gold or silver, etc.). The adult should put the treasure in a paper bag marked with a large X. The adult should hide it somewhere where it is not visible, but will not be overly difficult for children to find. Then, the adult should make a treasure map, using few words and many pictures, sketching landmark objects in the area (trees, houses, etc. if the activity will be done outdoors, and furniture, walls, etc. if the activity will be done indoors). The adult should ensure the map is developmentally appropriate for young children, and that they will be able to read it independently. Adults with time and motivation can make the map look authentic by soaking it in tea/coffee, drying it in a 200° oven, or even charring its edges. Adults should include a dotted line on the map that reinforces the simple directions and indicates the path to the treasure, which is indicated on the map by a large X. Children have fun, use their imaginations, make connections between symbols and images to corresponding real-world physical objects, and begin learning to read maps.

Pasta Necklace

Stringing beads/noodles is an activity that helps young children develop hand-eye coordination, which they will need for writing and other everyday activities that require fine motor coordination. Noodles are typically the perfect size for young children's hands. They are inexpensive, usually costing less than comparably-sized beads. Moreover, pasta is non-toxic, an advantage when working with little persons who put things in their mouths. Hollow, tubular noodles like penne, ziti, wagon wheels, etc. are ideal. Fishing line/craft beading string/other stiff string is best; soft, limp string/yarn is harder for young children to manipulate. Using multicolored vegetable pasta removes the need to use markers or dye to add color. If using white pasta, children can color the noodles with markers, but adults should keep in mind that the ink can bleed onto skin/clothes even when it is dry. Adults should cut pieces of string that are long enough to allow children to easily slip the necklaces on and off after they are tied. Adults should also use a knot to secure a noodle to one end of the string. By providing more than one noodle shape, adults can invite children to string the noodles to create patterns, which develops pattern recognition and pattern creation abilities. These abilities also inform repetition, rhythm, categorization, and sequencing skills, which are important in math, music, art, literature, clothing design, etc.

Number Dash

A game for young children that some educators call "Number Dash" (Miller, ed. Charner, 2009) builds foundational math concepts and skills, while providing physical activity. It can involve small or large groups (the referenced authors say "the more the merrier"). Help children write large numbers on a paved area with sidewalk chalk. Make sure numbers are spread far enough apart so children will not collide while running. There should be one of each number for each child (e.g., six "1s," "2s," "3s," etc. if there are six children). Use chalk colors that contrast with the pavement color to ensure the numbers will be highly visible. Tell children to run ("dash") to whichever number you call out and stand on it until you call another number. Call out numbers randomly. Encourage children who have located the number to help their classmates/playmates. This game develops gross motor skills, number writing skills, and number recognition skills. It also provides experience with playing organized games, following rules, following directions, and cooperating with and helping others. This game can also be played with letters, colors, and/or shapes.

Introducing Standard Measurement Using a Ruler

A teacher is introducing standard measures to her class as part of a unit on measurement, one of the early math skills. She shows the children a ruler, explaining that it is one foot long, and that we can use it to measure inches and parts of inches. She demonstrates placing the ruler on paper to measure a given length, explaining that the ruler can also be used as a straight edge for drawing lines. One child asks, "How come you started with zero? Why don't you start with one like when we count?" The teacher responds, "That's a very good question! Zero means none/nothing. When we count, we start with one because we already have at least one of something. When you were born, you were not one year old; your age began at zero. After a year, on your first birthday, you were one year old. We also begin measuring distances at zero/none/nothing. The first piece/unit of measurement is one, not two. The distance from zero to one is equal to one. To get to one inch, for example, we need to start at zero."

Learning About Geometric Shapes and Their Properties

A teacher has been working with students to help them develop their shape identification skills. They can recognize shapes by sight, and have also learned the defining properties of different shapes (number of sides, etc.). The teacher shows the class this figure:

———

She asks how many rectangles they can find in the figure. One student answers, "There is one rectangle," which is incorrect because a square is a rectangle; this figure has four rectangles that are squares. Moreover, the entire figure is itself a rectangle. Another student therefore says, "There are five rectangles." This response is also incorrect. Two adjacent squares also form a rectangle; this means there are three additional rectangles. Three adjacent squares also form a rectangle; this means there are two additional rectangles. Thus, the figure has a total of 10 rectangles. Solving this puzzle requires the use of many skills, including analyzing visual information, synthesizing visual information, recognizing patterns, recognizing shapes, and identifying the properties of shapes.

Collecting, Organizing, and Displaying Data Using Sticky Notes and a Teacher-Made Chart

A preschool teacher is teaching her group of ten children about basic data collection, data arrangement, and data display. She shows children yellow, blue, and green sticky notes, and has each child select his/her favorite color. Five children choose yellow notes, three select blue, and two choose green. By choosing one of three colors, each child has participated in data collection. The teacher draws lines to divide a sheet of paper into three columns, and labels each column with one of the colors. She helps the children place their chosen sticky notes in the correct columns. By arranging the colored sticky notes into columns, the teacher and children have organized the data they gathered. Once all notes are in their proper color columns, the completed chart is an example of how collected, organized data can be displayed.

	Yellow sticky note	
	Yellow sticky note	
Blue sticky note	Yellow sticky note	
Blue sticky note	Yellow sticky note	Green sticky note
Blue sticky note	Yellow sticky note	Green sticky note
BLUE	**YELLOW**	**GREEN**

<u>Selecting One of Three Colors of Sticky Notes, Organizing Them by Color, and Displaying Them</u>

The teacher had ten children each choose one of three colors of sticky notes, an example of basic data collection. She used a chart with three columns to organize the children's choices as follows:

	Yellow sticky note	
	Yellow sticky note	
Blue sticky note	Yellow sticky note	
Blue sticky note	Yellow sticky note	Green sticky note
Blue sticky note	Yellow sticky note	Green sticky note
BLUE	**YELLOW**	**GREEN**

The chart displays the collected and organized data. The teacher asks the children which color was chosen the most. Seeing five yellow notes, they answer, "yellow." She asks which color was chosen the least, and they say, "green." She asks them to use numbers to arrange the color choices from most popular to least popular. They arrive at, "five yellow, three blue, and two green." Together, the teacher and the children point to and count ten children. She tells them five equals half of ten, and asks which color half of the children chose. Together, they figure out it was yellow. These are examples of analyzing and interpreting data.

Science Concepts Young Children Learn During Everyday Activities

Science entails asking questions, conducting investigations, collecting data, and seeking answers to the questions asked by analyzing the data collected. Natural events that can be examined over time and student-centered inquiry through hands-on activities that require the application of problem solving skills are most appropriate for helping young children learn basic science. In their everyday lives, young children develop concepts of 1:1 correspondence through activities like fitting pegs into matching holes or distributing one item to each child in a class. They also develop counting concepts by counting enough items for each child in the group or counting pennies in a piggy bank. They develop classification concepts when they sort objects into separate piles according to their shapes or some other type of category (e.g., toy cars vs. toy trucks). When children transfer water, sand, rice, or other substances from one container to another, they develop measurement concepts. As they progress, children will apply these early concepts to more abstract scientific ideas during grade school.

Science Concepts Infants and Toddlers Learn in Normal Developmental Processes

Infants use their senses to explore the environment, and are motivated by innate curiosity. As they develop mobility, children gain more freedom, allowing them to make independent discoveries and think for themselves. Children learn size concepts by comparing the sizes of objects/persons in the environment to their own size, and by observing that some objects are too large to hold, while others are small enough to hold. They learn about weight when trying to lift various objects. They learn about shape when they see that some objects roll away, while others do not. Babies learn temporal sequences when they wake up wet and hungry, cry, and have parents change and feed them. They also learn this concept by playing, getting tired, and going to sleep. As soon as they look and move around, infants learn about space, including large/small spaces. Eventually, they develop spatial sense through experiences like being put in a playpen/crib in the middle of a large room.

Toddlers naturally sort objects into groups according to their sizes/shapes/colors/uses. They experiment with transferring water/sand among containers of various sizes. They learn part-to-whole relationships by building block structures and then dismantling them.

Naturalistic, Informal, and Structured Learning Experiences

Children actively construct their knowledge of the environment through exploring it. Young children's learning experiences can be naturalistic (i.e. spontaneously initiated by the child during everyday activities). During naturalistic learning, the child controls his/her choices and actions. Informal learning experiences also allow the child to choose his or her actions and activities, but they include adult intervention at some point during the child's engagement in naturalistic pursuits. In structured learning experiences, the adult chooses the activities and supplies some direction as to how the child should perform the associated actions. One consideration related to EC learning that teachers should keep in mind is that within any class or group of children, there are individual differences in learning styles. Additionally, children from different cultural groups have varying learning styles and approaches. EC teachers can introduce science content in developmentally appropriate ways by keeping these variations in mind.

Naturalistic Learning Experiences

Motivated by novelty and curiosity, young children spontaneously initiate naturalistic experiences during their everyday activities. Infants and toddlers in Piaget's sensorimotor stage learn by exploring the environment through their senses, so adults should provide them with many objects and substances they can see, hear, touch, smell, and taste. Through manipulating and observing concrete objects/substances, preschoolers in Piaget's preoperational stage begin learning concepts that will enable them to perform mental operations later on. Adults should observe children's actions and progress, and should give positive reinforcement in the form of looks, facial expressions, gestures, and/or words encouraging and praising the child's actions. Young children need adult feedback to learn when they are performing the appropriate actions. For example, a toddler/preschooler selects a tool from the toolbox, saying, "This is big!" and the mother responds, "Yes!" A four-year-old sorting toys of various colors into separate containers is another example of a naturalistic experience. A five-year-old who observes while painting that mixing two colors yields a third color is yet another example.

Informal Learning Experience

Informal learning experiences involve two main components. First, the child spontaneously initiates naturalistic learning experiences during everyday activities to explore and learn about the environment. Second, the adult takes advantage of opportunities during naturalistic experiences to insert informal learning experiences. Adults do not plan these in advance, but take advantage of opportunities that occur naturally. One way this happens is when a child is on the right track to solve a problem, but needs some encouragement or a hint from the adult. Another way is when the adult spots a "teachable moment" during the child's naturalistic activity, and uses it to reinforce a basic concept. For example, a three-year-old might hold up three fingers, declaring, "I'm six years old." The parent says, "Let's count fingers: one, two, three. You're three years old." Or, a teacher asks a child who has a box of treats if s/he has enough for the whole class, and the child answers, "I don't know." The teacher then responds, "Let's count them together," and helps the child count.

Structured Learning Experiences

Naturalistic learning experiences are spontaneously initiated and controlled by children. Informal learning experiences involve unplanned interventions by adults during children's naturalistic experiences, which is when adults offer suitable correction/assistance/support. Structured learning experiences differ in that the adult pre-plans and initiates the activity/lesson, and provides the child with some direction. For example, a teacher who observes a four-year-old's need to practice counting can give the child a pile of toys, and then ask him/her how many there are. To develop size concepts, a teacher can give a small group of children several toys of different sizes, and then ask the children to inspect them and talk about their characteristics. The teacher holds up one toy, instructing children to find one that is bigger/smaller. If a child needs to learn shape concepts, the teacher might introduce a game involving shapes, giving the child instructions on how to play the game. Or, a first grade teacher, recognizing the importance of the concept of classification to the ability to organize scientific information, might ask students to bring in bones to classify during a unit on skeletons.

Kindergarten Activity for Collecting and Organizing Data

Preschoolers and kindergarteners continue their earlier practices of exploration to learn new things, and they apply fundamental science concepts to collect and organize data in order to answer questions. To collect data, children must have observation, counting, recording, and organization skills. One activity kindergarteners and teachers enjoy is growing bean sprouts. For example, the teacher can show children two methods: one using glass jars and paper towels saturated with water, the other using cups of dirt. The children add water daily as needed, observe developments, and report to the teacher, who records their observations on a chart. The teacher gives each child a chart that they add information to each day. The children count how many days their beans took to sprout in the glass jars and in the cups of dirt. They then compare their own results for the two methods, and they compare their results to those of their classmates. The children apply concepts of counting, numbers, time, 1:1 correspondence, and comparison of numbers. They also witness the planting and growing process.

Science Process Skills

Science process skills include observation (using the senses to identify properties of objects/situations), classification (grouping objects/situations according to their common properties), measurement (quantifying physical properties), communication (using observations, classifications, and measurements to report experimental results to others), inference (finding patterns and meaning in experiment results), and prediction (using experimental experience to formulate new hypotheses). Inferences and predictions must be differentiated from objective observations. Classification, measurement, and comparison are basic math concepts which, when applied to science problems, are called process skills. The other science process skills named, as well as defining and controlling variables, are equally necessary to solve both science and math problems. For example, using ramps can help young children learn basic physics concepts. Teachers ask children what would happen if two balls were rolled down a ramp at the same time, if two balls were rolled down a ramp of a different height/length, if two ramps of different heights/lengths were used, etc. In this activity, children apply the scientific concepts of observation, communication, inference, and prediction, as well as the concepts of height, length, counting, speed, distance, and comparison.

Scientific Method

Children are born curious, and naturally engage in problem solving to learn. Problem solving and inquiry are natural child behaviors. EC teachers can use these behaviors to promote children's scientific inquiry. Scientific inquiry employs the scientific method. The first step in the method is to ask a question, which is another natural child behavior. Just as adult scientists formulate research questions, the first step of the scientific method for children is asking questions they want to answer. Next, to address a question, both adults and children must form a hypothesis (i.e. an educated guess about what the answer will be). The hypothesis informs and directs the next steps: designing and conducting an experiment to test whether the hypothesis is true or false. With teacher instruction/help, children experiment. For example, they might drop objects of different weights from a height to see when each lands, as Galileo did. Teachers help record outcomes. The next steps are deciding whether the results prove/disprove the hypothesis and reporting the results and conclusions to others.

Review Video: The Scientific Method
Visit mometrix.com/academy and enter code: 191386

Physical Science and Matter

Physical science is the study/science of the physical universe surrounding us. Everything in the universe consists of matter (i.e. anything that has mass and takes up space) or energy (i.e. anything that does not have mass or occupy space, but affects matter and space). Three states of matter are solid, liquid, and gas. Solids preserve their shape even when they are not in a container. Solids have specific, three-dimensional/crystalline atomic structures and specific melting points. Liquids have no independent shape outside of containers, but have specific volumes. Liquid molecules are less cohesive than solid molecules, but more cohesive than gas molecules. Liquids have flow, viscosity (flow resistance), and buoyancy. Liquids can undergo diffusion, osmosis, evaporation, condensation, solution, freezing, and heat conduction and convection. Liquids and gases are both fluids, and share some of the same properties. Gases have no shape, expanding and spreading indefinitely outside of containers. Gases can become liquid/solid through cooling/compression/both. Liquids/solids can become gaseous through heating. Vapor is the gaseous form of a substance that is solid/liquid at lower temperatures. For example, when water is heated it becomes steam, a vapor.

Review Video: States of Matter
Visit mometrix.com/academy and enter code: 742449

Liquids

Of the three states of matter—solid, liquid, and gas—liquids have properties that fall somewhere in between those of solids and gases. The molecules of solids are the most cohesive (i.e. they have the greatest mutual attraction). Gas molecules are the least cohesive, and liquid molecules are in between. Liquids have no definite shape, while solids do. Liquids have a definite volume, whereas gases do not. The cohesion of liquid molecules draws them together, and the molecules below the surface pull surface molecules down, creating surface tension. This property can be observed in containers of water. Liquid molecules are also attracted to other substance's molecules (i.e. adhesion). Surface tension and adhesion combined cause liquids to rise in narrow containers, a property known as capillarity. Liquids are buoyant (i.e. they exert upward force so objects which have more buoyancy than weight float in liquids, while objects which have more weight than buoyancy sink in liquids). Liquids can be made solid by freezing, and can be made gaseous by heating/evaporation. Liquids can diffuse, which means they can mix with other molecules. Liquid diffusion across semi-permeable membranes is known as osmosis.

Solids

Solids are one of the three forms of matter. The other two are liquids and gases. Solids maintain their shape when they are not inside of containers, whereas liquids and gases acquire the shapes of containers holding them. Containers also prevent liquids and gases from dispersing. Of the three forms of matter, solids have the most cohesive molecules. Solid molecules are most attracted to each other, and solid molecules are held together most strongly. Solid atoms are organized into defined, three-dimensional, lattice-shaped patterns (i.e. they are crystalline in structure). Solids also have specific temperatures at which they melt. Some substances that seem solid, such as plastic, gel, tar, and glass, are actually not true solids. They are amorphous solids because their atoms do not have a crystalline structure, but are amorphous (i.e. the positions of their atoms have no long-range organization). They also have a range of melting temperatures rather than specific melting points.

> **Review Video:** Amorphous Solids
> Visit mometrix.com/academy and enter code: 121001
>
> **Review Video:** Balance of Forces That Make a Solid
> Visit mometrix.com/academy and enter code: 519967

Gases

Gas, liquid, and solid are the three states of matter. Gases have the least cohesive (i.e. mutually attracted) molecules of the three states of matter, while solids have the most cohesive molecules. Gases do not maintain a defined shape, while solids do. If not contained within a receptacle, gases spread and expand indefinitely. Gases can be elementary or compound. An elementary gas is composed of only one kind of chemical element. At normal temperatures and pressures, 12 elementary gases are known: argon*, chlorine, fluorine, helium*, hydrogen, krypton*, neon*, nitrogen, oxygen, ozone, radon*, and xenon*. Compound gases have molecules containing atoms of more than one kind of chemical element. Carbon monoxide (which contains one carbon and one oxygen atom) and ammonia (which contains nitrogen and hydrogen atoms) are common compound gases. Heating gas molecules/atoms charges them electrically, making them ions. Plasma combines positive gas ions and electrons. Some gases are colorless and odorless, while others are not. Some burn with oxygen, while others do not. *Noble/inert gases have single atoms that do not normally form compounds with other elements.

Light

Reflection and Scattering

When a beam of light hits a smooth surface like a mirror, it bounces back off that surface. This rebounding is reflection. In physics, the law of reflection states that "the angle of incidence equals the angle of reflection." This means that when light is reflected, it always bounces off the surface at the same angle at which it hit that surface. When a beam of light hits a rough rather than a smooth surface, though, it is reflected back at many different angles, not just the angle at which it struck the surface. This reflection at multiple and various angles is scattering. Many objects we commonly use every day have rough surfaces. For example, paper may look smooth to the naked eye, but actually has a rough surface. This property can be observed by viewing paper through a microscope. Because light waves striking paper are reflected in every direction by its rough surface, scattering enables us to read words printed on paper from any viewing angle.

Absorption

When light strikes a medium, the light wave's frequency is equal or close to the frequency at which the electrons in the medium's atoms can vibrate. These electrons receive the light's energy, making them vibrate. When a medium's atoms hang on tightly to their electrons, the electrons transmit their vibrations to the nucleus of each atom. This makes the atoms move faster and collide with the medium's other atoms. The energy the atoms got from the vibrations is then released as heat. This process is known as absorption of light. Materials that absorb light, such as wood and metal, are opaque. Some materials absorb certain light frequencies but transmit others. For example, glass transmits visible light (and therefore appears transparent to the naked eye), but absorbs ultraviolet frequencies. The sky looks blue because the atmosphere absorbs all colors in the spectrum except blue, which it reflects. Only blue wavelengths/frequencies bounce back to our eyes. This is an example of subtractive color, which we see in paints/dyes and all colored objects/materials. Pigments absorb some frequencies and reflect others.

Refraction

When light moves from one transparent medium to another (e.g., between water and air/vice versa), the light's speed changes, bending the light wave. It bends either away from or toward the normal line, an imaginary straight line running at right angles to the medium's surface. We easily observe this bending when looking at a straw in a glass of water. The straw appears to break/bend at the waterline. The angle of refraction is the amount that the light wave bends. It is determined by how much the medium slows down the light's speed, which is the medium's refraction index. For example, diamonds are much denser and harder than water, and thus have a higher refraction index. They slow down and trap light more than water does. Consequently, diamonds sparkle more than water. Lenses, such as those in eyeglasses and telescopes, rely on the principle of refraction. Curved lenses disperse or concentrate light waves, refracting light as it both enters and exits, thus changing the light's direction. This is how lenses correct (eyeglasses) and enhance (telescopes) our vision.

Magnetism

Magnetism is the property some objects/substances have of attracting other materials. The form of magnetism most familiar to us is certain materials attracting iron. Magnets also attract steel, cobalt, and other materials. Generators supplying power include magnets, as do all electric motors. Loudspeakers and telephones contain magnets. Tape recorders use magnets. The tape they play is magnetized. Magnets are used in compasses to determine the location of north and various corresponding directions. In fact, the planet Earth is itself a giant magnet (which is why compasses point north). Hence, like the Earth, all magnets have two poles: a north/north-seeking pole and a south/south-seeking pole. Opposite poles attract, and like poles repel each other. Magnets do not need to touch to attract/repel each other. A magnet's effective area/range is its magnetic field. All materials have some response to magnetic fields. Magnets make nearby magnetic materials into magnets, a process known as magnetic induction. Materials that line up parallel to magnetic force field lines are paramagnetic, while materials that line up perpendicular to magnetic force field lines are diamagnetic.

Modern Theory of Magnetism and What Scientists Do/Do Not Know

Scientists have known about the effects of magnetism for hundreds of years. However, they do not know exactly what magnetism is, or what causes it. French physicist Pierre Weiss proposed a theory of magnetism in the early 20th century that is widely accepted. This theory posits that every magnetic material has groups of molecules—domains—that function as magnets. Until a material is magnetized, its domains have a random arrangement, so one domain's magnetism is cancelled out by another's. When the material comes into a magnetic field—the range/area wherein a magnet is effective—its domains align themselves parallel to the magnetic field's lines of force. As a result, all of their north-seeking/north poles point in the same direction. Removing the magnetic field causes like poles to repel one another as they normally do. In easily magnetized materials, domains revert to random order. In materials that are harder to magnetize, domains lack sufficient force to disassemble, leaving the material magnetized. Later versions of Weiss's theory attribute domain magnetism to spinning electrons.

> **Review Video: Magnets**
> Visit mometrix.com/academy and enter code: 570803

Insulation, Conduction, and the Flow of Electricity

The smallest units of all matter are atoms. The nuclei of atoms are orbited by negatively charged electrons. Some materials have electrons that are strongly bound to their atoms. These include air, glass, wood, cotton, plastic, and ceramic. Since their atoms rarely release electrons, these materials have little or no ability to conduct electricity, and are known as electrical insulators. Insulators resist/block conduction. Metals and other conductive materials have free electrons that can detach from the atoms and move around. Without the tight binding of insulators, materials with loose electrons enable electric current to flow easily through them. Such materials are called electrical conductors. The movements of their electrons transmit electrical energy. Electricity requires something to make it flow (i.e. a generator). A generator creates a steady flow of electrons by moving a magnet close to a wire, creating a magnetic field to propel electrons. Electricity also requires a conductor (i.e. a medium through which it can move from one place to another).

Movement of Electrical Currents by a Generator

Magnetism and electricity are related, and they interact with each other. Generators work by using magnets near conductive wires to produce moving streams of electrons. The agent of movement can range from a hand crank, to a steam engine, to the nuclear fission process. However, all agents of movements operate according to the same principle. A simple analogy is that a generator magnetically pushes electrical current the way a pump pushes water. Just as water pumps apply specific amounts of pressure to specific numbers of water molecules, generator magnets apply specific amounts of "pressure" to specific numbers of electrons. The number of moving electrons in an electrical circuit equals the current, or amperage. The unit of measurement for amperage is the ampere, or amp. The amount of force moving the electrons is the voltage. Its unit of measurement is the volt. One amp equals 6.24×10^{18} electrons passing through a wire each second. For example, a generator could produce 1 amp using 6 volts when rotating 1,000 times per minute. Today's power stations rely on generators.

Positions and Motions of Objects and Newton's Laws of Physics

Moving physical objects changes their positions. According to Newton's first law of motion, an object at rest tends to stay at rest and an object in motion tends to stay in motion, unless/until an opposing force changes the object's state of rest/motion. For example, an object at rest could be a small rock sitting on the ground. If you kick the rock into the air, it moves through the air. The rock will continue to move, but when a force like gravity acts on it, it falls/stops moving. The resulting motion from kicking the rock illustrates Newton's third law of motion: for every action there is an equal and opposite reaction. The acceleration or increase in velocity (a) of an object depends on its mass (m) and the amount of force (F) that is applied to the object. Newton's second law of motion states that F = ma (force equals mass times acceleration). Thus, moving objects maintain their speeds unless some force(s) cause acceleration or slowing/stopping, as frictional forces do.

Heat

Heat is transmitted through conduction, radiation, and convection. Heat is transmitted in solids through conduction. When two objects at different temperatures touch each other, the hotter object's molecules are moving faster. They collide with the colder object's molecules, which are moving slower. As a result of the collision, the molecules that are moving more rapidly supply energy to the molecules that are moving more slowly. This speeds up the movement of the (previously) slower moving molecules, which heats up the colder object. This process of transferring heat through contact is called thermal conductivity. An example of thermal conductivity is the heat sink. Heat sinks are used in many devices. Today, they are commonly used in computers. A heat sink transfers the heat building up in the computer processor, moving it away before it can damage the processor. Computers contain fans, which blow air across their heat sinks and expel the heated air out of the computers.

Acoustical Principles and the Human Hearing Process

When any physical object moves back and forth rapidly, this is known as vibration. The movements that occur during vibration disturb the surrounding medium, which may be solid, liquid, or gaseous. The most common sound conducting medium in our environment is gaseous: our atmosphere (i.e. the air). An object's vibratory movements represent a form of energy. As this acoustic energy moves through the air, it takes the form of waves, sound waves specifically. The outer ear receives and amplifies the sound and transmits it to the middle ear, where tiny bones vibrate in response to the sound energy and transmit it to the inner ear. The inner ear converts the acoustic energy into electrical energy. The electrical impulses are then carried by nerves to the brain. Structures in the brain associated with hearing receive these electrical signals and interpret them (i.e. make sense of them) as sounds. The ears' reception of sound waves is auditory sensation, and the brain's interpretation of them is auditory perception.

Solar System

Solar System's Location and Components

The universe is composed of an unknown (possibly infinite) number of galaxies or star systems, such as the Spiral Nebula, the Crab Nebula, and the Milky Way. Our sun, Sol, is one of billions of stars in the Milky Way. The solar system's planets are held in position at varying distances (according to their size and mass) from the Sun by its gravitational force. These planets orbit or revolve around the Sun. From the closest to the Sun to the farthest away, the solar system's planets are Mercury, Venus, Earth, Mars, Jupiter, Saturn, Uranus, and Neptune. Pluto was historically included as the ninth planet, but was demoted to a "dwarf planet" by the International Astronomical Union in 2006. Due to angular momentum, planets rotate on their axes, which are imaginary central lines between their north and south poles. One complete Earth rotation equals what we perceive as one 24-hour day. As the Earth turns, different portions face the Sun. These receive daylight, while the portions turned away from the Sun are in darkness. One complete revolution of the Earth around the Sun represents one calendar year.

Pluto

Since more powerful observatories have enabled greater detection and measurement of celestial objects, the International Astronomical Union has defined three criteria for defining a planet. First, it must orbit the Sun. Pluto meets this criterion. Second, it must have enough gravitational force to shape itself into a sphere. Pluto also meets this criterion. Third, a planet must have "cleared the neighborhood" in its orbit. This expression refers to the fact that as planets form, they become the strongest gravitational bodies within their orbits. Therefore, when close to smaller bodies, planets either consume these smaller bodies or repel them because of their greater gravity, clearing their orbital area/"neighborhood." To do this, a planet's mass must sufficiently exceed the mass of other bodies in its orbit. Pluto does not meet this criterion, having only 0.07 times the mass of other objects within its orbit. Thus, astronomers reclassified Pluto as a "dwarf planet" in 2006 based on its lesser mass and the many other objects in its orbit with comparable masses and sizes.

Earth

Earth is roughly spherical in shape. Its North and South Poles at the top and bottom are farthest away from and least exposed to the Sun, so they are always coldest. This accounts for the existence of the polar ice caps. The Equator, an imaginary line running around Earth at its middle exactly halfway between the North and South Poles, is at 0° latitude. Sunrises and sunsets at the Equator are the world's fastest. Days and nights are of virtually equal length at the Equator, and there is less seasonal variation than in other parts of the world. The equatorial climate is a tropical rainforest. Locations close to the North Pole, like Norway, are at such high latitudes that their nights are not dark in summertime, hence the expression "Land of the Midnight Sun." They also have very little light in wintertime. As Earth revolves around the Sun over the course of a year, the distance and angle of various locations relative to the Sun change, so different areas receive varying amounts of heat and light. This is what accounts for the changing seasons.

Rocks Found on the Earth's Surface

Sedimentary Rocks

Earth's rock types are sedimentary, igneous, and metamorphic. These categories are based on the respective processes that form each type of rock. Igneous rocks are formed from volcanoes. Metamorphic rocks are formed when igneous and sedimentary rocks deep inside the Earth's crust are subjected to intense heat and/or pressure. Sedimentary rocks are formed on Earth's surface, and characteristically accumulate in layers. Erosion and other natural processes deposit these layers. Some sedimentary rocks are held together by electrical attraction. Others are cemented together by chemicals and minerals that existed during their formation. Still others are not held together at all, but are loose and crumbly. There are three subcategories of sedimentary rock. Clastic sedimentary rocks are made of little rock bits—clasts—that are compacted and cemented together. Chemical sedimentary rocks are frequently formed through repeated flooding and subsequent evaporation. The evaporation of water leaves a layer of minerals that were dissolved in the water. Limestone and deposits of salt and gypsum are examples. Organic sedimentary rocks are formed from organic matter, such as the calcium left behind from animal bones and shells.

Metamorphic Rocks

Sedimentary rocks are formed on the Earth's surface by layers of eroded material from mountains that were deposited by water, minerals like lime, salt and gypsum deposited by evaporated floodwater, and organic material like calcium from animal bones and shells. Igneous rocks are formed from liquid volcanic rock—either magma underground or lava on the surface—that cools and hardens. Metamorphic rocks are formed from sedimentary and igneous rocks. This happens when sedimentary and/or igneous rocks are deep inside the Earth's crust, where they are subjected to great pressure or heat. The process of metamorphism does not melt these rocks into liquid, which would happen inside a volcano. Rather, the pressure and/or heat change the rocks' molecular structure. Metamorphic rocks are thus more compact and denser than the sedimentary or igneous rocks from which they were formed. They also contain new minerals produced either by the reconfiguration of existing minerals' structures or by chemical reactions with liquids infiltrating the rock. Two examples of metamorphic rocks are marble and gneiss.

Igneous Rocks

Igneous or volcanic rocks are formed from the magma emitted when a volcano erupts. Magma under the Earth's surface is subject to heat and pressure, keeping it in liquid form. During a volcanic eruption, some magma reaches the surface, emerging as lava. Lava cools rapidly in the outside air, becoming a solid with small crystals. Some magma does not reach Earth's surface, but is trapped underground within pockets in other rocks. Magma cools more slowly underground than lava does on the surface. This slower cooling forms rocks with larger crystals and coarser grains. The chemical composition and individual cooling temperatures of magma produce different kinds of igneous rocks. Lava that cools rapidly on the Earth's surface can become obsidian, a smooth, shiny black glass without crystals. It can also become another type of extrusive rock, such as andesite, basalt, pumice, rhyolite, scoria, or tuff (formed from volcanic ash and cinders). Magma that cools slowly in underground pockets can become granite, which has a coarse texture and large, visible mineral grains. It can also become another type of intrusive rock, such as diorite, gabbro, pegmatite, or peridotite.

Erosion

Erosion is a natural process whereby Earth's landforms are broken down through weathering. Rain, wind, etc. wear away solid matter. Over time, rain reduces mountains to hills. Rocks break off from mountains, and in turn disintegrate into sand. Weathering and the resulting erosion always occur in downhill directions. Rain washes rocks off mountains and down streams. Rains, rivers, and streams wash soils away, and ocean waves break down adjacent cliffs. Rocks, dirt, and sand change their form and location through erosion. They do not simply vanish. These transformations and movements are called mass wasting, which occurs chemically (as when rock is dissolved by chemicals in water) or mechanically (as when rock is broken into pieces). Because materials travel as a result of mass wasting, erosion can both break down some areas and build up others. For example, a river runs through and erodes a mountain, carrying the resulting sediment downstream. This sediment gradually builds up, creating wetlands at the river's mouth. A good example of this process is Louisiana's swamps, which were created by sediment transported by the Mississippi River.

Living Organisms

All living organisms have fundamental needs that must be met. For example, plants that grow on land need light, air, water, and nutrients in amounts that vary according to the individual plant. Undersea plants may need less/no light. They need gases present in the water, but not in the air above the water. Like land plants, they require nutrients. Like plants, animals (including humans) need air, water, and nutrients. They do not depend on light for photosynthesis like most plants, but some animals require more light than others, while others need less than others or none at all. Organisms cannot survive in environments that do not meet their basic needs. However, many organisms have evolved to adapt to various environments. For example, cacti are desert plants that thrive with only tiny amounts of water, and camels are desert animals that can also go for long periods of time with little water. Penguins and polar bears have adapted to very cold climates. Internal cues (e.g., hunger) and external cues (e.g., environmental change) motivate and shape the behaviors of individual organisms.

Types of Animal Life Cycles

Most animals, including mammals, birds, fish, reptiles, and spiders, have simple life cycles. They are born live or hatch from eggs, and then grow to adulthood. Animals with simple life cycles include humans. Amphibians like frogs and newts have an additional stage involving a metamorphosis, or transformation. After birth, they breathe through gills and live underwater during youth (e.g., tadpoles). By adulthood, they breathe through lungs and move to land. Butterflies are examples of animals (insects) that undergo complete metamorphosis, meaning they change their overall form. After hatching from an embryo/egg, the juvenile form, or larva, resembles a worm and completes the majority of feeding required. In the next stage, the pupa does not feed, and is typically camouflaged in what is called an inactive stage. Mosquito pupae are called tumblers. The butterfly pupa is called a chrysalis, and is protected by a cocoon. In the final stage, the adult (imago) grows wings (typically) and breeds. Some insects like dragonflies, cockroaches, and grasshoppers undergo an incomplete metamorphosis. There are egg, larva, and adult stages, but no pupa stage.

Ecology

Ecology is defined as the study of interactions between organisms and their environments. Abiotic factors are the parts of any ecosystem that are not alive, but which affect that ecosystem's living members. Abiotic factors also determine the locations of particular ecosystems that have certain characteristics. Abiotic factors include the sunlight; the atmosphere, including oxygen, hydrogen, and nitrogen; the water; the soil; the temperatures within a system; and the nutrient cycles of chemical elements and compounds that pass among living organisms and their physical environments. Biotic factors are the living organisms within any ecosystem, which include not only humans and animals, but also plants, microorganisms, etc. The definition of biotic factors also includes the interactions that occur between and among various organisms within an ecosystem. Sunlight determines plant growth and, hence, biome locations. Sunlight, in turn, is affected by water depth. Ocean depths where sunlight penetrates, called photic zones, are where the majority of the photosynthesis on Earth occurs.

> **Review Video: Photosynthesis**
> Visit mometrix.com/academy and enter code: 227035

Organism Reproduction

A few examples of the many ways in which organisms reproduce include binary fission, whereby the cells of prokaryotic bacteria reproduce; budding, which is how yeast cells reproduce; and asexual reproduction. The latter occurs in plants when they are grafted, when cuttings are taken from them and then rooted, or when they put out runners. Plants also reproduce sexually, as do humans and most other animals. Animals, including humans, produce gametes (i.e. sperm or eggs) in their gonads through the process of meiosis. Gametes are haploid, containing half the number of chromosomes found in the body's cells. During fertilization, the gametes combine to form a zygote, which is diploid. It has the full number of chromosomes (half from each gamete), which are arranged in a genetically unique combination. Zygotes undergo mitosis, reproducing their gene combination with identical DNA sequences in all new cells, which then migrate and differentiate into organizations of specialized organs and tissues. These specialized organs in biologically mature organisms, alerted by signals such as hormonal cues, undergo meiosis to create new haploid gametes, beginning the cycle again.

Plant Reproduction

Most plants can reproduce asexually. For example, cuttings can be rooted in water and planted. Some plants put out runners that root new growths. Many plants can be grafted to produce new ones. Plants also reproduce sexually. Plants' sexual life cycles are more complex than animals', since plants alternate between haploid form (i.e. having a single set of chromosomes) and diploid form (i.e. having two sets of chromosome) during their life cycles. Plants produce haploid cells called gametes* (equivalent to sperm and egg in animals) that combine during fertilization, producing zygotes (diploid cells with chromosomes from both gametes). Cells reproduce exact copies through mitosis (asexual reproduction), becoming differentiated/specialized to form organs. Mature diploid plants called sporophytes—the plant form we usually see—produce spores. In sporophytes' specialized organs, cells undergo meiosis. This is part of the process of sexual reproduction, during which cells with half the normal number of chromosomes are produced before fertilization occurs. The spores produced by the sporophyte generation undergo mitosis, growing into a haploid plant of the gametophyte generation that produces gametes*. The cycle then repeats.

Ecological Relationships

Organisms interact, both with other organisms and their environments. Relationships wherein two differing organisms regularly interact so that one or both of them benefit are known as ecological relationships. In mutualistic relationships, both organisms benefit. For example, bacteria live in termites' digestive systems. Termites eat wood. However, they cannot digest the cellulose (the main part of plant cell walls) in wood. The bacteria in termites' guts break down the cellulose for them, releasing the wood's nutrients. Reciprocally, the termites as hosts give the bacteria a home and food. In commensalistic relationships, one organism benefits and the other one is unaffected. One example is barnacles attaching to whales. Barnacles, which are filter feeders, benefit from the whales' swimming, which creates currents in the water that bring the barnacles food. The whales are not disturbed by the barnacles. In parasitic relationships, the parasite benefits, but the host suffers. For example, tapeworms inside animals' digestive tracts get nutrients. The hosts lose the nutrients stolen by the worms, and can sustain tissue damage because of the presence of the tapeworms.

Levels of Self-Awareness

Even newborns demonstrate differentiation of body through rooting and orienting responses, which are triggered by touching the cheek. (1) <u>Differentiation</u>: At this level, children recognize correspondence between their movements and those in the mirror, and differentiate their mirror images from other individuals. They differentiate the self. (2) <u>Situation</u>: At this level, beyond matching the surface properties of what they feel and what they see in the mirror, and beyond differentiating the self, children realize that their reflection is unique to their self. They also realize that their body/self and other things are situated in space. (3) <u>Identification</u>: At this level, beyond differentiating and situating the self, children now identify their reflection as "me." When psychologists place a dot/sticky note on a child's face before s/he looks in a mirror, the child reaches toward his or her own face to touch/remove it, demonstrating self-recognition and an emerging self-concept. (4) <u>Permanence</u>: At this level, children identify a permanent self across time and space, recognizing themselves in photos and home movies regardless of year/age/clothing/location/setting, etc. (5) <u>Self-consciousness/"meta" self-awareness</u>: At this level, children recognize their self from others' perceptions/perspectives as well as their own. They experience pride, shame, and other "self-conscious" feelings.

Progression of Self-Awareness Between Birth and Two Years of Age

From birth, infants differentiate their bodies from the environment, and differentiate internal from external stimuli (i.e. self-touch/stimulation vs. non-self/others' touch/stimulation). From two months old, babies show a sense of their body's position relative to other things in their environment. They systematically imitate others' facial expressions and movements. They also explore and consider the environment's responses to their own actions. Additionally, they smile and socially interact face-to-face with others, showing a new sense of shared experiences. By four months, infants systematically reach for and touch objects they see, showing hand-eye coordination. From four to six months, they regulate their reaching based on their sitting/posture and balance. By six months, babies can differentiate video of themselves from that of other, identically dressed babies. Babies between the ages of four and seven months can differentiate live video of themselves from that of experimenters imitating the same behaviors. By two years, children develop an understanding of symbolic representation, and know that mirror images and pictures of themselves stand for themselves. They also start to develop language skills and develop the ability to engage in pretend play.

Factors Contributing to the Development of Interpersonal Relationships

(1) The first basic factor that contributes to the development of interpersonal relationships in early childhood is child-adult relationships. These are the earliest interpersonal interactions, and start to develop at birth. When children's needs are consistently met by adults, children learn to trust adults. In his famous theory of development, Erikson called the first stage of psychosocial development and the central conflict of infancy basic trust vs. mistrust. (2) The second factor is autonomy, which refers to making decisions and doing things for oneself. Toddlers develop autonomy. Erikson called his second stage of psychosocial development and the central conflict of toddlerhood autonomy vs. shame and self-doubt. Children who are consistently given developmentally appropriate autonomy are more likely to respect others' autonomy, a key feature of interpersonal development. (3) The third basic factor is pretend play, which emerges as children's understanding of symbolic representation develops and they begin to use things to stand for other things. Pretending to be grown-ups engaging in adult activities helps children learn about adult skills and roles. Interacting with peers in make-believe scenarios prepares children for real-life adult interactions. Constructive ECE approaches do not involve punishing children who have not developed sufficient interpersonal relationship awareness. Instead, they encourage adults to teach children socially acceptable behaviors and reward positive interpersonal interactions.

Interactions and Relationships with Peers

By the time they are a year old, most babies have begun to interact with their peers, particularly when it comes to activities involving concrete objects. The development of walking and talking abilities in normally developing toddlers by the time they are two years old enables them to coordinate their behavior when playing with peers. They can imitate one another's behaviors, and can alternate roles during play, as they understand symbolic representation and can create make-believe scenarios. Pretend play increases from the ages of three to five years, as do prosocial behaviors, which include helping and caring for others. At the same time, egocentrism and aggressive behaviors decrease, as children are more able to consider others' viewpoints and feelings. Emergent social interaction skills such as these form the foundation for children's early peer relationships. When children demonstrate preferences for certain peers and choose to play and otherwise interact with them over others, this is the beginning of what will develop into preschool friendships, which are based mostly upon mutual play activities and exchanges of concrete things. Children tend to form daycare friendships with members of their own sex only over time.

Current Views on Conflict Resolution

ECE experts find that while many elementary and secondary schools have implemented conflict resolution programs, children should start learning how to resolve conflicts at younger ages. For example, experts associated with the successful HighScope EC curriculum have designed an approach to conflict resolution for children from 18 months to six years old. The steps in EC conflict resolution are similar to those used to resolve adult conflicts in education, law, labor relations, and

138

diplomacy. Such problem solving steps have also been found to be effective in daycares, Head Start programs, preschools, nursery schools, and kindergartens. While the steps are the same regardless of the age of the children, they are applied differently according to children's developmental levels. Adults supply much of the language to describe problems and solutions for toddlers; preschoolers can often do this themselves. After experiencing the conflict resolution process, elementary school students can frequently function as mediators for classmates. Even very young children with limited language skills should be encouraged to agree and participate through nodding, pointing, and answering yes/no questions. Conflict mediation and resolution skills help children develop lifelong problem solving and social skills.

Conflict Resolution Approach Designed for Children Between the Ages of 18 Months and 6 Years

The steps used to mediate EC conflicts resemble the steps used in adult mediation. For example, EC experts at the HighScope Educational Research Foundation designed a conflict resolution approach for children aged 18 months to 6 years that consists of these six steps: (1) Calmly approach the children who are in conflict and stop any harmful behaviors. (2) Acknowledge what the children are feeling. (3) Collect information about the conflict. (4) Restate what the problem is. (5) Ask children to suggest possible solutions, and help them choose one together. (6) Follow up by providing support as needed. Experts find that children as young as 18 months demonstrate emergent problem solving skills. They observed young children's abilities to immediately and honestly express emotions. They noted that with adult support, children can frequently generate simple and creative problem solutions. While school conflict resolution is typically aimed at preventing violence, teaching conflict resolution skills can also help children develop the social skills needed to grow into independent, productive members of society.

Parenting Styles Identified by Psychologists

Psychologists (Baumrind, 1967; Maccoby & Martin, 1983) have identified four parenting styles: (1) Authoritarian These parents are strict, punitive, demanding, and unresponsive. They do not explain reasons for their rules to children. Their children are obedient and proficient at completing academic/technical tasks, but they are less competent socially and less happy. They also have lower self-esteem. (2) Authoritative This is the ideal parenting style. These parents are responsive, nurturing, and forgiving. They are assertive without being restrictive or intrusive. They set rules, but explain them. They are democratic, address children's questions and input, and use supportive rather than punitive discipline. Their children tend to be competent, successful, and happy. (3) Permissive These parents are indulgent, lenient, nontraditional, and undemanding. They are nurturing, responsive, and communicative with children, but do not expect their children to show much maturity and/or self-control. They avoid confrontation and seldom use discipline, often acting more like friends than parents. Their children's self-regulation skills are deficient and they are not as happy as many of their peers. They tend to have difficulty with authority and perform poorly in school. (4) Uninvolved These parents are undemanding, unresponsive, and uncommunicative. They meet their children's basic needs, but are relatively detached from their children's lives. In extreme cases, these parents may neglect/reject children. Their children have low self-esteem and lack self-control.

Family Systems Theory

Characteristics of Families Affecting the Early Development of Children

Family systems theory studies the behavior of the family unit rather than the behavior of individual family members. Family behavior includes the interactions among family members and how the family unit responds to stress. Some family characteristics have been identified as particularly pertinent to ECE (Christian/NAEYC, 2006). They are boundaries, roles, rules, hierarchy, climate, and equilibrium. Hierarchy is a family's balance of power, control, and decision making. Culture, religion, age, gender, and economic status influence the family hierarchy, which shifts whenever changes occur in the family's composition. Climate refers to a family's emotional quality, and includes the physical and emotional environments in which families raise children. These environments reflect a family's belief about families and children. Family climate determines whether a child feels safe/loved/supported or frightened/rejected/unhappy in his/her family. Equilibrium refers to the family's balance and consistency. It is disrupted by stress and change, and is maintained or protected by family traditions, customs, and rituals.

Family Influences on Early Childhood Development

Family systems theory examines not individual behavior but family behavior, including communication, interaction, connection/separation, loyalty/autonomy, and responses to stress within the context of the family unit. Family system components particularly influential in early childhood development include the following: (1) Boundaries This refers to limits, separateness, and togetherness (i.e. what/whom the family includes/excludes). "Disengaged" families value independence over belonging, and are open to new input. "Enmeshed" families value togetherness over autonomy, and have more closed/restrictive boundaries. (2) Roles Each family member has a role (e.g., helper, clown, peacemaker, victim, rescuer, etc.). Family members also tend to assume these roles in social, school, and work contexts. (3) Rules Family interaction rules have long-term influences (e.g., parents who view life as predictable are likely to plan ahead, while those who view life as less controllable may not prevent/avoid problems, but rather address them as they occur). Family rules can be unspoken. Also, the rules of family cultures and school cultures can conflict. The other three of the six prominent influences on EC are hierarchy, climate, and equilibrium.

Human Socialization and Major Socializing Agencies

Socialization is the process by which individuals learn their society's norms, values, beliefs, and attitudes; and what behaviors society expects of them relative to those parameters. This learning is imparted by agencies of socialization. The family, peer groups, and leaders of opinion are considered primary socializing agencies. The family is probably the most important because it has the most significant influence on individual development. Families influence the self-concept, feelings, attitudes, and behaviors of each individual member. As children grow, they encounter peer groups throughout life, which also establish norms and values to which individual group members conform. Schools, workplaces, religions, and mass media are considered secondary socializing agencies. Schools dictate additional academic and behavioral norms, values, beliefs, and behaviors. Workplaces have their own cultures that continue, modify, and/or add to the values and behaviors expected of their members. Religions also regulate members' behavior through beliefs, values, goals, and norms that reflect moral principles within a society. Mass media communicate societal conventions (e.g., fashion/style), which enables individuals to learn and adopt new behaviors and/or lifestyles.

Influence of Institutions on the Development of Individual Identity, Relationships, Beliefs, and Behaviors

Family is the first and most important socializing agent. Infants learn behavioral patterns from mothers. Their primary socialization is enabled through such early behaviors as nursing, smiling, and toddling. Babies soon interact with other family members. All the infant's physiological and psychological needs are met within the family. Babies learn their sleeping, eating, and toileting habits within the family environment. Babies' personalities also develop based on their early experiences, especially the amounts and types of parental love and affection they receive. School is also a critical socializing agent. Children extend family relationships to society when they go to school. Cognitive and social school experiences develop children's knowledge, skills, beliefs, interests, attitudes, and customs, and help determine the roles children will play when they become adults. In addition to family relationships, receiving reinforcements at school and observing and imitating teachers influence personality development. Peer groups that are based on friendships, shared ideas, and common interests in music, sports, etc. teach children/teens about conforming to rules and being rejected for not complying with these rules. Mass media like TV profoundly influence children, both negatively and positively.

Culture

While no single definition of culture is universally embraced, one from the cultural anthropology perspective is "...a system of shared beliefs, values, customs, behaviors and artifacts that members of society use to cope with their worlds and with one another, and that are transmitted from generation to generation through learning." (Bates and Fratkin, 2002) Cultural groups are based on a wide range of factors, including geographic location, occupation, religion, sexual orientation, income, etc. Individuals may follow the beliefs and values of more than one culture concurrently. For instance, recent immigrants often espouse values and beliefs from both their original and adopted countries. Traditionally, social systems like education and healthcare have approached cultural diversity by focusing on race/ethnicity and common beliefs about various racial/ethnic group customs. These are frequently generalizations (e.g., lumping Mexican, Cuban, and Puerto Rican cultures together and describing them as "Latino" culture). This type of practice can lead to oversimplified stereotypes, and therefore to unrealistic behavioral expectations. Service professionals need more detailed knowledge of cultural complexities and subtleties to effectively engage and interact with families.

Collectivism and Individualism

Certain world cultures are oriented more toward collectivism, while others are oriented more toward individualism. Native American, Latin American, Asian, and African cultures are more often collectivistic, focusing on interdependence, social interactions, relationships, and connections among individuals. North American, Canadian, European, and Australian cultures are more commonly individualistic, focusing on independence, uniqueness, self-determination, and self-actualization (realizing one's full potential). Individualism favors competition and distinguishing oneself as an individual, while collectivism favors cooperation that promotes and contributes to the harmony and well-being of the group. Individualist cultures value teaching young children object manipulation and scientific thinking, while collectivist cultures value social and relational behaviors. For example, adults in collectivist cultures may interpret a child's first steps as walking toward the adult, while adults in individualist cultures interpret them as developing motor skills and autonomy. These interpretations signify what each culture values most, forming the child's cultural orientation early in life. The planning and design of educational and other programs should be informed by a knowledge of these and other cultural differences.

Cultural Competence

Culturally Competent Professionals

A culturally competent professional demonstrates the ability to enable "...mutually rewarding interactions and meaningful relationships in the delivery of effective services for children and family whose cultural heritage differs from his or her own." (Shonkoff, National Research Council and Institute of Medicine, 2000) Providing interpreters and/or translators does not on its own constitute cultural competence. Hiring racially diverse educational staff in schools is also not enough. Culturally competent educators demonstrate highly developed self-awareness of their own cultural values and beliefs. They must also have and/or develop communication skills that allow them to elicit information from students and families regarding their own cultural beliefs. Further, they must be able to understand how diverse cultural views may affect a child's education, as well as how parents/families receive, comprehend, interpret, and respond to educators' communications. Therefore, educators must develop communication skills to meet educational goals.

Aspects of Cultural Competence

It is important for educational professionals to acquire and demonstrate cultural competence at the individual level to effectively interact with individual children and their families. Moreover, cultural competence is also important at the program level, the school level, and the system level. According to the National Center for Cultural Competence (NCCC), system level cultural competence is a continuing process that includes "...valuing diversity, conducting self-assessments (including organizational assessments), managing the dynamics of differences, acquiring and institutionalizing cultural knowledge, and adapting to the diversity and cultural contexts of the individuals and communities served." (Goode, 2001) Individual educational interactions are informed by a knowledge of cultural diversity and of the importance of such diversity in educational settings, an ability to adapt to the population's cultural needs, and a willingness to engage in ongoing self-reflection. This same set of knowledge and skills is also applied at the system level. Family engagement is important in EC care and education. This includes understanding the developmental needs of families as well as their children, especially when families and/or children speak different languages.

Acculturation Versus Assimilation

Acculturation describes the process whereby people adapt or change their cultural traditions, values, and beliefs as a result of coming into contact with and being influenced by other cultures over time. Some cultures adopt certain characteristics from other cultures they are exposed to, and two or more separate cultures may sometimes virtually fuse. However, assimilation, wherein various ethnic groups unite to form a new culture, is different from acculturation. One dominant culture may assimilate others. A historical example is the Roman Empire, which forced many members of ancient Greek, Hebrew, and other cultures to abandon their own cultures and adopt Roman law, military allegiance, traditions, language, religion, practices, and customs (including dress). The extent of a diverse cultural group's acculturation influences how it interacts with social systems like education and healthcare. Groups that are strongly motivated to maintain their cultural identity may interact less with mainstream systems that significantly conflict with or vary from their own cultural beliefs.

Measuring the Acculturation of Immigrants and Diverse Cultural Groups in America

Social scientists currently use indices such as people's country of birth, how long they have lived in America, their knowledge of the English language, and their level of English language use to study acculturation. However, these factors are measured not because they are the core elements of acculturation, but because they are easier to validly and reliably measure than the underlying cultural beliefs, attitudes, and behaviors they reflect, which are harder to quantify. The interactions between American educators and culturally diverse families can be problematic on both sides. Educators have difficulty interacting, communicating, and collaborating with families that come from a variety of other countries, speak various other languages, and differ in their degree of acculturation to American culture. On the other hand, immigrant and culturally diverse families encounter a foreign language, different cultural customs and practices, and an unfamiliar

142

educational system with different methods of assessment, placement, curriculum planning and design, instruction, and evaluation—not to mention different special education laws and procedures. Thus, the acculturation challenges related to interactions between American educators and culturally diverse families are bilateral.

Cultural Differences in Parents' Goals for Raising Their Children

Depending on their cultural group, parents have varying goals for their children, and use different practices to achieve those goals. For example, research on four different cultural groups in Hawaii found the following differences related to what parents visualized when they pictured their children as successful adults: Native Hawaiians most wanted their children to have social connections, be happy in their social networks, and demonstrate self-reliance as adults. Caucasian American parents most valued self-reliance, happiness, spontaneity, and creativity as developmental outcomes for their children. Filipino American parents most valued the development of traits related to obedience, citizenship, respect for authority, and good conduct and manners in their children. Japanese American parents placed priority on their children's achievement, as well as their ability to live well-organized lives, stay in contact with family, and master the demands of life. Such distinct, significant differences imply that these parent groups would vary in how they would respond to young children's assertive behaviors, in their disciplinary styles (e.g., permissive, authoritative, authoritarian), and in the emphasis they would place on activities focusing on physical and cognitive skill mastery vs. social competence and connection.

Educational Services Accessed by Different Cultures

Parents in America have been found to show distinct preferences for the kinds of care and educational services they access for their children. For example, Caucasian parents in America are more likely to turn to preschool centers for help with their young children's care and instruction. This preference is influenced not only by custom, but also by scientific evidence that center-based preschool experience improves children's skills and prepares them for school. Hispanic parents in America are more likely to use home-based and/or family-based care settings. This preference probably reflects the more collectivist Hispanic perspective, which places more importance on social relationships than on structured learning in early childhood. Educators can take a culturally competent approach to such cultural diversity by looking for ways in which young children's school readiness skills can be promoted in family and home-based child care settings.

Different Views on Care, Education, and the Nature of Their Cognitive Abilities

Depending on their native culture, parents vary in terms of the early experiences they select for their young children. For example, Latino parents tend to prefer family-based/home-based care. White parents tend to prefer center-based daycare and education designed to promote school readiness. Another cultural difference is parental beliefs about children's learning capacities. For example, research in California found that the majority of Latino parents believed their children's learning capacity is set at birth; only a small minority of white parents held this belief. Parents subscribing to a transactional child development model view the complex interaction between child and environment as creating a dynamic developmental process. These parents are more likely to value the stimulation of early childhood development, seek/implement activities that will provide such stimulation, and access early intervention services for children with developmental delays/difficulties. Parents subscribing to a view of fixed, innate cognitive capacity are less likely to believe their children's cognitive abilities can be influenced by educational experiences, and may not see the benefits of or seek out early learning stimulation and intervention.

<u>Cultural and Other Influences and How Much Parents in America Read to Their Children</u>

Researchers analyzing national early childhood surveys have identified significant variations in how often white, Asian, and Hispanic parents read to their young children. This variation is not solely due to varying cultural values. Additional factors include parents' financial limitations; time limitations; familiarity and comfort with accessing libraries and other government resources, websites, etc.; and literacy levels in both English and their native languages. Educators must realize that trying to encourage or even teach parents to read to their children earlier and/or more often is unlikely to be successful if parents do not place value or priority on the benefits of being read to, or do not view the outcomes of reading aloud to children as benefits. Reading to children is known to promote school readiness and academic success. Educators should also understand that some children, despite not being read to in early childhood, become successful adults. Additionally, some cultures, including African Americans, emphasize oral learning traditions more than written ones, developing different skills, such as the basic understanding of story flow.

Factors Affecting Parents Who Are Immigrants to America

Parents educated in other countries may not know a great deal about the American educational system, and may not be aware of the educational demands made on their children, even in early childhood. Educators need to work with these parents to find common ground by identifying shared goals for children. While culturally diverse parents may disagree with some educators' goals, they can collaborate with educators to promote those on which they do agree. Immigrant parents may also be unaware of additional services available in America for children with developmental and/or learning problems. Educators can help parents by providing this information. Another consideration is that some other cultures have more paternalistic educational systems. Parents from such cultures, rather than vocally advocating for their children who need services, tend to wait for teachers/specialists to voice concerns before communicating any problems they have observed. Thus, they could miss out on the chance to obtain helpful services. Even worse, educators could misconstrue their behavior as a lack of interest in children's progress, or as resistance to confronting problems.

Developmental Milestones Varying by Culture

Research has found that different cultures have different age expectations for many early childhood developmental milestones. For example, Filipinos expect children to eat using utensils at 32.4 months. Anglo families expect children to do this at 17.7 months, and Puerto Ricans expect children to reach this milestone at 26.5 months. Filipino cultures expect children to sleep all night by 32.4 months; Puerto Rican and Anglo cultures expect this at 14.5 and 14.4 months, respectively. Similarly, while Anglos expect children to sleep by themselves at around 13.8 months and Puerto Ricans at around 14.6 months, Filipinos do not expect this until 38.8 months. Filipinos expect children to eat solid food by 6.7 months; Anglos by 8.2 months; and Puerto Ricans by 10.1 months. In Anglo families, an 18-month-old not drinking from a cup could indicate developmental delay if parents introduced the cup when s/he was one year old and regularly continued encouraging cup use. But, Filipino parents of an 18-month-old have likely not even introduced the child to a cup yet, so the fact that the child is not using a cup would not be cause for concern from a development standpoint.

When EC researchers investigated the average expectations of different cultural groups of when children would reach various developmental milestones, some of the milestones they examined included: eating solid food, weaning from nursing, drinking from a cup, eating with the fingers, eating with utensils, sleeping alone, sleeping through the night, choosing one's own clothes, dressing oneself, and playing alone. They also looked at daytime and nighttime toilet training.

Educators must become aware of different cultures' different socialization goals before assuming culturally diverse children have developmental delays. On the other hand, they must also avoid automatically attributing variations in milestone achievement to cultural child rearing differences when full developmental assessments might be indicated. Family expectations and values influence the complex process of developmental assessment. When families and assessors share common cultures, it is more likely that valid data will be collected and interpreted. When their cultures differ, however, it is more likely that the assessment information will be misinterpreted. Employing EC teachers/care providers who are familiar with the child, family, and assessment setting as mediators can make developmental assessments more culturally competent.

Essential Geographical Concepts

Ten concepts considered essential to the study of geography are: location, distance, achievability, pattern, morphology, agglomeration, utility value, interaction, area differentiation, and spatial interrelatedness. (1) Location: This concept identifies "where" a place is and examines the positive and negative properties of any place on the surface of the Earth. Absolute location is based upon latitude and longitude. Relative location is based upon changing characteristics of a region, and is influenced by surrounding areas. For example, urban areas have higher land prices than rural ones. (2) Distance: This identifies "how far" a place is, and is often described in terms of location. It is also related to the effort required to meet basic life needs. For example, the distance of raw materials from factories affects transportation costs and hence product prices. In another example, land costs less the farther it is from highways. (3) Achievability: The conditions on the Earth's surface dictate how accessible a geographic area is. For example, villages on beaches are easier to reach. Villages surrounded by forests or swamps are harder to reach. As its economy, science, technology, and transportation develop, a region's level of dependency on other areas changes.

(4) Patterns These are found in geographical forms and in how geographical phenomena spread, which affect dependency on those phenomena. For example, in fold regions (areas where the folding of rocks forms mountains), the rivers typically form trellis patterns. Patterns are also seen in human activity that is based on geography. For example, in mountainous regions, settlements predominantly form spreading patterns. (5) Morphology This is the shape of our planet's surface resulting from inner and outer forces. For example, along the northern coast of Java, sugarcane plantations predominate on the lowlands. (6) Agglomeration This is defined as collecting into a mass, and refers to a geographic concentration of people, activities, and/or settlements within areas that are most profitable and relatively narrow in size. (7) Utility value This refers to the existence and relative usefulness of natural resources. For example, fishermen find more utility value in the ocean than farmers do, and naturalists perceive more utility value in forests than academics would.

(8) Interaction This is the reciprocal and interdependent relationship between two or more geographical areas, which can generate new geographical phenomena, configurations, and problems. For example, a rural village produces raw materials through activities like mining ores or growing and harvesting plant crops, while a city produces industrial goods. The village needs the city as a market for its raw materials, and may also need the city's industrial products. The city needs the village for its raw materials to use in industrial production. This interdependence causes interaction. (9) Area differentiation This informs the study of variations among regional geographical phenomena. For example, different plants are cultivated in highlands vs. lowlands due to their different altitudes and climates. Area differentiation also informs the study of regional variations in occupation (farming vs. fishing, etc.). (10) Spatial interrelatedness This shows the relationship between/among geographic and non-physical phenomena, like rural and urban areas. The example above of village-city interaction also applies here.

145

Geographical Maps

General Features and Purposes

Maps can be drawn to show natural or man-made features. For example, some maps depict mountains, elevations (altitudes), average rainfall, average temperatures, and other natural features of an area. Other maps are made to depict countries, states, cities, roads, empires, wars, and other man-made features. Some maps include both natural and man-made features (e.g., a map showing a certain country and its elevations). Different types of maps are described according to their purposes. For example, political maps are made to depict countries, areas within a country, and/or cities. Physical maps are drawn to display natural features of the terrain in an area, such as rivers, lakes, and mountains. Thematic maps are drawn to focus on a more specific theme or topic, such as the locations and names of battles during a war or the average amounts of rainfall a country, state, or region receives in a given year or month. Some maps are made for more than one purpose, and indicate more than one of the types of information described above.

Basic Tools Supplied on Maps

On maps depicting local, national, and world geography, cartographers supply tools for navigating these maps. For example, the compass rose indicates the directions of north, south, east, and west. By looking at the compass, people can identify the locational relationships of places (e.g., in South America, Chile is west of Argentina). The scale of miles indicates how distances on a map correspond to actual geographical distances, enabling us to estimate real distances. For example, the scale might show that one inch is equal to 500 miles. By placing a piece of paper on the map, we can mark it to measure the distance between two cities (e.g., Washington, DC, in the USA and Ottawa in Canada) on the map, and then line the paper up with the scale of miles to estimate an actual distance of approximately 650 miles between the two cities. Map keys/legends identify what a map's symbols and colors represent.

Grids

Maps show absolute geographic location (i.e. the precise "address" of any place on the planet) using a grid of lines. The lines running from east to west are called parallels or latitudes, and they correspond to how many degrees away from the equator a place is located. The lines running from north to south are called meridians or longitudes, and they correspond to how many degrees away from the prime meridian a place is located. To determine the absolute location of a place, we find the spot on the map where its latitude and longitude intersect. This intersection is the place's absolute location. For example, if we look at Mexico City on a map, we will find that its latitude is 19° north and its longitude is 99° west, which is expressed in cartography as 19° N, 99° W. Numbers of latitudes and longitudes like these are also referred to as coordinates.

Reading and Analyzing a Special Purpose Map

(1) First, read a map's title and look at the overall map. This provides a general idea of what the map shows. For example, a map entitled "Battles of the Punic Wars" would not be a good choice if someone was looking for the political boundaries of modern day Greece, Italy, and Spain. (2) Next, read the map's legend/key to see what symbols and colors the map uses, and what each represents. For example, some lines represent divisions between countries/states; some, roads; some, rivers; etc. Different colors can indicate different countries/states, elevations, amounts of rainfall, population densities, etc. These are not uniform across all maps, so legends/keys are necessary references. (3) Use the legend/key to interpret what the map shows. For example, by looking at colors representing elevations, one can determine which area of a country has the highest/lowest altitude. (4) Draw conclusions about what the map displays. For example, if a country map mainly

has one color that indicates a certain elevation range, it can be concluded that this is the country's most common elevation.

Graphs

Graphs display numerical information in pictorial forms, making it easier to view statistics quickly and draw conclusions about them. For example, it is easier to see patterns/trends like increases/decreases in quantities using visual graphs than columns of numbers. Line graphs, bar graphs, and pie charts are the most common types of graphs. Line graphs depict changes over time by plotting points for a quantity measured each day/week/month/year/decade/century etc. and connecting the points to make a line. For example, showing the population of a city/country each decade in a line graph reveals how the population has risen/fallen/both. Bar graphs compare quantities related to different times/places/people/things. Each quantity is depicted by a separate bar, and its height/length corresponds to a number. Bar graphs make it easy to see which amounts are largest/smallest within a group (e.g., which of several cities/countries has the largest population). Pie charts/circle graphs divide a circle/"pie" into segments/"slices" showing percentages/parts of a whole, which also facilitates making comparisons. For example, the city/country with the largest population is the largest segment on a pie chart or circle graph.

Review Video: Bar Graph
Visit mometrix.com/academy and enter code: 226729

Review Video: Line Graphs
Visit mometrix.com/academy and enter code: 480147

Review Video: Pie Chart
Visit mometrix.com/academy and enter code: 895285

Review Video: Identifying Units and Trends in a Chart
Visit mometrix.com/academy and enter code: 638347

Importance of Chronological Thinking to Understanding History

To see cause-and-effect relationships in historical events and explore and understand relationships among those events, students must have a solid grasp of when things happened and in what time sequence (chronology). Teachers can help students develop chronological thinking by using and assigning well-constructed/well-written narratives. These include histories written in the same style as stories, works of historical literature, and biographies. These hold students' attention, allowing them to focus on authors' depictions of temporal relationships among antecedents, actions, and consequences; of historical motivations and deeds of individuals and groups; and of the time structure of sequential occurrences. By middle school, students should have the skills needed to measure time mathematically (e.g., in years/decades/centuries/millennia), interpret data displayed in timelines, and calculate time in BCE and CE. High school students should be able to analyze patterns of historical duration (e.g., how long the U.S. Constitutional government has lasted) and patterns of historical succession (e.g., the development of expanding trade and communication systems, from Neolithic times through ancient empires and from early modern times to modern global interaction).

Educational Standards That Demonstrate Skills in Historical and Chronological Thinking

Students should be able to differentiate among past, present, and future. They should be able to identify the beginning, middle, and end/outcome of historical narratives/stories. They also should be able to construct their own historical narratives, including working forward and backward in time from some event to explain causes and temporal development of various events, issues, etc. Students should be able to calculate and measure calendar time, including days/dates, weeks, months, years, centuries, and millennia. They should be able to describe time periods using BCE/BC and CE/AD. They should be skilled at comparing calendar systems (e.g., Roman, Gregorian, Julian, Hebrew, Muslim, Mayan, and others) and at relating the calendar years of major historical events. They should be able to look at timelines and interpret the information they contain, and make their own timelines using equidistant time intervals and recording events sequentially. Students should be able to explain change and continuity in history through reconstructing and applying patterns of historical duration and succession. They should be able to identify the structural principles that are the bases of alternative periodization models, and to compare these models.

Reasons/Purposes for Our Country's Laws and Teaching Citizenship

Young children must understand the purposes of rules/laws: They identify acceptable/unacceptable citizen behaviors; make society and life predictable, secure, and orderly; designate responsibilities to citizens; and prevent persons in authority positions from abusing their roles by limiting their power. Understanding these functions of laws/rules enables children to realize that our government consists of individuals and groups authorized to create, implement, and enforce laws and manage legal disputes. Some creative EC teachers have used children's literature to illustrate these concepts. Children can relate personally to stories' characters, and story situations make the concepts real and concrete to children. Stories can be springboards for discussing rules and when they do/do not apply. One activity involves children in small groups making class rules (e.g., "No talking" and "Stay in your seat"), and then rewriting these to be more realistic (e.g., "Talk softly in class; listen when others talk" and "Sit down and get right to work"). Children consider issues of safety and fairness, and develop an understanding of judicial and legislative roles.

MTEL Practice Test

Language and Literacy

1. Children develop phonological awareness:
   a. Only through direct training given by adults.
   b. Only naturally, through exposure to language.
   c. Via both natural exposure and direct training.
   d. Via neither incidental exposure nor instruction.

2. Young children are more likely to respond to analogies in stories than to metaphors because
   a. They are old enough to understand the abstract thinking and symbolism that analogies express
   b. The ability to understand the kinds of abstraction expressed in metaphors is not developed until later in childhood
   c. They can apply the concepts expressed in analogies to their own daily lives, but metaphors do not compare things that children are familiar with
   d. Metaphors and symbols are usually found only in books that children find boring because of their abstractions

3. Young children's skills in phonological awareness are focused on:
   a. Morphologies.
   b. Speech sounds.
   c. Word meanings.
   d. Word sequence.

4. Which of the following is the earliest phonological feature to be independently recognizable in a typically developing child?
   a. Syllables
   b. Alliteration
   c. Rhyming
   d. Letter-sound relationships

5. Which of the following has research found most predictive of children's future long-term literacy performance?
   a. Their scores on standardized intelligence tests
   b. Their family's relative socioeconomic status
   c. Their phonological and phonemic awareness
   d. Their early knowledge of vocabulary words

6. What statement is accurate regarding normally developing oral language in children?
   a. There is a considerable range of ages within normal individual growth.
   b. There are no individual differences among developmental milestones.
   c. Individual children achieve oral language milestones at specified ages.
   d. Individual children all develop spoken language skills at the same rates.

7. To support EC language development, experts advise which of the following teacher practices?
   a. Asking children linear or one-way questions
   b. Doing most of the talking in their classrooms
   c. Focusing on durations of verbal interactions
   d. Asking children more open-ended questions

8. A student learning English as a second language (ESL) who has limited comprehension of English and can speak one- to two-word English answers, essential English words, present-tense English verbs, and some familiar English phrases is in which stage of second-language acquisition?
   a. Preproduction
   b. Early Production
   c. Speech Emergence
   d. Intermediate Fluency

9. A child who omits, substitutes, or distorts certain speech sounds beyond the usual age-range norms is most likely to have:
   a. An articulation disorder.
   b. A type of voice disorder.
   c. One specific type of aphasia.
   d. Delayed language development.

10. A four-year-old child who does not correctly or clearly produce the speech sounds /r/ and /s/:
   a. Likely has delayed language development.
   b. Likely has normal articulatory development.
   c. Likely has some degree of hearing impairment.
   d. Likely needs early intervention for stuttering.

11. The Alphabetic Principle is *best* defined as the concept that:
   a. The letters of the alphabet are arranged in a specific sequence.
   b. The letters of the alphabet are combined to spell various words.
   c. The letters of the alphabet represent corresponding phonemes.
   d. The letters of the alphabet are used to create matching sounds.

12. Which is true about instruction to improve preschoolers' alphabetic knowledge as needed?
   a. Teachers should give only explicit instruction in isolated letter-sound matches.
   b. Teachers should only integrate letter-sound correspondences into curriculum.
   c. Teachers should provide opportunities for practice, but not isolated instruction.
   d. Teachers should combine explicit instruction, integration, and ways to practice.

13. What is true about teaching ESL students English-language reading, including alphabetic knowledge?
   a. Formal instruction in a second language can accelerate students' acquisition of English.
   b. Teachers should require ESL students to master each curriculum element consecutively.
   c. Providing students with linguistic activities meaningful to them promotes ESL acquisition.
   d. Letter-to-sound correspondences are the same across languages, so they transfer easily.

14. Which of these is accurate regarding young children's development of print awareness?

    a. The most common age for children to develop print awareness is between five and seven years.

    b. Research finds that four-year-olds are likely to acquire print concepts before word concepts.

    c. Preschoolers who attain print literacy skills are no more likely to read better at later ages.

    d. Print awareness is knowing that print has meaning, but not necessarily its form/function.

15. The Interactive Book Reading teaching method promotes early literacy development and reading comprehension by incorporating all EXCEPT which of these strategies?

    a. Curriculum-embedded assessments

    b. The 3S strategy (See, Show, and Say)

    c. Asking the students "Wh-" questions

    d. The Expanded Book Reading strategy

16. Which of the following is true about the 3N (Notice, Nudge, Narrate) instructional strategy for developing early childhood literacy?

    a. It does not incorporate any informal assessment of literacy levels.

    b. It uses scaffolding to promote further literacy skills development.

    c. It is a strategy that does not integrate any reflective components.

    d. This strategy is not found adaptable to games for young children.

17. Which of the following reading comprehension strategies is *most* applicable to differentiating between homonyms without knowing their exact spellings?

    a. Pictures

    b. Phonics

    c. Context

    d. Grammar

18. Which of these is an example of attributes to seek in good children's literature?

    a. Stable story characters who do not change

    b. Books featuring overtly moralistic themes

    c. Concise summaries of race/gender types

    d. Original yet believable plot constructions

19. Which genre of children's literature is most likely to begin "Once upon a time..." and conclude with a happy ending?

    a. Modern fantasy

    b. Picture books

    c. Traditional

    d. Poetry books

20. Which of these is true regarding early signs of reading difficulties in young children?

    a. A child's inability to form rhymes is not a concern, as long as s/he can identify rhymes.

    b. A child's inability to separate words into individual phonemes can indicate a problem.

    c. A child's inability to blend individual phonemes to form words is not a sign of trouble.

    d. A child's inability to count word syllables or spell new words phonetically is immaterial.

21. Which of the following is accurate regarding conversational vs. academic English for ESL students?
    a. Conversational English is not as cognitively demanding of ESLs as academic English.
    b. Conversational English deficits are the causes for ESL academic underachievement.
    c. Conversational English is harder for ESL students to develop than academic English.
    d. Conversational English takes the same time for ESLs to develop as academic English.

22. Of the following activities that promote building vocabulary for young children, which one is *most* dependent on the teacher?
    a. Repeatedly singing the same familiar song over and over
    b. Reciting the same familiar rhymes and chants repeatedly
    c. Listening to repeated readings of the same favorite story
    d. A word wall in the classroom to illustrate words/concepts

23. Which of the following is true regarding children's reading fluency?
    a. The lack of reading fluency is always due to word-decoding deficits.
    b. Children's motivation to read is unaffected by their reading fluency.
    c. Some children need only more reading practice to develop fluency.
    d. Fluency has equal impact on school performance at all grade levels.

24. Which of these is an indication that a child has problems with reading comprehension?
    a. The child wonders about why the characters in a story did some things.
    b. The child can tell how a story s/he read ended, but cannot explain why.
    c. The child makes predictions about what will happen next in a narrative.
    d. The child associates things in the reading with things in his/her own life.

25. Regarding student problems that teachers may observe which can indicate dyslexia, which is true?
    a. Dyslexic students perform worse on objective tests than their IQ and knowledge.
    b. Students with dyslexia typically have more trouble reading long than short words.
    c. Students who have dyslexia lack fluidity, but fare much better with rote memory.
    d. Dyslexic students have equal trouble understanding words in isolation or context.

26. Concerning spelling, what statement is correct about how children learn?
    a. Children must be taught spelling patterns as they will not learn them incidentally.
    b. Children who know basic spelling rules can deduce spellings for words they hear.
    c. Children may be able to spell words, but this does not mean they can read them.
    d. Children's reading and writing skills promote spelling, but the reverse is not true.

27. According to linguists, what do invented spellings by young children best signify?
    a. Children who invent spellings lack phonemic and phonetic awareness.
    b. Children's selections of phonetic spellings are due to adult influences.
    c. Inventing spellings for words is evidence of phonetic comprehension.
    d. Diverse children choosing the same phonetic spellings is just chance.

28. In which stage of writing development do children understand that written forms symbolize meanings?
   a. Scribbling and drawing
   b. Letters
   c. Letters and spaces
   d. Letter-like forms and shapes

29. According to literacy experts, what is true about student writing for various purposes and audiences?
   a. The primary purpose of student writing is expressing their ideas, thoughts, and emotions.
   b. The primary purpose of student writing is persuading their readers to agree/believe them.
   c. Improving student reading skills improves their writing skills, but not the other way around.
   d. Improving student writing skills as well as their reading skills improves their learning ability.

30. In the POWER instructional strategy for teaching students the writing process, the P stands for:
   a. Purpose
   b. Program
   c. Planning
   d. Partners

31. One simple rating scale for assessing young children's early writing (Clay, 1993) divides skills into three areas: Language Level, Message Quality, and Directional Principles. Which of the following achievements falls into the Message Quality category?
   a. The child can write two related sentences with punctuation.
   b. The child attempts to set down his/her own ideas in writing.
   c. The child can write a story with paragraphs and two themes.
   d. The child writes showing correct spacing between the words.

32. Which of these correctly shows the normal developmental sequence of children's writing with regard to directional principles?
   a. No knowledge; partial knowledge; reverses the direction; correct direction; correct spacing
   b. No knowledge; reverses the direction; partial knowledge; correct spacing; correct direction
   c. No knowledge; partial knowledge; correct spacing; reverses the direction; correct direction
   d. No knowledge; reverses the direction; correct direction; correct spacing; partial knowledge

33. Regarding the standard conventions for written English when evaluating student writing, which of the following reflects the function of writing rather than its form?
   a. The length of the student's composition
   b. Appropriate content in the composition
   c. Word usage in a student's composition
   d. The spelling in a student's composition

34. Of the following writing examples, which one reflects an error in grammar?
   a. "She is without a doubt the very best freind I have ever had in my life."
   b. "He said we should wait two hours, we waited two hours and returned."
   c. "A great animal lover, his pets included dogs, cats, horses, and chickens."
   d. "They were traveling South at first, but later in the trip they went West."

35. Which of the following is most accurate about teacher strategies to promote young children's motivation to write?

    a. Children's enthusiasm is sustained by sticking with the same writing activities.
    b. Children are less motivated to write about subjects that are familiar to them.
    c. Children display greater writing motivation with predictable, routine activities.
    d. Children are more motivated to participate in activities that they find exciting.

36. In selecting literature for children, the most important first step a teacher should perform is to evaluate

    a. Whether the characters are interesting
    b. Whether the plots are appealing
    c. Class composition and preferences
    d. The reading level of the material

Mathematics

37. Regarding the relationship of cognitive problem-solving skills to mathematics, which of these is true?

    a. Problem-solving skills inform mathematical thinking but not social skills.
    b. Developing problem-solving skills aids math rather than language skills.
    c. Students apply logical reasoning to solve every day and novel problems.
    d. Children must be taught to have interest in solving everyday problems.

38. Which of the following correctly describes a characteristic of students with effective problem-solving skills?

    a. Students develop hypotheses via repeated trial-and-error tests.
    b. Students have developed demonstrated skills for self-regulation.
    c. Students are cautious in solving problems and avoid taking a risk.
    d. Students quickly switch to another problem if their solution fails.

39. Which of these is correct about mental math games adults can initiate with young children to promote their problem-solving skills for learning math?

    a. Adults should always use concrete objects within oral story problems.
    b. Adults should plan mental math games to adhere to child grade levels.
    c. Adults should always keep problems simple with only whole numbers.
    d. Adults should always tell young children correct answers to questions.

40. To support children's development of reasoning skills for comprehending and applying early math and science concepts, which of these is the best adult behavior?

    a. Asking children "why?" questions and waiting until they find the expected answers
    b. Asking children "why?" questions and disregarding both expected and real answers
    c. Asking children "why?" questions and requiring them to answer them immediately
    d. Asking children "why?" questions, giving time to think, and listening to the answers

41. Which of these is true about children's transition from intuitive thinking to formal math education?
    a. Children do not use mathematical thinking until they begin their formal school education.
    b. Children may see math as a set of rules and procedures, not as practical problem solving.
    c. Children will automatically apply their formal math learning to useful solutions in real life.
    d. Children are less likely to see connections between math and life using concrete objects.

42. What is the most effective way to facilitate children's comprehension of mathematics?
    a. To preserve mathematics as a discipline separate from other academic subjects and everyday life
    b. To allow children to find their own activities applying math rather than providing activities for them
    c. To help them connect and apply common math rules to many different life activities and processes
    d. To ask/answer questions and explain during formal math lessons, not confusing math with real life

43. Which of the following is true regarding children's development of the concept of symbolic representation?
    a. When young children engage in make-believe and pretend play, this is symbolic representation.
    b. Children do not develop this ability until they are old enough to engage in fully abstract thinking.
    c. Children first show this concept by reading, writing, and connecting written with spoken language.
    d. When young children first begin counting on their fingers, they have not yet developed this concept.

44. Suppose that a child in a preschool learning center enjoys sorting different rocks by color. Which of the following teacher practices is the best example of emphasis on connecting the informal math activity with formal math vocabulary?
    a. Telling the child s/he is classifying the rocks
    b. Asking the child how s/he is sorting the rocks
    c. Asking after s/he finishes other ways to sort
    d. These all exemplify the vocabulary emphasis

45. Which of these is true about having an awareness of patterns and relationships in the real world?
    a. Our understanding the basic structure of things is uninformed by it.
    b. It helps us understand series of events, but not predict future ones.
    c. It is unrelated to our basic feeling of confidence in the environment.
    d. It increases our self-efficacy about interacting with our environment.

46. The property of numbers that states that 1 + 3 is the same as 3 + 1 is called
    a. Associative
    b. Distributive
    c. Inverse
    d. Commutative

47. A number system in which the position of a digit in a number determines its value is called a
    a. Relationship system
    b. Place value system
    c. Regrouping system
    d. Tens and hundreds system

48. Which of the following is most accurate regarding young children's development of numeracy skills?
    a. Young children typically learn all of the number names before they learn to count.
    b. Young children typically learn to name all of the numbers and count simultaneously.
    c. Young children typically learn to count before they have learned all number names.
    d. Young children typically learn these two numeracy skills in individually varying order.

49. What is a correct statement about the development of number sense in young children?
    a. Children with developed number sense can count forward, but cannot necessarily count backward.
    b. Counting ability, number familiarity, and a good number sense enable children to add and subtract.
    c. Children who have developed number sense can break numbers down, but not reassemble them.
    d. Being able to identify relationships between/among numbers is an ability outside of number sense.

50. For three days, Mr. Hanson had his students keep track of how many times each of them used a pencil during the school day. What is the best kind of graph to use to display these data?
    a. Bar graph
    b. Circle graph
    c. Pictograph
    d. Line graph

51. Which of the following would be most effective to help young children learn geometry?
    a. Giving them hands-on activities manipulating concrete objects
    b. Giving the earliest geometric theorems for them to memorize
    c. Giving them everyday life activities only after they learn basics
    d. Giving them instructions for drawing geometric shape diagrams

52. Of the following, what statement is correct regarding practice in measurement for young children?
    a. Measurement is exclusively a formal method for quantifying sizes, time durations, weights, etc.
    b. Measurement is for both formal quantification and recognizing and finding real-life relationships.
    c. Measurement can only be accomplished by young children with standard measurement devices.
    d. Measurement practice for young children is unlikely to help them in learning about comparisons.

53. Which of these is correct regarding young children and the measurement of time?
    a. Young children typically develop an understanding of the abstract concept of time very early.
    b. Adults should not refer to periods of time with young children before they understand them.
    c. Using activities involving counting allows children to generalize these to the counting of time.
    d. Adults can say "yesterday, today, tomorrow" with young children and they will understand it.

54. Regarding young children's early comprehension of fractions, which of these is accurate?
    a. Children must know how many parts a unit is divided into, but not what comprises the unit.
    b. Children must know what makes a whole unit, but not into how many pieces it was divided.
    c. Children must know how many pieces a unit is divided into, but not if they are of equal size.
    d. Children must know what a whole unit is, how many parts there are, and if part sizes match.

55. Of the following, which is prerequisite for young children to understand before they can engage in accurately estimating basic measurements of quantities?
    a. Knowledge of math vocabulary words indicating estimation
    b. Knowledge of how to make predictions that are appropriate
    c. Knowledge of how to achieve estimates that are reasonable
    d. Knowledge of what relative quantities and comparisons are

56. Which of these is/are most representative of using statistics in everyday life to predict probabilities?
    a. An actuarial table in an insurance company
    b. A weather forecast for the chances of rain
    c. A chart comparing results of interventions
    d. Answers (A) and (B) represent probability

57. A teacher asks ten preschoolers to choose their favorite among four colors of foil stars. Five children pick gold; three choose silver; two select blue; and one picks red. The teacher then helps the student to stick the stars onto a paper chart with a separate row for each color:

This activity supports which of the following early mathematics skills?
    a. Determining various properties of figures
    b. Applying mathematical formulas to shapes
    c. Collecting, organizing, and displaying data
    d. Intuitively identifying probability concepts

58. A teacher presents this figure and asks the class how many different rectangles they can find in it.

Which student response is correct?
a. Andrea's answer, "Only one."
b. Billy's answer, "There are four."
c. Charlie's answer, "I found ten."
d. Darlene's answer, "I count five."

59. Which of the following statements is an example of using ordinal numbers?
a. "I am four years old and my brother Timmy is two years old."
b. "I sit at the first table for lunch and my sister sits at the third."
c. "I play on the junior soccer team. My shirt says number six."
d. "Two-thirds of my math class are boys and one-third is girls."

60. A group of five- and six-year-olds watch a teacher demonstrate measuring things with a standard ruler. Some students want to know why the teacher aligns the number 0 on the ruler with the first edge of an object, instead of starting with the number 1 as they do when they count. Which choice is the best answer for the teacher to give?
a. To tell them this is how the teacher learned to do it in school
b. To tell them this is how we include the first inch on the ruler
c. To tell them this is how we can use the most space on rulers
d. To tell them this is how we follow standard ruler convention

61. Which level of shape perception do young children typically develop first?
a. Recognizing shapes
b. Naming the shapes
c. Analysis of shapes
d. All develop at once

62. A teacher regularly integrates math into everyday EC activities. By asking young children to help at snack time by putting one snack on each plate, which math skill is the teacher primarily engaging?
a. 1:1 correspondence
b. Practice in counting
c. Shapes recognition
d. Comparison of size

63. How can an EC teacher best facilitate children's development of math communication and literacy?
a. By asking the children questions
b. By observing children's behaviors
c. By lecturing to model language use
d. By having children write about math

64. Preschoolers' development of spatial awareness will later support their comprehension of which areas of math the most?
    a. Arithmetic and algebra
    b. Geometry and physics
    c. Arithmetic and physics
    d. Geometry and algebra

65. Of the following, which preschool activity is most related to learning 1:1 correspondence?
    a. Being able to name all printed numbers on sight
    b. The ability to count numbers both up and down
    c. Counting out pennies to match a written number
    d. These all relate the same to 1:1 correspondence

66. Which of the following is a rational number?
    a. The value of pi (π)
    b. Square root of 2 ($\sqrt{2}$)
    c. Any decimal number
    d. 9,731,245/42,754,021

Social Studies

67. Which of the following levels of self-awareness do children tend to develop earliest?
    a. Situation
    b. Permanence
    c. Identification
    d. Differentiation

68. Of the following, which can babies typically do from birth?
    a. Recognize photos and mirror images as themselves
    b. Systematically imitate facial expressions of others
    c. Distinguish between internal and external stimuli
    d. Systematically reach for and touch seen objects

69. In EC development in the area of interpersonal interactions, which do children typically develop first?
    a. Autonomy/independence
    b. Trusting/mistrusting others
    c. A sense of initiative or guilt
    d. Make-believe/pretending

70. What is true about instructing children in conflict resolution skills and processes?
    a. Conflict resolution can be taught to children who are as young as eighteen months.
    b. Children can only understand these concepts at school ages (six years and up).
    c. Conflict resolution instruction has never been attempted with young children.
    d. Children taught conflict mediation/resolution are unlikely to generalize these.

71. Of these four parenting styles described by psychologists, which is considered the ideal?
    a. Authoritative
    b. Authoritarian
    c. Permissive
    d. Uninvolved

72. According to family systems theory, when one member of a family is consistently identified as the family peacemaker and another is viewed as the family clown, these most reflect which system component?
    a. Boundaries
    b. Roles
    c. Rules
    d. Equilibrium

73. A child whose family comes from a collectivist culture is most likely to value:
    a. Competition.
    b. Independence.
    c. Cooperation.
    d. Uniqueness.

74. A family moves to America from another country with a very different culture. They discard their native cultural practices and adopt American customs. This is an example of:
    a. Accommodation
    b. Adaptation
    c. Acculturation
    d. Assimilation

75. Which of the following is most accurate about cultural competence in educational professionals?
    a. Hiring language interpreters and translators will assure cultural competence.
    b. Hiring educational staff with racial diversity will ensure cultural competence.
    c. Hiring highly culturally self-aware educators will create cultural competence.
    d. Hiring these plus educator communication skills creates cultural competence.

76. Research comparing American Latino and White parent beliefs has found that:
    a. Most White parents believe that children's learning capacities are set at birth.
    b. Most White and Latino parents share the same beliefs about learning capacity.
    c. Most Latino parents believe children's learning capacities are fixed from birth.
    d. Most Latino parents highly value early intervention and stimulation of learning.

77. Which statement is most accurate regarding variations among culturally diverse U.S. parents in whether or how often they read to their young children?
    a. Parents who succeeded despite not being read to as children value reading to children even more.
    b. Some cultures with oral traditions tell stories and sing to their children more than reading to them.
    c. Educators can easily influence parents whose culture does not value/prioritize reading to children.
    d. Parents not seeing school readiness and success as benefits can still be taught to read to children.

78. Which statement is true of findings about culturally diverse parental views of child development milestones in America?

    a. Parents in America from different cultures expect their children to reach milestones at different ages.

    b. Anglo, Filipino, and Puerto Rican parents in America differ in age expectations only for sleeping lone.

    c. Anglo, Filipino, and Puerto Rican parents in America expect children to eat solid food at the same age.

    d. The only age expectation shared by all parents is when their children should sleep through the night.

79. Land is typically more expensive in urban areas than in rural areas. Which geography concept does this reflect?

    a. Location
    b. Distance
    c. Pattern
    d. Interaction

80. As used in geographical maps, which of the following is a synonym for the term *latitude?*

    a. Longitude
    b. Parallel
    c. Meridian
    d. Coordinate

81. Which of the following is correct regarding common types of graphs?

    a. A pie chart shows differences in quantities over time.
    b. A bar graph can compare quantities but not over time.
    c. A line graph clarifies how amounts change over time.
    d. A number column makes patterns and trends clearer.

82. Of these materials, which can teachers use to help students develop chronological thinking?

    a. Only history books can be used for this.
    b. Biographies can also serve this function.
    c. Historical literature can be used for this.
    d. These are all good chronology materials.

83. To teach citizenship at the EC level, what purposes of laws and rules should teachers help young children to understand?

    a. People who are employed in positions of authority wield unlimited powers.
    b. Individual citizens determine their own responsibilities separately from laws.
    c. Individuals and groups make up our government to create and enforce laws.
    d. Life and society are unpredictable, insecure and disorderly, despite any laws.

Science

84. Young children develop many basic science concepts through everyday activities. Of the following, which activity is most related to the development of measurement concepts?
    a. Fitting wooden pegs into holes with matching shapes in a toy
    b. Pouring sand from one container into a differently sized one
    c. Seeing how many coins they have accrued in their piggy bank
    d. Separating toys into piles of cars, trucks, animals, people, etc.

85. Which is the best definition of an informal learning experience for learning basic science concepts?
    a. A child chooses what to do, and an adult provides some intervention
    b. A child chooses what to do spontaneously without adult intervention — *Naturalistic Learning*
    c. A child engages in an activity which is chosen and directed by an adult
    d. A child engages in a group activity assigned by the preschool teacher

86. Of the following actions, which best represents the science process skill of Inference?
    a. Formulating new hypotheses based on experimental results
    b. Finding patterns and meaning in the results of experiments   *infering*
    c. Identifying properties of things/situations using the senses
    d. Reporting experimental results and conclusions to others

87. Which of the following gases is known as a compound gas?
    a. Oxygen
    b. Nitrogen
    c. Ammonia
    d. Hydrogen

88. When we look at a straw in a glass of water, the straw appears broken or bent at the waterline. This appearance is a function of:
    a. Scattering.
    b. Absorption.
    c. Reflection.
    d. Refraction.

89. When materials that are attracted by magnets align at right angles to the lines of the magnetic force field, the name for this is:
    a. Magnetic induction
    b. Ferromagnetism
    c. Paramagnetism
    d. Diamagnetism

90. Which statement is correct regarding the phenomenon of magnetism?
    a. Opposite poles of magnets repel each other.
    b. The like poles of magnets attract each other.
    c. Magnets can attract/repel without touching.
    d. Magnets work beyond their magnetic fields.

91. For electricity to flow and move, it requires which of these?
    a. A generator and an insulator
    b. A generator and a conductor
    c. A conductor and an insulator
    d. Electricity needs all of these

92. Heat is transmitted through solid materials via:
    a. Conduction.
    b. Convection.
    c. Radiation.
    d. All three.

93. Newton's First Law of Motion states that:
    a. An object at rest tends to stay at rest unless an opposing force changes this.
    b. An object stays at rest or in motion unless/until an opposing force changes it.
    c. An object in motion tends to stay in motion until an opposing force changes it.
    d. For every action that take place, there is an equal and opposite reaction to it.

94. Which of the following will not conduct sound waves?
    a. solids
    b. liquids
    c. gases
    d. vacuum

95. Which type of rock typically forms on the surface of the earth in cumulative layers?
    a. Igneous
    b. Obsidian
    c. Metamorphic
    d. Sedimentary

sed rocks shells

96. Which organisms depend *most* on light to survive?
    a. Undersea plants
    b. Mammalians
    c. Land plants
    d. Humans

97. Which of the following have a simple life cycle, without a metamorphosis?
    a. Frogs
    b. Newts
    c. Grasshoppers
    d. Human beings

98. Of the following insects, which undergo a complete metamorphosis during their life cycle?
    a. Mosquitos
    b. Butterflies
    c. Dragonflies
    d. Grasshoppers

99. The way that plants reproduce is:
   a. Asexual.
   b. Sexual.
   c. Both.
   d. Neither.

100. In an ecosystem, its <u>abiotic factors</u>:
   a. Are alive.
   b. Are not alive.
   c. Do not affect living organisms.
   d. Include some microorganisms.

Constructed Response Questions

Overview

On your official test, you will have to prepare an organized, developed analysis that relates child development to two or more of the following: language arts, mathematics, history and social science, and science. 150-300 words for each assignment

A strong response to these constructed response questions must:

- Fully answer the question, leaving no portions unanswered.
- Provide an appropriate application of the subject matter knowledge to the scenario.
- Provide sound evidence for the reasoning given, with relevant examples.
- Demonstrate a strong knowledge of the content matter.

Constructed Response Question 1

An important learning standard for first-grade students is to develop skills related to literature, including recognition and use of rhetorical and literary devices (eg. analogies, metaphor, symbolism, and point of view).

Using your knowledge of rhetorical and literary devices, prepare a response in which you.

- Describe the meaning and importance of two literary skills;
- Summarize an experience that would help develop these two skills.
- Explain why this experience would help to develop the skills.

Constructed Response Question 2

An important learning standard for second-grade students is to develop foundations of scientific thought, such as reliance on evidence and reasoning, logical arguments, and experimental design.

Using your knowledge of scientific thought prepare a response in which you

- Describe the meaning of an element of scientific thought.
- Summarize an experience that would help develop a broader understanding of that element of scientific thought;
- Explain why this experience would help to develop the skill.

Answer Key and Explanations

Language and Literacy

1. C: Children develop phonological awareness through a combination of incidental learning via being naturally exposed to language in their environments, and receiving direct instruction from adults. They do not develop it solely through one or the other, or neither.

2. B: The ability to understand the abstract concept expressed in metaphors is not developed until later in childhood. Analogies are easier for children to understand because they compare known items, whereas metaphors require abstract thinking.

3. B: Speech sounds or phonemes are the focus of phonological awareness skills, as well as the relationships of speech sounds to written language symbols. Morphologies (A) are the structural aspects of letters, syllables, and words that reflect grammatical changes. Word meanings (C) are called semantics, not morphology or phonology. Word sequences (D) or sentence structures are called syntax.

4. C: Phonological awareness skills are developed over the course of several years, and where there may be overlap in development, recognition of rhymes (C) comes rather early, between 2 and 3 years of age. Recognition of alliteration comes shortly thereafter, whereas syllables are recognizable between 3 and 6 years old. Phonic understanding is much more complex, as it requires a coordination between auditory and visual understanding.

5. C: Many educational research studies find that having strong phonological and phonemic awareness in early childhood is more predictive of later successful literacy performance than intelligence (A), socioeconomic status (B), or vocabulary knowledge (D) are.

6. A: Within normal development, individual children do vary (B) as to when they reach developmental milestones in spoken language. Due this variance, normal oral language development is represented in ranges rather than specific ages (C). In addition to developing at different ages within ranges, normally developing children also vary in the rates (D) at which they develop oral language skills.

7. D: Researchers advise EC teachers to ask children more open-ended questions, the kind that allow the children and the teacher to give two- and three-way responses in conversations, rather than the more common but less desirable practice of asking linear questions that demand one-way responses (A). They also criticize teachers' tendency to do most of the talking (B) in classrooms rather than encouraging children to use conversational language, which is preferable. Experts advise teachers not to focus only on the quantity of conversations (C), but equally on their quality.

8. B: Early Production, with the characteristics named, is the second stage of ESL acquisition. Preproduction (A), the first stage, involves no English speech; minimal listening comprehension; and the abilities to draw pictures of and/or point at objects represented by some English words. Speech Emergence (C) is the third stage, characterized by good English comprehension; English speech using simple sentences, but still showing pronunciation and grammatical errors; and frequently misunderstanding English-language jokes. Intermediate Fluency (D), the fourth stage, features excellent English listening comprehension and few spoken grammatical errors.

9. A: Articulation is the correct pronunciation of speech sounds (phonemes), and articulation disorders are characterized by incorrectly pronouncing one or multiple phonemes beyond the usual age range norms for the speech sound (age norms are older for more difficult sounds). Voice disorders (B) affect voice qualities like nasality, pitch, volume, and tone rather than pronunciation of specific phonemes. Aphasias (C) are cognitive language-processing disorders that affect language comprehension and/or production, e.g., word retrieval, grammatical sentence composition, etc. Delayed language development (D) falls behind normal developmental ranges for understanding and producing language, but not necessarily speech sounds.

10. B: The age norms for correctly pronouncing these most difficult of phonemes, /r/ and /s/, are around seven to eight years old. Thus a four-year-old who substitutes /w/ for /r/, lisps on /s/ or otherwise distorts it, or omits either/both of these sounds likely has normal development in speech articulation. Delayed language development (A) is not signaled by mispronouncing phonemes but by being significantly behind age norms for comprehending and constructing language. Hearing impairment (C) often causes misarticulations; however, errors in only two difficult phonemes when far below the age norms do not indicate it. Misarticulating phonemes is not a symptom of stuttering (D).

11. C: The best definition of the Alphabetic Principle is that the letters of the alphabet are symbols to represent the various phonemes (speech sounds) we use in our language. While it is true that the alphabet has a sequence (A), this does not define the Alphabetic Principle. The sequence serves as a master mnemonic to help us remember all the letters, but we could still identify letters and associate them with phonemes without it. Similarly, (B) is true but is not the definition. (D) is the reverse of the correct answer (sounds => letters, not letters => sounds).

12. D: Teachers' instructional plans for preschoolers with inadequate alphabetic knowledge should include NOT ONLY explicit instruction in isolated letter-sound correspondences (A); NOT ONLY curricular lessons and activities that integrate letter-sound relationships (B); and NOT ONLY regular opportunities for children to practice their newly developing alphabetic knowledge (C), but all of these together.

13. C: When teachers provide language-related activities for ESL students that are relevant to them personally, this is found to help them acquire English. Formal instruction does NOT speed up English acquisition (A): it can facilitate and inform the process and expand ESL students' knowledge, but because language learning is not linear, formal instruction will not make it happen faster. For this reason, teachers also should NOT require ESL students to master every individual curriculum element before starting another (B). Teachers must also realize that letter-sound correspondences are NOT the same across languages (D). For example, Spanish letters correspond better to their sounds than in English; therefore, native Spanish speakers are apt to be confused at the multiple sounds of many English letters/letter combinations (e.g., "-ough" as in *through, though, rough, ought, bough*).

14. B: Studies do show that although four-year-olds are unlikely to have mastered either print or word concepts, they may have learned many print concepts earlier than word concepts. The most common age for normally developing children to develop print awareness is between three and five years, not five and seven years (A). Studies show that preschoolers who attain print literacy skills ARE more likely to read better when they are older (C). Print awareness is defined as not only knowing that print has meaning, but also understanding the form and function of print (D).

15. A: Using curriculum-embedded assessments is another instructional strategy to enhance early literacy development and reading comprehension, but it is not included in Interactive Book Reading. The Interactive Book Reading method incorporates three primary strategies: the 3S (See,

Show, and Say) strategy (B); the strategy of asking "Wh-" questions (C); and the strategy of Expanded Book Reading (D).

16. B: The 3N strategy does use scaffolding, i.e., temporary support that the teacher provides to help young students achieve tasks at levels higher than their current literacy status. Scaffolding is gradually withdrawn as students become more proficient until they can achieve these tasks independently. 3N *does* incorporate informal assessment of literacy levels (A): the first, "Notice" step involves the teacher's noticing each individual student's current level of literacy skills. It *does* integrate reflection (C): the third, "Narrate" step involves the teacher's reflecting on what the student does. This strategy *is* adaptable to young children's games (D): various literacy games designed for young children apply the 3N strategy.

17. C: The most helpful strategy for discerning which of two homonyms (sound-alike words) is correct without knowing the spelling is its surrounding context of the sentence, paragraph, and/or book and subject matter. For example, "Mexico cedes land" and "Mexico seeds land" sound the same, but if the context continues "to the United States," the meaning of "cedes" applies. Pictures (A) help children identify unknown words rather than differentiate homonyms. Phonics (B) help students sound out unfamiliar words, not differentiate meanings. Grammar (D) can help when one homonym is a verb and the other a noun, for example; but "cedes" and "seeds" are the same part of speech with different meanings, so grammar alone does not help as much as context.

18. D: Good children's books should feature plots that are well-constructed, and are original but not incredible. Narrative books should feature story characters who are believable, which includes their changing (A) and growing as a result of their experiences like real people do, rather than staying the same throughout the story. Adults choosing children's literature should seek books with themes of value to children, but avoid books with overtly moralistic themes (B). Likewise they should avoid books that promote racial, gender, and other stereotypes (C).

19. C: These features are most characteristic of traditional literature, which has been adapted by authors from oral traditions including folklore, epics, fables, proverbs, and fairy tales. The modern fantasy (A) genre, which includes modern-day fairy tales and tells imaginative tales, may use traditional literature themes as its foundation, but is original writing by authors such as Hans Christian Andersen, Lewis Carroll, and E.B. White. Picture books (B) combine text and pictures, which help beginning students learn to read by supplementing words with illustrations. Poetry books (D) contain poems rather than prose writing.

20. B: If a young child cannot break down a word into its component phonemes, this represents a deficit in phonological and/or phonemic awareness, which will cause reading difficulties. Likewise, the inability to do the reverse and blend individual phonemes to form words (C) is a sign the child will have trouble reading. Young children with good phonological and phonemic awareness can both identify *and* form rhymes (A). To learn to read well, they should also be able to count the syllables in a word and use phonetic spellings (by sound) for new/unfamiliar words (D).

21. A: Conversational English is much *less* difficult (A) for ESL students to learn because it is much less demanding of them cognitively. Most often, academic underachievement in ESL students is caused by deficits in academic, not conversational English (B). The disparity in ease of developing these separate skill sets—basic, everyday-life interpersonal communication skills in conversational English vs. the complex-compound syntax and vocabularies specific to math, science, social studies, and other content areas in academic English—is apparent in the fact that while most ESL children develop conversational English within about two years of living in English-speaking settings, they take at least five to seven years to develop academic English (D).

22. D: A word wall uses visual illustrations of vocabulary words and the concepts they represent, and includes additional words, concepts, and pictures related to the main words and pictures to enrich vocabulary and relational thinking. The teacher would be most responsible for creating the word wall, using it in lessons/activities, and instructing/assisting young children in its use. The children themselves can and will repeatedly sing the same familiar song (A) and repeat the same rhymes and chants (B), which enhance vocabulary development for both native English-speaking and ESL students. Stories (C) may be read live by teachers, or readings may be recorded. Either way, the children play the same role of listening to repeated readings.

23. C: While *some* children's reading lacks fluency due to deficits in their word-decoding abilities, this is not *always* (A) the case: some children simply need more reading practice to develop fluency. Children's motivation to read (B) *is* affected by their reading fluency: when reading is laborious, children do not enjoy it and avoid reading; when reading is easy, children enjoy it and want to read. Fluency has much *greater* impact (D) on the performance of students in higher grades, when the volume of reading required of them in school is exponentially greater.

24. B: If a child can repeat the factual elements of how a story ended, but cannot explain why this ending occurred, this may show that the child cannot reason about cause and effect, logic, and sequencing in the material s/he has read; and/or lacks the expressive language skills to explain. Wondering about characters' reasons for their actions (A) indicates comprehension, not its lack: readers with good comprehension will speculate about character motivations, and will also try to predict future events in a book (C) before reading of them. Relating reading matter to one's own life (D) and pre-existing knowledge also does not indicate comprehension problems, but rather good reading comprehension.

25. A: Students with dyslexia tend to perform much worse than their intelligence and knowledge would indicate on objective formats like multiple-choice tests. They are likely to have *equal* amounts of difficulty with reading short function words (e.g., *an, on, in*) as with reading long, multisyllabic words (B). While they do have trouble with fluid thinking, e.g., thinking "on the spot" to produce spoken and/or written verbal responses, they also have equal difficulty with retaining and/or retrieving names, dates, random lists, phone numbers, and other information through rote memorization and recall (C). Students with dyslexia typically have more trouble understanding words in isolation than in context (D), because they rely on the surrounding context to comprehend word meanings.

26. B: Once children have learned the basic rules and principles for spelling in their native language, they can usually figure out how to spell words that are new to them when they hear them spoken. As children accrue experience in communicating with language, they notice basic patterns in letter combinations, syllables, common word roots, prefixes, suffixes, endings, etc., so much of their knowledge of spelling patterns comes through incidental learning (A). Also, children usually can read words that they can spell (C). Therefore, not only do their reading and writing skills support correct spelling, but reciprocally, good spelling skills also support children's reading and writing (D).

27. C: Linguists have found through research studies that not only do preschool children invent spellings for words before they have learned their actual spellings, but moreover, preschoolers from diverse backgrounds all choose the same phonetic spellings, at a rate higher than can be attributed to chance (D) or adult influences (B). The researchers have concluded that through these common invented, phonetic spellings, young children demonstrate comprehension—not a lack thereof (A)—of the phonetic characteristics of words, and of how conventional word spellings symbolize these characteristics.

28. D: Five stages identified in children's writing development are: Scribbling and drawing (A), wherein they hold crayons/pencils in their fists and explore line, space, and form; Letter-like forms and shapes (D), wherein they understand that written forms symbolize meanings and begin drawing circles, squares, and other shapes, drawing figures and asking parents what they "say." In the Letters (B) stage, children can form letter shapes, usually starting with consonants, and enjoy writing their own name initials. They only gradually develop understanding of the sounds represented by the letters. In the Letters and spaces (C) stage, children develop word concepts and space correctly between words. The fifth stage is Conventional writing and spelling, including correct punctuation and purposeful writing.

29. D: Research into literacy development reveals that improvement in students' writing skills improves their overall learning ability, just as improvement in their reading skills also does. Expressing ideas, thoughts, and feelings (A) is *one* purpose of student writing, but not the only or main one. Another purpose is persuasion of the reader audience to agree with the writer's point of view and/or believe the writer's assertions—again, not the only or main purpose (B), but one of various purposes. Research also finds not only that improving student reading skills improves their writing, but *also* that, reciprocally, improving student writing skills improves their reading (C).

30. C: POWER stands for Planning, Organization, Writing, Editing, and Rewriting. The first, Planning, step is particularly important because many students tend simply to plunge into writing without making any plans in advance for choosing a good topic, researching and/or reading on the topic, considering which information will appeal to the reader audience, and writing down all their ideas on the topic.

31. B: The category of Message Quality includes understanding the concepts of signs and symbols, of communicating a message; copying messages; repeating formulaic sentence patterns (e.g., "This is a...."); attempting to use writing to record one's own ideas; and successfully composing writing. Writing two related sentences with punctuation (A) and writing a story with paragraphs and two themes (C) are progressive levels of development falling into the Language Level category. Spacing correctly between written words (D) is a level of the Directional Principles category.

32. A: First, a child typically shows no knowledge of the correct direction in which to write (left-right, top-bottom in English); then partial knowledge, e.g., *either* left-right *or* top-bottom *or* moving from the upper right at the end of one line to the left for the next line; then reversed writing direction; then correct directionality; then correct direction plus correct spacing between words.

33. B: How appropriate the content of a student's composition is reflects function rather than form. Composition length (A), word usage (C), and spelling (D) in a student's composition are all reflections of the composition's form rather than its function.

34. C: This sentence contains the grammatical error of a misplaced modifier. The modifying phrase "a great animal lover" does NOT modify "his pets" but him (e.g., "A great animal lover, *he had* pets including...."). Choice (A) contains a spelling error: "friend" is misspelled. A common student error is to transpose vowel combinations like this. Choice (B) has a punctuation error: these two independent clauses should be separated by a semicolon, not a comma. (In this example, a colon would also be acceptable, but not a comma, which creates a run-on sentence.) Choice (D) has a capitalization error: "South" and "West" are only capitalized when used as names, e.g., "the wild West" or "the sunny South," but when used as directions are lowercase.

35. D: Educational experts find that children, like adults, are more motivated to participate in activities that are exciting to them than to engage in activities they find uninteresting or boring.

They also advise that to sustain children's enthusiasm for writing, teachers should provide diverse writing activities rather than getting stuck in a predictable routine (C) of always using the same ones (A). They note that children's familiarity with the subject they write about increases their motivation rather than decreasing it (B).

36. C: Class composition and preferences. Before selecting literature for the classroom, the teacher needs to assess the class, considering where they are with their reading skills and what their current interests are. After determining these things, the teacher would next evaluate books that seem appropriate for this particular group of children in terms of plot, character, and reading level.

Mathematics

37. C: Students apply logical reasoning to solve both usual, everyday problems and unusual, novel problems they encounter. Developing problem-solving skills not only helps students to think mathematically; it also develops their social skills (A) and language skills (B) when they collaborate to solve problems in math questions, in other school subjects, and in real life; and when they communicate, compare, and discuss their solutions. Children are naturally curious about how everyday problems can be solved: rather than having to teach them this interest (D), teachers can take advantage of this naturally existing motivation by asking them to propose problems; to propose solutions to problems and explain how they reached them; and asking questions about problems and solutions.

38. B: Emotional and behavioral self-regulation skills are important components of problem-solving abilities in students. Without these, students would not have the patience, persistence, and flexibility to keep trying alternative solutions if their first solution fails (D). Another characteristic of problem-solving behavior is to formulate hypotheses first and then test them for accuracy, not vice versa (A). An additional characteristic of good problem-solvers is to be willing to take reasonable risks (C).

39. A: Whether they actually introduce physical objects for the youngest children, or simply describe concrete objects in oral story problems, adults should always ask young children these in terms of concrete objects. For example, asking, "two + two = what?" may be too abstract; but asking, "If you have two grapes and I give you two more, how many will you have?" facilitates children's ability to manipulate numbers via seeing them as familiar items. Adults can start with favorite foods and then add problems using toys, cars, grocery items, etc. According to experts, adults should not restrict such games to grade levels (B): young children can address any scenario for which they can form mental images. Adults are also advised to include occasional harder problems, e.g., involving division remainders, bigger numbers, negative number results, etc., rather than making 100 percent of them simple (C). They should also ask young children guiding questions (the Socratic method) to help them solve problems themselves, rather than just telling them an answer (D).

40. D: Experts recommend asking children "why?" questions; *not* expecting certain answers (A) but being open to whatever ideas they may produce; *not* asking questions without permitting or attending to children's answers (B); allowing children enough time to think about what their answers might be rather than demanding immediate responses (C); and listening attentively to the original, sometimes unique, answers that the children come up with on their own by thinking through the questions. This supports children in developing their reasoning skills, which are vital to problem solving, math, and science.

41. B: One common event when children begin school is that, through formal math lessons, they view academic math as a group of rules and steps to follow rather than a body of knowledge they can apply to solve real-life problems. Children *do* mathematical thinking before school (A); it is just intuitive rather than formal mathematical thought. As evidenced by the accuracy of (B), children will *not* automatically apply their formal math learning to useful solutions in real life (C); however, teachers can help them learn to do this. One way they can facilitate this transition and application is to provide children with familiar concrete objects that they can manipulate during math lessons, which makes them *more,* not less (D) likely to see connections between math and real life.

42. C: Parents and other adults can best help children understand math concepts and procedures by helping them realize how these are applied in many different activities, including other academic subjects like the sciences, arts, and music and a variety of everyday life activities. They should NOT isolate math from life and other school subjects (A). They should NOT just let children do whatever they please and hope that they apply math in these activities (B); instead, they can engage them in activities applying math concepts, like sorting when putting away groceries or setting the table. They should not restrict working on math comprehension to formal math lessons (D), but seek and find math concepts and practices in everyday life routines and events. This will help them understand math better, as well as apply it in practical ways.

43. A: One of the earliest evidences of children's developing the idea of symbolic representation—i.e., the concept that things like numbers, letters, words, and objects can be used to represent other things—is their engaging in make-believe and pretend play (e.g., a toy horse represents a real horse; a block is used to represent a cell phone; a stick becomes a laser sword, etc.). Children develop this ability long before they develop fully abstract thought (B). Make-believe and pretend play develop *sooner than* reading, writing, and the alphabetic principle (C), which also employs the concept of symbolic representation. Another example that young children *have* developed symbolic representation is their counting on their fingers (D).

44. A: When the teacher supplies the student with the formal math vocabulary word "classifying", s/he is emphasizing the connection of the child's informal math activity of sorting rocks with the formal math vocabulary word that describes it. Asking the child how s/he is sorting the rocks (B) is a better example of the teacher's emphasizing math communication than vocabulary (by having the child explain). Asking, after the child finishes sorting rocks, what other ways s/he could sort them (C) is a better example of emphasizing problem-solving skills than math vocabulary. Therefore (D) is incorrect.

45. D: Being aware that patterns (regular repetitions) and relationships (associations between/among things) exist in the world affords us greater self-efficacy about our interacting with the environment, as well as increasing our sense of confidence in the environment itself (C). This awareness not only helps us to understand sequences of events; it moreover enables us to predict the next event in the series before it occurs (B). Having an awareness of patterns and relationships in things also informs our understanding of the basic structure of those things (A).

46. D: Commutative. The property that states that the order in which numbers are added does not change the answer is called the commutative property.

47. B: A place value system. That is the system that requires the position of a digit in a number to determine the digit's value. For example, in the number 123, the digit two is in ten's place, and its value is 20. **48. C:** Normally developing young children typically learn to count before they have learned the names of all of the numbers. They do NOT typically learn all number names before

172

learning to count (A). They do NOT typically acquire both skills at the same time (B). And they do NOT typically vary individually in the order (D) of acquiring these skills.

49. B: When young children have learned how to count, have become familiar with numbers, and have developed good number sense, these three achievements will enable them to add and subtract numbers—i.e., to do beginning arithmetic computations. Children with developed number sense are able to count both forward *and* backward (A). They can also break numbers down into their components, *and* reassemble them (C). Being able to identify relationships between or among numbers *is* an ability that is included in number sense (D).

50. A: Bar graph. A bar graph is used to compare quantities. A circle is used to compare parts of a whole. A pictograph shows comparison of quantities using symbols. A line graph shows trends over a period of time.

51. A: Young children need concrete objects to manipulate to learn geometry concepts. In early childhood, they think concretely and thus need to see, touch, and manipulate real things to help them understand abstract concepts. Therefore, their memorizing theorems (B) at this age, when most children cannot even read let alone understand them, would be ineffective. Children should be given everyday life activities that teach geometric concepts—e.g., cutting their sandwiches into different geometric shapes, naming these for them, and letting them assemble and/or rearrange the pieces—*before* rather than after (C) they learn formal geometry basics, as activities that are part of daily life are relevant to young children and an effective way to teach concepts. Instructions to draw geometric diagrams (D) are more appropriate when children are older and have learned geometry concepts from interacting with solid objects, and also have better-developed fine motor skills. Certainly adults can help them draw shapes, but this should not be a first and/or isolated exercise.

52. B: Measurement is not only a formal system for quantifying amounts and numbers that specify sizes, times, weights, etc. (A). It is also used informally in everyday life. As such, it is a valuable skill that young children can use to recognize and find relationships among real-world objects, outside of academic exercises. Young children are not restricted to standardized rulers, scales, clocks, calendars, etc. (C). They also practice measuring things using whatever is available, e.g., comparing objects to the length of their fingers, hands, feet, etc., or to pieces of string; comparing the heft of an object to that of a block or other toy for weight; comparing how long someone is gone to the duration of a TV show, etc. Measuring practice *does* help children learn to compare object sizes/weights and time periods (D).

53. C: Adults can help young children understand the concepts that time passes and is counted and measured by engaging them in counting activities, getting them used to counting in general, telling them how much time various activities took, and showing them the second hand on a clock or watch and counting "One second, two seconds, three...." Young children typically have NOT yet developed understanding of the abstract concept of time (A). However, adults *should* refer to time periods with young children, even before they understand these (B). For example, they can tell children, "You may play for five more minutes before bedtime." Making such references will aid young children's eventual realization of the passage of time. But young children will typically *not* understand such abstract concepts as yesterday/today/tomorrow (D); adults can use more concrete referents, e.g., "after supper" or "before bedtime" until children are older.

54. D: To understand fractions, children must know all of these things: what makes up a particular whole unit; how many pieces that unit is divided into; and whether the pieces are all of the same size or not. Knowing the number of parts but not what makes up the unit (A); knowing what comprises the whole unit, but not how many pieces into which it has been divided (B); or knowing both what makes up the whole unit and how many pieces it has been divided into, but not knowing whether the pieces are equal in size or not (C) will not allow children to comprehend the concept of fractions. For example, a child will not understand the idea of thirds if something is divided into three parts of *unequal* size, because each piece is not equal to one-third of the whole.

55. D: To be able to make accurate estimates of quantities, children must first understand relative and comparative concepts such as bigger than, smaller than, more of, less of, etc. The process of estimating numbers and amounts in lieu of actual exact measurements helps young children to *learn* math vocabulary words (A) like *around, about, more than, less than,* etc., rather than vice versa. By practicing estimation, children also learn how to make predictions appropriately (B) and attain reasonable estimates (C), rather than the other way around.

56. D: Both an insurance company's actuarial table (A) and a weather forecast for the chances of rain (B) predict the probability or likelihood of something happening—for an individual's illness, injury, or death by a given age (A), or for precipitation to occur in a given day or week (B). A chart comparing the results of different interventions (C) organizes and allows people to interpret data related to which method was more or less effective with certain populations rather than predicting the likelihood of any occurrence.

57. C: By having each child select his/her favorite star color, the teacher is giving the children experience with collecting things the way adults collect data (i.e., pieces of information). By having them place all stars of each color in separate columns, the teacher gives the children experience with organizing the data they have collected. By labeling each column with one color and placing each star in the corresponding color column, the teacher is giving the children experience with displaying the data they have collected and organized. Determining figure properties (A) would be better illustrated by an activity involving differentiating triangles, octagons, circles, etc. Applying formulas to shapes (B) would work better with school-age children; for example, practice in multiplying length by width to find area. Intuitively identifying probability (D) might involve having the children predict how many of them will choose each star color with the example given.

58. C: Charlie's response of ten rectangles is correct. The entire figure is itself a rectangle, making one (A). The four squares within it (B) that Billy saw are also rectangles, making the five (D) that Darlene counted. In addition, connected squares create more rectangles: there are three two-square rectangles and two three-square rectangles. Three and two make five more, for a total of ten.

59. B: Ordinal numbers do not indicate the quantity of things but rather their order in a series or set, i.e., the rank or position of each member—the first and third tables here. Choice (A) is an example of cardinal numbers, which indicate quantity or how many—here, four years and two years old. Choice (C) is an example of a nominal number, i.e., one that indicates neither rank nor quantity, but rather a number used as a name to identify something—here, the shirt number of a team player (six). Choice (D) is an example of using rational numbers, i.e., divisions/ratios of integers, or more simply, fractions—two-thirds and one-third here.

60. B: The most accurate, and therefore the best answer in this case, is to tell the students that only starting the measurement with zero allows the first inch to be included/counted. Telling them this is how the teacher learned to do it (A) or that this is a convention of standard rulers to be followed (D) do not offer any explanation of the logic behind measurement; moreover, it is not accurate to say this is done merely to conform. It is equally inaccurate to tell young students this is a way to maximize the use of ruler space (C). Such answers fail to address the central concept that measuring quantities does not begin with a pre-existing quantity of 1.

61. A: Children develop shape perception in a chronological sequence, rather than all at once (D). At their youngest, children can identify simple shapes by sight. Only once their linguistic and cognitive skills develop further do they learn the words to name these shapes (B). When they reach the third level of shape perception, children no longer rely only on intuition and appearances, but can also analyze shapes (C), so that they can recognize even a triangle, for example, which is crooked, distorted, taller/thinner/wider than usual, by its constant properties (e.g., three sides, which may be of equal or different lengths).

62. A: The teacher is engaging the math skills of 1:1 correspondence by directing the children to place one object on each plate. Practice in counting (B) would be engaged more by, for example, asking children when they line up for an activity, "Who is first? Second? Third?" etc., or by asking them to "count off" in line ("One, two, three...."). Recognizing shapes (C) could be engaged by, for example, asking children when they play with blocks what shape each block has. Size comparison (D) could be engaged by asking children which block or other toy is bigger or smaller than another one.

63. A: EC teachers can learn much about how young children are learning new mathematical concepts through observing their behaviors (B); but to help them develop math communication, realize the linguistic functions of math, and develop overall literacy, teachers must also elicit spoken expressions from children about their own knowledge and thought processes. They can do this by asking children questions (e.g., "What shape is this? How about this one? How are these shapes different? Why/how do you think they are different?" etc.). They can then use children's responses to elicit additional expressions from them. While teachers can certainly model language use for children (C) in their speech, including conversations, discussions, directions, and lessons, lecturing (C) is not the best method, especially with young children. Assigning writing about math (D) supports children's reading and writing development and supports literacy too, but is not a substitute for questioning and eliciting further responses.

64. B: Spatial awareness is a foundation most related to later understanding the mathematical areas of geometry, which deals with shapes, lines, and other forms and their movements, and physics, which deals with the laws of objects in motion, at rest, etc. Arithmetic {(A), (C)} deals with basic numerical computations, and algebra {(A), (D)} deals with sets of numbers and their relationships, including letter symbols, equations, and formulas, as for solving unknown quantities, etc.

65. C: Young children's learning to name numbers (A) is comparable to their learning to name alphabet letters. This reflects the understanding that written/printed symbols represent numerical or alphabetic concepts. Learning to count (B) reflects an additional math skill. But neither of these is the same as understanding that symbols also represent concrete objects found in the real world, which constitutes a major cognitive progression. This understanding is demonstrated by young children when they can view a printed/written number and then count out the corresponding number of objects (like pennies). Therefore, (D) is not true.

66. D: 9,731,245/42,754,021 is a fraction. Any number that can be written as a ratio or fraction is rational. The value of pi (π) (A) is an irrational number, as is the square root of 2 ($\sqrt{2}$) (B), because their numbers to the right of the decimal point continue indefinitely without resolution. Therefore, any decimal number (C) is NOT rational; only decimal numbers that end, and thus can be written as fractions or ratios, are rational.

Social Studies

67. D: Newborns demonstrate body differentiation in their rooting and orienting responses for nursing, and young children learn to differentiate their mirror images from other people. Typically, situation (A) follows differentiation: children progress from differentiating self to realizing that their bodies/selves are physically situated in space, and that their mirror reflections are unique to their selves. Subsequently, children develop identification (C), e.g., knowing one's mirror image is "me" as demonstrated by their touching something applied to their face when they see it in a mirror. Thereafter, they develop permanence (B), the recognition that their self is permanent across space and time. (The fifth level of self-awareness is "meta"-self-awareness or self-consciousness, allowing perception of the self from others' perspectives.)

68. C: From birth, infants can tell the difference between their own bodies and the environment around them. They can differentiate between internal stimulation from touching themselves and external stimulation from others touching them. Children typically develop the recognition of photos and mirror images as symbolic representations of themselves (A) by the time they are around two years old. Babies typically develop systematic imitation of others' facial expressions (B), gestures, and other movements around the age of two months. They usually develop the ability of systematically reaching for and touching things they see (D), which requires eye-hand coordination, around the age of four months.

69. B: According to Erikson's theory of psychosocial development, the earliest stage in a child's first year of life is when s/he develops a basic sense of trust or mistrust in parents and the environment. Having their needs met sufficiently and consistently engenders trust, while having needs met inadequately and/or irregularly spawns mistrust. The second stage, in toddlerhood, involves developing a sense of autonomy or independence (A) versus one of shame and self-doubt. According to Piaget's theory of cognitive development, it is during this time period that children also develop an understanding of symbolic representation, evidenced by their engaging in make-believe or pretend play (D). According to Erikson, preschool children aged around three to five years develop a sense of initiative through exploring and exercising power over their environment, or develop a sense of guilt (C) if they garner disapproval for exerting excessive power.

70. A: It is true that conflict resolution steps have been taught successfully to children as young as eighteen months. For example, the HighScope EC curriculum, well known for its effectiveness, has sponsored the expert design of a conflict resolution approach for children aged eighteen months to six years. Conflict mediation and resolution have been taught in such settings as daycare centers, Head Start programs, preschools, nursery schools, and kindergartens. Therefore, (C) is not true. Instruction features the same steps used with adults, but adjusted commensurately with various EC developmental levels. Preschoolers are found to understand these concepts (B) when presented age appropriately. Teaching conflict mediation and resolution to young children is found to develop lifelong social skills and problem-solving skills; hence, children *do* generalize this learning (D).

71. A: Authoritative parents are nurturing, responsive, and forgiving; they are assertive but not punitive. They make rules but explain them to children. Authoritarian (B) parents are overly strict, unresponsive, and demanding, and do not explain rules. Permissive (C) parents are nurturing, responsive, and communicative; but are also undemanding, overly indulgent, and avoid discipline. Uninvolved (D) parents are undemanding *and* unresponsive; meeting only basic child needs, they are detached from their children's lives.

72. B: Family peacemaker, clown, as well as victim, rescuer, etc., are examples of the family system component of roles. Each member's family role generalizes to school, workplace, and social settings. Boundaries (A) reflect whom and what the family includes or excludes. Rules (C) in families, spoken and unspoken, affect family life in the long term, such as planning ahead to avert problems vs. meeting these as they occur. Equilibrium (D) reflects the consistency and balance in a family.

73. C: Collectivist cultures value group harmony and cooperation, while individualist cultures value competition (A), independence (B), and uniqueness (D). World cultures that tend to espouse collectivism include Asian, Latin American, African, and Native American. Those tending to embrace individualism include North American, Canadian, European, and Australian cultures.

74. D: Assimilation is the process whereby members of one cultural group (voluntarily or involuntarily) give up their own traditions to adopt those of another culture, often one which is dominant. Acculturation (C) can mean gradual cultural modifications to a person or group through adopting some elements of another culture; the merging of cultures via long-term interaction; or a person's acquiring a society's culture from birth. Accommodation (A) as a general vocabulary word means providing a service (as in hospitality services) or adjustment (as in schools) to meet a need. As a term used by Piaget, it means forming a new schema (concept) or altering an existing one to include new input. Piaget also used assimilation (D) to mean fitting new input into an existing schema without changing the schema. Adaptation (B) in general vocabulary means adjustment; for Piaget, it meant the learning process of assimilation and accommodation combined.

75. D: Experts find that cultural competence in educational professionals is not achieved simply by hiring foreign language interpreters and translators (A), or only by hiring racially diverse personnel (B), or just by hiring educators with high self-awareness of their own cultural values (C). Rather, schools must do all three of these things; plus, the educators hired must have and/or develop the communication skills to be able to deliver effective educational services to culturally diverse children and their families, and to conduct meaningful, mutually beneficial interactions and relationships with them.

76. C: Researchers in California found that the majority of Latino parents believed their children's capacity for learning was set at birth and would not change, but that only a small minority of White parents held this belief. Hence choices (A) and (B) are incorrect. More White parents are likely to embrace transactional models of child development, seeing their children's learning as a dynamic process involving complex interactions between child and environment. This view is conducive to valuing early childhood stimulation to enhance normal learning, and early intervention to remediate developmental delays. However, the view that a child's cognitive capacity is fixed is conducive to seeing less or no benefit in early stimulation and/or intervention rather than valuing these (D), and hence to not pursuing them.

77. B: Various cultures, including African-American as an example, have strong oral traditions. Educators must take this into account rather than focusing on their not reading to their children, or reading to them less often. Telling stories and singing songs is an oral version of developing children's language skills (though it does not confer the same benefits for reading and writing language). Educators must also consider that parents who were not read to themselves as children, and grew up to succeed regardless, are unlikely to value reading to their own children (A). Educators must realize they are unlikely to influence parents whose culture does not value or prioritize reading to children (C). Educators are also unlikely to be able to teach parents to read to their children when the parents do not view children's school readiness and success as benefits of reading to them (D).

78. A: Researchers have found that parents from diverse cultures in America vary in their age expectations for many different EC developmental milestones—not just for sleeping alone (B). For instance, Anglo, Filipino, and Puerto Rican parents in the U.S. vary in the ages when they expect their children to eat solid food (C). They also have different ages when they expect their children to sleep through the night (D).

79. A: In geography, location—specifically, relative location—determines things like land prices based on the characteristics of an area, which are affected by nearby regions. An example of distance (B) is that land that is close to major highways is more expensive, while land far from main thoroughfares costs less. One example of pattern (C) in geography is that where rock folds form mountains (fold regions), the rivers accordingly form trellis patterns. Another example of pattern, in geographically oriented human behavior, is that settlements in mountainous areas form mainly spreading patterns. An example of interaction (D) in geography is when an industrial city needs raw materials from a rural village for production, and the village needs the city both as a market to buy its resources and for its industrial products: their mutual interdependence creates interaction between them.

80. B: Latitudes are lines that run east and west on geographical maps, and are also called parallels. Longitudes (A) are lines that run north and south, so longitude is not a synonym for latitude. Longitudes are also called meridians (C), so meridian is a synonym for longitude, not latitude. Coordinates (D) are the numbers of degrees assigned to various latitudes and latitudes.

81. C: A line graph makes clearest how quantities vary across periods of time, by drawing a line connecting each data point so we can see how many/much of something there was each second, minute, hour, day, week, month, year, etc. A pie chart (A) is excellent for clearly visualizing different percentages or proportions, by dividing a "pie" (circle) into "slices" representing what part of the whole each amount represents; however, pie charts do not show change across time the way line graphs do. But a bar graph (B) *can* compare quantities over time: for example, each bar could show the amount of rainfall in a given month. A column of numbers (D) is not a type of graph, and it does not make patterns and trends as clear visually as graphs do.

82. D: Teachers can use not only history books (A); they can also assign students to read well-constructed and well-written biographies (B) of famous figures in history and works of historical literature (C), which set even fictionalized stories within real historical periods and events. Historical narratives written in "storytelling" style are also good for engaging student attention while establishing chronological sequences in history.

83. C: To help young children understand citizenship concepts, teachers should help them understand the purposes and functions of laws and rules. Understanding these will help them realize that our government is made up of individuals and groups who create and enforce laws. Teachers should also help young children understand that laws limit the powers of authorities (A), preventing them from abusing their roles. Teachers should explain that laws determine the responsibilities of individual citizens (B) like themselves and their family members. They should also point out to young children that laws and rules help to make life and society more predictable, secure, and orderly (D).

Science

84. B: When young children pour sand, water, rice, etc., from one container to another, differently sized (or shaped) container, they are developing basic measurement concepts. Children fitting pegs into matching holes (A) are developing basic 1:1 correspondence concepts. Seeing how many coins they have put into their piggy bank (C) helps children develop basic counting concepts. Separating toys into piles according to type (D), color, shape, size, or any other characteristic helps children develop basic classification/categorization concepts.

85. A: When young children learn basic science concepts, an informal learning experience is defined as one wherein the child has choice and control over the activity, but at some point during the activity an adult provides some kind of intervention. When the child has complete choice and control of the activity and no adult intervenes at all (B), this is the definition of a naturalistic learning experience. If the child's activity is chosen and directed by an adult (C), or assigned to a group of children in preschool by the teacher (D), these are examples of structured learning experiences.

86. B: When scientists and students are able to identify patterns and find meaning in the results of their experiments, they are using the process skill of Inference. When they use the results of their experiments to formulate new hypotheses (A), they are using the process skill of Prediction. When they identify the properties of objects or situations using their senses, they are using the process skill of Observation. When they report the results of their experiments and their conclusions based on these results to others (D), they are using the process skill of Communication. These skills are required for solving both math and science problems.

87. C: Ammonia is known as a compound gas because its molecules contain atoms of more than one of the chemical elements—nitrogen (B) and hydrogen (D) atoms in the case of ammonia gas. Oxygen (A) as well as nitrogen and hydrogen are elementary gases rather than compound gases because their molecules contain only one chemical element.

88. D: Refraction is the process whereby the speed of light is changed as it passes from one transparent medium, like air, to another, like water. The change in speed bends the light wave. Scattering (A) is the process whereby light bounces back at multiple angles when it strikes a rough or uneven surface (instead of bouncing back at a single angle as when it strikes a smooth surface). When light bounces back off a surface, this is reflection (C). Materials that do not reflect *any* light waves (smoothly or scattered) or refract any light waves appear opaque, i.e., we cannot see through them, because they take in all frequencies of light; this is absorption (B).

89. D: Diamagnetic materials align perpendicularly to magnetic field lines, and do not retain magnetic properties when the external magnetic field is removed. These include copper, silver, gold, and most other elements in the periodic table. Paramagnetic (C) materials align parallel to magnetic field lines, and also do not retain magnetic properties upon removal of the external field. These include lithium, magnesium, molybdenum, and tantalum. Ferromagnetic (B) materials retain their magnetic properties even when the external magnetic field is removed. These include iron, nickel, and cobalt. Magnetic induction (A) is the name for the process whereby magnets turn magnetic substances near them into magnets as well.

90. C: Magnets do not have to be touching to attract or repel materials; they are able to do this from a distance. However, magnets do NOT work beyond their magnetic fields (D): the magnetic field is defined as the effective range or area of a magnet, so magnets only work within their magnetic fields by definition. Opposite poles of magnets do NOT repel (A), but instead attract each other. Conversely, the like poles of magnets do NOT attract (B), but instead repel one another.

91. B: Electricity requires a generator to make it flow. It needs a conductor as a medium through which it can travel from place to place. An insulator {(A), (C)} is a material that *blocks* the conduction of electricity. Insulation is used to prevent electricity from going where we do not want it to go—for example, into our bodies. Therefore, (D) is incorrect.

92. A: Three ways of transmitting heat are conduction (A), convection (B), and radiation (C). When heat is transmitted through solids, this is done via conduction. Conduction occurs between solid materials directly contacting one another. Convection (B) is how heat travels through liquids and gases. Heat makes them expand, lowering their density so they rise. When they cool, they recover density and fall. This heating-rising and cooling-falling process creates a current known as convection. Radiation (C), like the heat from the sun, occurs when electromagnetic waves travel through space and transfer heat to objects, like the Earth, that they touch. Therefore, (D) is incorrect.

93. B: Newton's First Law of Motion states *both* that an object at rest tends to stay at rest (A), and an object in motion tends to stay in motion (C), unless or until an opposing force changes this. Newton's *Third* Law of Motion states that for every action there is an equal and opposite reaction (D).

94. D: Sound waves require a physical medium to travel through. This can be a solid, liquid, or gas, but cannot be a vacuum, which is defined as a space lacking matter.

95. D: Sedimentary rock is formed on the surface of the earth, deposited in layers as the result of natural processes like erosion. Igneous (A) rocks are formed from volcanic eruptions. Obsidian (B) is just one type of igneous rock. Metamorphic (C) rocks form deep in the earth's crust through heavy pressure and/or heat, which metamorphose or change sedimentary and igneous rocks far below the surface.

96. C: Plants growing on land depend on sunlight to perform photosynthesis, the process whereby they convert sunlight's energy to chemical energy as fuel for their life functions. Undersea plants (A) need water and nutrients like land plants; they do not need all gases in the atmosphere but need the gases in the water, and they need less light than land plants, or no light at all, to survive. Mammals (B) need air, water, and nutrients; some mammals need more or less light, but none need light for photosynthesis as land plants do. Humans (D) are also mammals.

97. D: Human beings, like other mammals, birds, fish, reptiles, and spiders, have simple life cycles in that they are either born live or hatched from eggs, and then grow to adulthood. Frogs (A), newts (B), and grasshoppers (C) undergo metamorphoses wherein their forms change. Frogs and newts are amphibians; they begin life underwater, breathing through gills, but breathe through lungs by adulthood and move from the water to live on the land. Grasshoppers hatch from eggs into larvae, wormlike juvenile forms that do most of the feeding they need; then they progress to adulthood.

98. B: Butterflies undergo a *complete* metamorphosis during their life cycle, i.e., they completely change in form. The stages of a complete metamorphosis are (1) egg, (2) larva, (3) pupa, and (4) imago. Mosquitos (A), dragonflies (C), and grasshoppers (D) all go through an *incomplete* metamorphosis in their life cycles, including the egg, larva, and imago (adult) stages, but not the pupa stage. The butterfly pupa, called a chrysalis, is protected by a cocoon, does not feed, and is inactive until the imago (adult) emerges.

99. C: Most plants reproduce both asexually (A) and sexually (B). Asexual reproduction occurs through runners that some plants extend to root new growth, through plant cuttings being rooted in water and then planted, and through grafts. Plants reproduce sexually through fertilization, wherein plant gametes combine, contributing chromosomes from both sides, similarly to how animals mate. Since (C) is correct, (D) is incorrect.

100. B: The abiotic factors of an ecosystem are not alive; hence (A) is incorrect. Abiotic factors include such things as the atmosphere, water, soil, sunlight, temperatures, nutrient cycles, etc. While not living themselves, abiotic factors *do* affect the living organisms (C) in the ecosystem. Living organisms are biotic factors, including humans, other animals, plants, *and* microorganisms; hence abiotic factors do NOT include microorganisms (D).

How to Overcome Test Anxiety

Just the thought of taking a test is enough to make most people a little nervous. A test is an important event that can have a long-term impact on your future, so it's important to take it seriously and it's natural to feel anxious about performing well. But just because anxiety is normal, that doesn't mean that it's helpful in test taking, or that you should simply accept it as part of your life. Anxiety can have a variety of effects. These effects can be mild, like making you feel slightly nervous, or severe, like blocking your ability to focus or remember even a simple detail.

If you experience test anxiety—whether severe or mild—it's important to know how to beat it. To discover this, first you need to understand what causes test anxiety.

Causes of Test Anxiety

While we often think of anxiety as an uncontrollable emotional state, it can actually be caused by simple, practical things. One of the most common causes of test anxiety is that a person does not feel adequately prepared for their test. This feeling can be the result of many different issues such as poor study habits or lack of organization, but the most common culprit is time management. Starting to study too late, failing to organize your study time to cover all of the material, or being distracted while you study will mean that you're not well prepared for the test. This may lead to cramming the night before, which will cause you to be physically and mentally exhausted for the test. Poor time management also contributes to feelings of stress, fear, and hopelessness as you realize you are not well prepared but don't know what to do about it.

Other times, test anxiety is not related to your preparation for the test but comes from unresolved fear. This may be a past failure on a test, or poor performance on tests in general. It may come from comparing yourself to others who seem to be performing better or from the stress of living up to expectations. Anxiety may be driven by fears of the future—how failure on this test would affect your educational and career goals. These fears are often completely irrational, but they can still negatively impact your test performance.

> **Review Video:** 3 Reasons You Have Test Anxiety
> Visit mometrix.com/academy and enter code: 428468

Elements of Test Anxiety

As mentioned earlier, test anxiety is considered to be an emotional state, but it has physical and mental components as well. Sometimes you may not even realize that you are suffering from test anxiety until you notice the physical symptoms. These can include trembling hands, rapid heartbeat, sweating, nausea, and tense muscles. Extreme anxiety may lead to fainting or vomiting. Obviously, any of these symptoms can have a negative impact on testing. It is important to recognize them as soon as they begin to occur so that you can address the problem before it damages your performance.

Review Video: 3 Ways to Tell You Have Test Anxiety
Visit mometrix.com/academy and enter code: 927847

The mental components of test anxiety include trouble focusing and inability to remember learned information. During a test, your mind is on high alert, which can help you recall information and stay focused for an extended period of time. However, anxiety interferes with your mind's natural processes, causing you to blank out, even on the questions you know well. The strain of testing during anxiety makes it difficult to stay focused, especially on a test that may take several hours. Extreme anxiety can take a huge mental toll, making it difficult not only to recall test information but even to understand the test questions or pull your thoughts together.

Review Video: How Test Anxiety Affects Memory
Visit mometrix.com/academy and enter code: 609003

Effects of Test Anxiety

Test anxiety is like a disease—if left untreated, it will get progressively worse. Anxiety leads to poor performance, and this reinforces the feelings of fear and failure, which in turn lead to poor performances on subsequent tests. It can grow from a mild nervousness to a crippling condition. If allowed to progress, test anxiety can have a big impact on your schooling, and consequently on your future.

Test anxiety can spread to other parts of your life. Anxiety on tests can become anxiety in any stressful situation, and blanking on a test can turn into panicking in a job situation. But fortunately, you don't have to let anxiety rule your testing and determine your grades. There are a number of relatively simple steps you can take to move past anxiety and function normally on a test and in the rest of life.

Review Video: How Test Anxiety Impacts Your Grades
Visit mometrix.com/academy and enter code: 939819

Physical Steps for Beating Test Anxiety

While test anxiety is a serious problem, the good news is that it can be overcome. It doesn't have to control your ability to think and remember information. While it may take time, you can begin taking steps today to beat anxiety.

Just as your first hint that you may be struggling with anxiety comes from the physical symptoms, the first step to treating it is also physical. Rest is crucial for having a clear, strong mind. If you are tired, it is much easier to give in to anxiety. But if you establish good sleep habits, your body and mind will be ready to perform optimally, without the strain of exhaustion. Additionally, sleeping well helps you to retain information better, so you're more likely to recall the answers when you see the test questions.

Getting good sleep means more than going to bed on time. It's important to allow your brain time to relax. Take study breaks from time to time so it doesn't get overworked, and don't study right before bed. Take time to rest your mind before trying to rest your body, or you may find it difficult to fall asleep.

> **Review Video: The Importance of Sleep for Your Brain**
> Visit mometrix.com/academy and enter code: 319338

Along with sleep, other aspects of physical health are important in preparing for a test. Good nutrition is vital for good brain function. Sugary foods and drinks may give a burst of energy but this burst is followed by a crash, both physically and emotionally. Instead, fuel your body with protein and vitamin-rich foods.

Also, drink plenty of water. Dehydration can lead to headaches and exhaustion, especially if your brain is already under stress from the rigors of the test. Particularly if your test is a long one, drink water during the breaks. And if possible, take an energy-boosting snack to eat between sections.

> **Review Video: How Diet Can Affect your Mood**
> Visit mometrix.com/academy and enter code: 624317

Along with sleep and diet, a third important part of physical health is exercise. Maintaining a steady workout schedule is helpful, but even taking 5-minute study breaks to walk can help get your blood pumping faster and clear your head. Exercise also releases endorphins, which contribute to a positive feeling and can help combat test anxiety.

When you nurture your physical health, you are also contributing to your mental health. If your body is healthy, your mind is much more likely to be healthy as well. So take time to rest, nourish your body with healthy food and water, and get moving as much as possible. Taking these physical steps will make you stronger and more able to take the mental steps necessary to overcome test anxiety.

> **Review Video: How to Stay Healthy and Prevent Test Anxiety**
> Visit mometrix.com/academy and enter code: 877894

Mental Steps for Beating Test Anxiety

Working on the mental side of test anxiety can be more challenging, but as with the physical side, there are clear steps you can take to overcome it. As mentioned earlier, test anxiety often stems from lack of preparation, so the obvious solution is to prepare for the test. Effective studying may be the most important weapon you have for beating test anxiety, but you can and should employ several other mental tools to combat fear.

First, boost your confidence by reminding yourself of past success—tests or projects that you aced. If you're putting as much effort into preparing for this test as you did for those, there's no reason you should expect to fail here. Work hard to prepare; then trust your preparation.

Second, surround yourself with encouraging people. It can be helpful to find a study group, but be sure that the people you're around will encourage a positive attitude. If you spend time with others who are anxious or cynical, this will only contribute to your own anxiety. Look for others who are motivated to study hard from a desire to succeed, not from a fear of failure.

Third, reward yourself. A test is physically and mentally tiring, even without anxiety, and it can be helpful to have something to look forward to. Plan an activity following the test, regardless of the outcome, such as going to a movie or getting ice cream.

When you are taking the test, if you find yourself beginning to feel anxious, remind yourself that you know the material. Visualize successfully completing the test. Then take a few deep, relaxing breaths and return to it. Work through the questions carefully but with confidence, knowing that you are capable of succeeding.

Developing a healthy mental approach to test taking will also aid in other areas of life. Test anxiety affects more than just the actual test—it can be damaging to your mental health and even contribute to depression. It's important to beat test anxiety before it becomes a problem for more than testing.

> **Review Video: Test Anxiety and Depression**
> Visit mometrix.com/academy and enter code: 904704

Study Strategy

Being prepared for the test is necessary to combat anxiety, but what does being prepared look like? You may study for hours on end and still not feel prepared. What you need is a strategy for test prep. The next few pages outline our recommended steps to help you plan out and conquer the challenge of preparation.

Step 1: Scope Out the Test

Learn everything you can about the format (multiple choice, essay, etc.) and what will be on the test. Gather any study materials, course outlines, or sample exams that may be available. Not only will this help you to prepare, but knowing what to expect can help to alleviate test anxiety.

Step 2: Map Out the Material

Look through the textbook or study guide and make note of how many chapters or sections it has. Then divide these over the time you have. For example, if a book has 15 chapters and you have five days to study, you need to cover three chapters each day. Even better, if you have the time, leave an extra day at the end for overall review after you have gone through the material in depth.

If time is limited, you may need to prioritize the material. Look through it and make note of which sections you think you already have a good grasp on, and which need review. While you are studying, skim quickly through the familiar sections and take more time on the challenging parts. Write out your plan so you don't get lost as you go. Having a written plan also helps you feel more in control of the study, so anxiety is less likely to arise from feeling overwhelmed at the amount to cover.

Step 3: Gather Your Tools

Decide what study method works best for you. Do you prefer to highlight in the book as you study and then go back over the highlighted portions? Or do you type out notes of the important information? Or is it helpful to make flashcards that you can carry with you? Assemble the pens, index cards, highlighters, post-it notes, and any other materials you may need so you won't be distracted by getting up to find things while you study.

If you're having a hard time retaining the information or organizing your notes, experiment with different methods. For example, try color-coding by subject with colored pens, highlighters, or post-it notes. If you learn better by hearing, try recording yourself reading your notes so you can listen while in the car, working out, or simply sitting at your desk. Ask a friend to quiz you from your flashcards, or try teaching someone the material to solidify it in your mind.

Step 4: Create Your Environment

It's important to avoid distractions while you study. This includes both the obvious distractions like visitors and the subtle distractions like an uncomfortable chair (or a too-comfortable couch that makes you want to fall asleep). Set up the best study environment possible: good lighting and a comfortable work area. If background music helps you focus, you may want to turn it on, but otherwise keep the room quiet. If you are using a computer to take notes, be sure you don't have any other windows open, especially applications like social media, games, or anything else that could distract you. Silence your phone and turn off notifications. Be sure to keep water close by so you stay hydrated while you study (but avoid unhealthy drinks and snacks).

186

Also, take into account the best time of day to study. Are you freshest first thing in the morning? Try to set aside some time then to work through the material. Is your mind clearer in the afternoon or evening? Schedule your study session then. Another method is to study at the same time of day that you will take the test, so that your brain gets used to working on the material at that time and will be ready to focus at test time.

Step 5: Study!

Once you have done all the study preparation, it's time to settle into the actual studying. Sit down, take a few moments to settle your mind so you can focus, and begin to follow your study plan. Don't give in to distractions or let yourself procrastinate. This is your time to prepare so you'll be ready to fearlessly approach the test. Make the most of the time and stay focused.

Of course, you don't want to burn out. If you study too long you may find that you're not retaining the information very well. Take regular study breaks. For example, taking five minutes out of every hour to walk briskly, breathing deeply and swinging your arms, can help your mind stay fresh.

As you get to the end of each chapter or section, it's a good idea to do a quick review. Remind yourself of what you learned and work on any difficult parts. When you feel that you've mastered the material, move on to the next part. At the end of your study session, briefly skim through your notes again.

But while review is helpful, cramming last minute is NOT. If at all possible, work ahead so that you won't need to fit all your study into the last day. Cramming overloads your brain with more information than it can process and retain, and your tired mind may struggle to recall even previously learned information when it is overwhelmed with last-minute study. Also, the urgent nature of cramming and the stress placed on your brain contribute to anxiety. You'll be more likely to go to the test feeling unprepared and having trouble thinking clearly.

So don't cram, and don't stay up late before the test, even just to review your notes at a leisurely pace. Your brain needs rest more than it needs to go over the information again. In fact, plan to finish your studies by noon or early afternoon the day before the test. Give your brain the rest of the day to relax or focus on other things, and get a good night's sleep. Then you will be fresh for the test and better able to recall what you've studied.

Step 6: Take a practice test

Many courses offer sample tests, either online or in the study materials. This is an excellent resource to check whether you have mastered the material, as well as to prepare for the test format and environment.

Check the test format ahead of time: the number of questions, the type (multiple choice, free response, etc.), and the time limit. Then create a plan for working through them. For example, if you have 30 minutes to take a 60-question test, your limit is 30 seconds per question. Spend less time on the questions you know well so that you can take more time on the difficult ones.

If you have time to take several practice tests, take the first one open book, with no time limit. Work through the questions at your own pace and make sure you fully understand them. Gradually work up to taking a test under test conditions: sit at a desk with all study materials put away and set a timer. Pace yourself to make sure you finish the test with time to spare and go back to check your answers if you have time.

After each test, check your answers. On the questions you missed, be sure you understand why you missed them. Did you misread the question (tests can use tricky wording)? Did you forget the information? Or was it something you hadn't learned? Go back and study any shaky areas that the practice tests reveal.

Taking these tests not only helps with your grade, but also aids in combating test anxiety. If you're already used to the test conditions, you're less likely to worry about it, and working through tests until you're scoring well gives you a confidence boost. Go through the practice tests until you feel comfortable, and then you can go into the test knowing that you're ready for it.

Test Tips

On test day, you should be confident, knowing that you've prepared well and are ready to answer the questions. But aside from preparation, there are several test day strategies you can employ to maximize your performance.

First, as stated before, get a good night's sleep the night before the test (and for several nights before that, if possible). Go into the test with a fresh, alert mind rather than staying up late to study.

Try not to change too much about your normal routine on the day of the test. It's important to eat a nutritious breakfast, but if you normally don't eat breakfast at all, consider eating just a protein bar. If you're a coffee drinker, go ahead and have your normal coffee. Just make sure you time it so that the caffeine doesn't wear off right in the middle of your test. Avoid sugary beverages, and drink enough water to stay hydrated but not so much that you need a restroom break 10 minutes into the test. If your test isn't first thing in the morning, consider going for a walk or doing a light workout before the test to get your blood flowing.

Allow yourself enough time to get ready, and leave for the test with plenty of time to spare so you won't have the anxiety of scrambling to arrive in time. Another reason to be early is to select a good seat. It's helpful to sit away from doors and windows, which can be distracting. Find a good seat, get out your supplies, and settle your mind before the test begins.

When the test begins, start by going over the instructions carefully, even if you already know what to expect. Make sure you avoid any careless mistakes by following the directions.

Then begin working through the questions, pacing yourself as you've practiced. If you're not sure on an answer, don't spend too much time on it, and don't let it shake your confidence. Either skip it and come back later, or eliminate as many wrong answers as possible and guess among the remaining ones. Don't dwell on these questions as you continue—put them out of your mind and focus on what lies ahead.

Be sure to read all of the answer choices, even if you're sure the first one is the right answer. Sometimes you'll find a better one if you keep reading. But don't second-guess yourself if you do immediately know the answer. Your gut instinct is usually right. Don't let test anxiety rob you of the information you know.

If you have time at the end of the test (and if the test format allows), go back and review your answers. Be cautious about changing any, since your first instinct tends to be correct, but make sure you didn't misread any of the questions or accidentally mark the wrong answer choice. Look over any you skipped and make an educated guess.

At the end, leave the test feeling confident. You've done your best, so don't waste time worrying about your performance or wishing you could change anything. Instead, celebrate the successful completion of this test. And finally, use this test to learn how to deal with anxiety even better next time.

Review Video: 5 Tips to Beat Test Anxiety
Visit mometrix.com/academy and enter code: 570656

Important Qualification

Not all anxiety is created equal. If your test anxiety is causing major issues in your life beyond the classroom or testing center, or if you are experiencing troubling physical symptoms related to your anxiety, it may be a sign of a serious physiological or psychological condition. If this sounds like your situation, we strongly encourage you to seek professional help.

Thank You

We at Mometrix would like to extend our heartfelt thanks to you, our friend and patron, for allowing us to play a part in your journey. It is a privilege to serve people from all walks of life who are unified in their commitment to building the best future they can for themselves.

The preparation you devote to these important testing milestones may be the most valuable educational opportunity you have for making a real difference in your life. We encourage you to put your heart into it—that feeling of succeeding, overcoming, and yes, conquering will be well worth the hours you've invested.

We want to hear your story, your struggles and your successes, and if you see any opportunities for us to improve our materials so we can help others even more effectively in the future, please share that with us as well. **The team at Mometrix would be absolutely thrilled to hear from you!** So please, send us an email (support@mometrix.com) and let's stay in touch.

If you'd like some additional help, check out these other resources we offer for your exam:

http://MometrixFlashcards.com/MTEL